Fundamentals of
Total Quality Management

Fundamentals of Total Quality Management

Process analysis and improvement

Jens J. Dahlgaard
Division of Quality and Human Systems Engineering,
Linköping University, Sweden

Kai Kristensen
Aarhus School of Business, Aarhus, Denmark

and

Gopal K. Kanji
Centre for Quality and Innovation, Sheffield Hallam University,
Sheffield, UK

Taylor & Francis
Taylor & Francis Group

LONDON AND NEW YORK

First published in 1998 by:
Taylor & Francis

Reprinted in 2002 by:
Taylor & Francis
2 Park Square, Milton Park,
Abingdon, Oxon, OX14 4RN

Transferred to Digital Printing 2005

02 03 04 05 / 10 9 8 7 6 5 4 3 2 1

A catalogue record for this book is available from the British Library

ISBN 0 7487 7293 6

Page make-up by Blackpool Typesetting Services Ltd

Printed and bound by Antony Rowe Ltd, Eastbourne

Contents

Preface

The principles of TQM have proven very valuable to individuals, groups of people and organizations and many organizations have now discovered a relationship between quality and profitability. It has now become important for organizations to develop a quality strategy by adopting the principles of TQM.

In the present changing environment of the business world, it is evident that education will play a vital role in coping with the change process. There is now a real need to incorporate the principles of TQM in any education and there is an even greater need to educate specialists in this field and to propagate new ideas.

The purpose of this textbook is to provide a framework for the development of understanding of some of the basic aspects of Total Quality Management. The aim is to provide students with deeper knowledge of various principles and core concepts of Total Quality Management. It will also help them to learn and appreciate the role of measurement, quality strategy and quality systems, etc. in the development of the Total Quality Management process.

This book will also provide the readers with a basic knowledge and understanding of various aspects of the effective organizational process and quality improvement plans for the development of the required change in the process of management. We believe that with the help of this book students will be able to use the process specification and analysis tools to create process-oriented organizations. They will also be able to understand the need to change the management process and required motivation to create a quality organization.

Finally this book is designed to help students towards an understanding of the problem-solving process and the tools to overcome the difficulties created by process development. It will also give them the know-how of various statistical methods which can be applied to the control and improvement of processes.

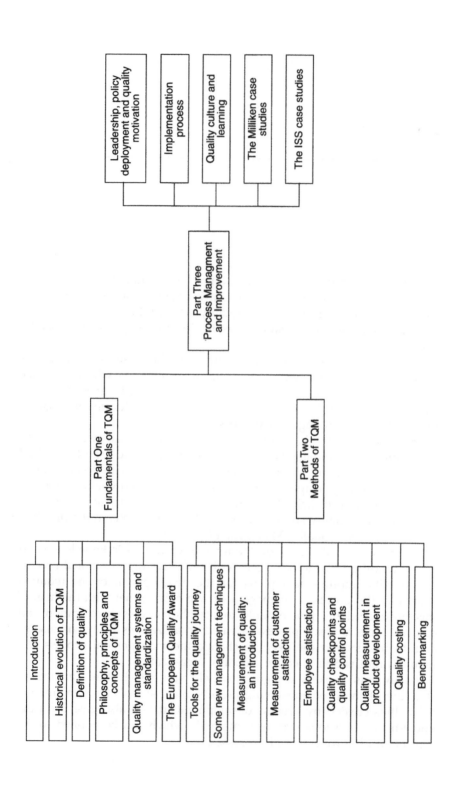

Introduction

Historical evolution of TQM

Definition of quality

Philosophy, principles and concepts of TQM

Quality management systems and standardization

The European Quality Award

Part One
Fundamentals of TQM

Tools for the quality journey

Some new management techniques

Measurement of quality: an introduction

Measurement of customer satisfaction

Employee satisfaction

Quality checkpoints and quality control points

Quality measurement in product development

Quality costing

Benchmarking

Part Two
Methods of TQM

Part Three
Process Managment and Improvement

Leadership, policy deployment and quality motivation

Implementation process

Quality culture and learning

The Milliken case studies

The ISS case studies

This book is divided into three parts but interlinked to each other in order to provide an integrated approach. The three parts of the book, i.e. Fundamentals of TQM, Methods of TQM and Process Management and Improvement, are linked together in a tree diagram to provide an overall understanding of the subject.

Jens J. Dahlgaard, Kai Kristensen (Aarhus)
and Gopal K. Kanji (Sheffield)
August, 1997

PART ONE
Fundamentals of Total Quality Management

PART ONE

Introduction

1

It is hard to believe that the current approach to Japan's quality improvement programme has changed the balance of the present trade situation between Japan and the rest of the world. It is evident that one of the most important aspects of Japanese quality improvement is the Japanese approach to quality management. Japanese companies have developed quality improvement (QI) in various stages, that is, from inspection after production to new product development through the stages of process control. The Japanese way of QI has been described by Ishikawa (1985), Sullivan (1986) and Yoshizawa (1987) who have pointed out the importance of the seven stages of QI. Even now, the value of effective QI has not been fully realized by many industries. In fact some people still think that it is the role of a quality department. They do not realize that QI is a way of life and the human aspect of it requires a great deal of education and training at all levels.

Improving quality is very often regarded as an activity which is going to increase cost. This view confuses the terms used in industry concerning quality and grade. Improving or raising the grade of products relates to the use of more expensive materials or processes to produce a product and will raise product costs. Improving quality means, among other things, making less faulty products with the same amount of effort or cost which usually gives a lower unit cost.

The cost of producing faulty products in the United Kingdom has been estimated as 10% of the gross national product: several thousand million pounds (Dale and Plunkett, 1991, p. 11). Improving quality aims to reduce this cost. This cannot be achieved overnight but requires an investment to be made in activities which are designed to avoid defective production, not activities designed to detect defects after they have been made.

The problem is knowing in what to invest (systems, technology, people) and it is this which seems to have bewildered Western industrialists. The search for the key to quality has been going on since the Japanese made us aware that we had missed something out along the way. Various analyses of Japanese success have attempted to condense the effect to one particular activity; hence fashions of 'quality circles' and 'statistical process control'. The latest analysis has developed the concept of 'Total Quality Management', which may well provide an answer to the problem. The keynote here is that the achievement of quality should not be considered to be a separate activity from the achievement of production.

Many large organizations are now trying to emulate that Japanese achievement in their commitment to quality. Each is developing its own approach and may give a different title to its efforts but each has similar elements to 'Total Quality Management' (TQM). The development of Total Quality Management in America started at the beginning of the 1980s when American companies realized that not only Japan but also Korea and Taiwan were coming forward with quality products and services to capture the American market.

In Europe even now, with some exceptions, it is not unfair to say that European organizations lag behind those of Japan and the United States and it will be many years before they catch up with them. For the development of TQM European organizations looked for real explanations of the Japanese quality improvement in their quality culture and consensus management. Further, like the Japanese, European industrialists also tried to develop TQM from the teaching of American experts. In doing so, they realized that for the proper implementation of TQM they must understand the quality culture of their organizations and the country.

Kristensen, Dahlgaard and Kanji (1993) noted the importance of product quality to various business parameters. In order to assess the importance of competitive parameters for the company they investigated three different countries and the results are presented in Table 1.1 below. The respondents were allowed to choose between the following answers:

- irrelevant (1)
- unimportant (2)
- modestly important (3)
- rather important (4)
- very important (5)

It appears from the table that among manufacturing companies 'product quality' is considered to be the most important competitive parameter in all three countries. At the other end of the scale, we find that advertising is considered the least important parameter in all countries. However, between these two extremes we have found that the market price is ranked 5 in Taiwan and Korea and 4 in Japan. There is

Table 1.1 Evaluation of business parameters

	Country					
	Taiwan		Japan		Korea	
Business parameter	Mean	Rank	Mean	Rank	Mean	Rank
Market price	4.11	5	4.20	4	4.08	5
Product quality	4.72	1	4.88	1	4.56	1
Delivery	3.98	7	4.48	2	4.32	3
Advertising	3.00	9	3.20	9	2.89	9
Service before sale	4.02	6	3.56	8	3.27	8
Service after sale	4.49	4	4.20	4	4.00	6
Assortment	3.94	8	3.68	7	3.73	7
Warranty	4.68	2	3.80	6	4.38	2
Handling of complaints	4.55	3	4.48	2	4.21	4

also reasonable consensus about the importance of assortment, which is ranked 8 in Taiwan and 7 in Japan and Korea.

Regarding delivery and warranty, opinions differ considerably among the three countries. For example, in Japan and Korea, delivery is considered very important with a rank of 2 and 3 respectively, whereas it plays a modest role in Taiwan. Since we were expecting delivery to be a very important parameter we were a bit surprised about the Taiwanese result. One explanation for this could be that the companies in Taiwan produce less goods to order than the companies in Japan and Korea.

The difference concerning the importance of warranty is much easier to explain. When the perception of quality is high, as is the case for Japanese products, warranty is not an important business parameter. On the other hand, when the quality level is unknown or is considered to be less than world class, as is the case for the newly industrialized countries of Taiwan and Korea, warranty becomes a very important selling point.

The authors' recent QED studies (Dahlgaard, Kanji and Kristensen, 1992) regarding the importance of product quality to various business parameters for nine countries can be seen in Figure 1.1. The result indicates the differences between the various countries with respect to quality and four business parameters.

It is evident that in this competitive world, organizations and countries as a whole must achieve recognition from consumers about their top quality activities at all times in order to conduct business successfully. According to a worldwide Gallup poll of 20 000 people conducted recently by Bozell Worldwide of America (Figure 1.2), world consumers believe the best quality goods are made by Japan.

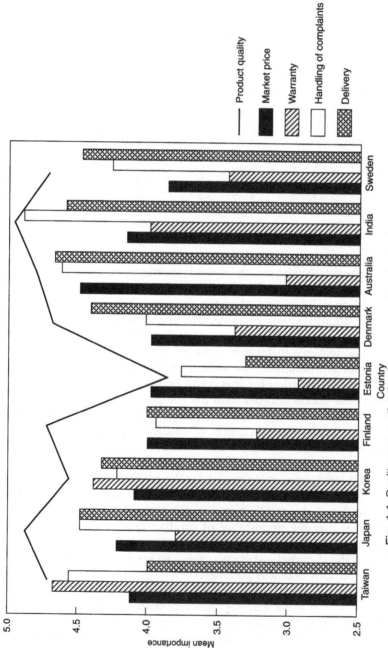

Fig. 1.1 Quality versus other business parameters. 1 = irrelevant; 5 = very important.

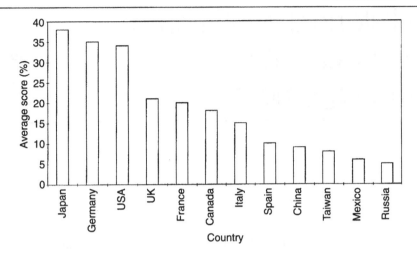

Fig. 1.2 Quality league. (Source: Bozell Gallup poll.)

REFERENCES

Dahlgaard, J.J., Kanji, G. K. and Kristensen, K. (1992) Quality and economic development project. *Total Quality Management*, **3**(1), 115–18.

Dale, B.G. and Plunkett, J.J. (1991) *Quality Costing*, Chapman & Hall, London.

Ishikawa, K. (1985) *What is Total Quality Control? – The Japanese Way*, Prentice Hall, Englewood Cliffs, USA.

Kristensen, K., Dahlgaard, J.J. and Kanji, G.K. (1993) Quality motivation in East Asian countries. *Total Quality Management*, **4**(1), 79–89.

Sullivan, L.P. (1986) The seven stages in company-wide quality control. *Quality Progress*, **19**, 77–83.

Yoshizawa, T. (1987) *Exploratory Data Analysis in the Development Stage of New Products*. Proceedings of the 46th session of the ISI invited papers, 5.3, 1–11.

Historical evolution of Total Quality Management

2

The historical evolution of Total Quality Management has taken place in four stages. They can be categorized as follows:

1. quality inspection
2. quality control
3. quality assurance
4. Total Quality Management.

Quality has been evident in human activities for as long as we can remember. However the first stage of this development can be seen in the 1910s when the Ford Motor Company's 'T' Model car rolled off the production line. The company started to employ teams of inspectors to compare or test the product with the project standard. This was applied at all stages covering the production process and delivery, etc. The purpose of the **inspection** was that the poor quality product found by the inspectors would be separated from the acceptable quality product and then would be scrapped, reworked or sold as lower quality.

With further industrial advancement came the second stage of TQM development and quality was controlled through supervised skills, written specification, measurement and standardization. During the Second World War, manufacturing systems became complex and the quality began to be verified by inspections rather than the workers themselves. **Statistical quality control** by inspection – the post-production effort to separate the good product from the bad product – was then developed. The development of control charts and accepting sampling methods by Shewhart and Dodge-Roming during the period 1924–1931 helped this era to prosper further from the previous inspection era. At this stage Shewhart introduced the idea that quality control can help to distinguish and separate two types of process variation; firstly the variation resulting from random causes and secondly the variation resulting from assignable or special causes. He also suggested that a process can be made to function predictably by separating the variation due to special causes. Further, he designed a control chart for monitoring such process variation in order to decide when to interact with the process.

The main processes which help products and services to meet customers' needs are inspection and quality control which require greater process control and lower evidence of non-conformance.

The third stage of this development, i.e. **quality assurance** contains all the previous stages in order to provide sufficient confidence that a product or service will satisfy customers' needs. Other activities such as comprehensive quality manuals, use of cost of quality, development of process control and auditing of quality systems are also developed in order to progress from quality control to the quality assurance era of Total Quality Management. At this stage there was also an emphasis of change from detection activities towards prevention of bad quality.

The fourth level, i.e. **Total Quality Management** involves the understanding and implementation of quality management principles and concepts in every aspect of business activities. Total Quality Management demands that the principles of quality management must be applied at every level, every stage and in every department of the organization. The idea of Total Quality Management philosophy must also be enriched by the application of sophisticated quality management techniques. The process of quality management would also be beyond the inner organization in order to develop close collaboration with suppliers. Various characteristics of the different stages in the development of Total Quality Management can be seen in Table 2.1. Here QI, QC, QA and TQM are abbreviations of Quality Inspection, Quality Control, Quality Assurance and Total Quality Management.

The development of total quality management from 1950 onwards can be credited to the works of various American experts. Among them, Dr Edward Deming, Dr Joseph Juran and Philip Crosby have contributed significantly towards the continuous development of the subject.

According to Deming (1982), organization problems lie within the management process and statistical methods can be used to trace the source of the problem. In order to help the managers to improve the quality of their organizations he has offered them the following 14 management points.

1. Constancy of purpose: create constancy of purpose for continual improvement of product and service.
2. The new philosophy: adopt the new philosophy. We are in a new economic age, created in Japan.
3. Cease dependence on inspection: eliminate the need for mass inspection as a way to achieve quality.

Table 2.1 Characteristics of the different stages in TQM

Stage	Characteristics
QI (1910)	Salvage Sorting Corrective action Identify sources of non-conformance
QC (1924)	Quality manual Performance data Self-inspection Product testing Quality planning Use of statistics Paperwork control
QA (1950)	Third-party approvals Systems audits Quality planning Quality manuals Quality costs Process control Failure mode and effect analysis Non-production operation
TQM (1980)	Focused vision Continuous improvements Internal customer Performance measure Prevention Company-wide application Interdepartmental barriers Management leadership

4. End 'lowest tender' contracts: end the practice of awarding business solely on the basis of price tag.
5. Improve every process: improve constantly and forever every process for planning, production and service.
6. Institute training on the job: institute modern methods of training on the job.
7. Institute leadership: adopt and institute leadership aimed at helping people and machines to do a better job.
8. Drive out fear: encourage effective two-way communication and other means to drive out fear throughout the organization.
9. Break down barriers: break down barriers between department and staff areas.
10. Eliminate exhortations: eliminate the use of slogans, posters and exhortations.

11. Eliminate targets: eliminate work standards that prescribe numerical quotas for the workforce and numerical goals for people in management.
12. Permit pride of workmanship: remove the barriers that rob hourly workers, and people in management, of the right to pride of workmanship.
13. Encourage education: institute a vigorous programme of education and encourage self-improvement for everyone.
14. Top management commitment: clearly define top management's permanent commitment to ever-improving quality and productivity.

At the same time Dr Joseph Juran (1980) through his teaching was stressing the customer's point of view of products' fitness for use or purpose. According to him a product could easily meet all the specifications and still may not be fit for use or purpose. Juran advocated 10 steps for quality improvements as follows:

1. Build awareness of the need and opportunity for improvement.
2. Set goals for improvement.
3. Organize to reach the goals (establish a quality council, identify problems, select projects, appoint teams, designate facilitators).
4. Provide training.
5. Carry out projects to solve problems.
6. Report progress.
7. Give recognition.
8. Communicate results.
9. Keep score
10. Maintain momentum by making annual improvement part of the regular systems and processes of the company.

Both Deming and Juran were in favour of using statistical process control for the understanding of total quality management.

However, Crosby (1982) on the other hand was not keen to accept quality which is related to statistical methods. According to him quality is conformance to requirement and can only be measured by the cost of non-conformance. Crosby provides four absolutes and the 14 steps for the quality improvement process. His four absolutes are:

1. Definition of quality – conformance to requirements.
2. Quality system – prevention.
3. Quality standard – zero defects.
4. Measurement of quality – price of non-conformance.

His 14 steps for quality improvement can be described as follows:

1. Management commitment: to make it clear where management stands on quality.

2. Quality improvement team: to run the quality improvement process.
3. Measurement: to provide a display of current and potential non-conformance problems in a manner thet permits objective.
4. Cost of quality: to define the ingredients of the cost of quality (COQ) and explain its use as a management tool.
5. Quality awareness: to provide a method of raising the personal concern felt by all employees toward the conformance of the product or service and the quality reputation of the company.
6. Corrective action: to provide a systematic method for resolving forever the problems that are identified through the previous action steps.
7. Zero defects: to examine the various activities that must be conducted in preparation for formally launching zero-defects day.
8. Employee education: to define the type of training all employees need in order actively to carry out their role in the quality improvement process.
9. Planning and zero-defects day: to create an event that will let all employees realize, through a personal experience, that there has been a change.
10. Goal setting: to turn pledges and commitments into action by encouraging individuals to establish improvement goals for themselves and their groups.
11. Error-cause removal: to give the individual employee a method of communicating to management the situations that make it difficult for the employee to meet the pledge to improve.
12. Recognition: to appreciate those who participate.
13. Quality councils: to bring together the appropriate people to share quality management information on a regular basis.
14. Do it all over again: to emphasize that the quality improvement process is continuous.

In this section we have only indicated a few detailed contributions to the historical evaluation of TQM. Many other people also (e.g. Ishikawa, Feigenbaum) have contributed and it is not our intention to present all the details of that development in this section.

REFERENCES

Crosby, P.B. (1982) *Quality is Free*, The New American Library Inc., New York, USA.

Deming, W.E. (1982) *Quality, Productivity and Competitive Position*, MIT, USA.

Juran, J.M. and Gryna, F.M. (1980) *Quality Planning and Analysis – From Product Development through Use*, McGraw-Hill, New York, USA.

Shewhart, W.A. (1931) *Economic Control of Quality and Manufactured Products*, D. van Nostrand & Co., Inc., New York, USA.

Some definitions of quality

3

Quality is an important issue in the modern competitive business world. Like the 'theory of relativity' quality is sometimes expressed as a relative concept and can be different things to different people (e.g. a Rolls Royce car is a quality car for certain customers whereas a VW Beatle can be a quality car for other customers).

Sometimes people visualize quality in absolute terms and for them it can be compared with beauty and sweetness. According to them it can be compared with certain absolute characteristics and the product and services must achieve a pre-set standard in order to obtain a quality rating.

Hence, one can find a variety of definitions of quality. For example, Garvin (1984, 1988) has given reasons why quality should have different meanings in different contexts. He suggested the following five co-existing definitions:

1. transcendent (excellence);
2. product-based (amount of desirable attribute);
3. user-based (fitness for use);
4. manufacturing-based (conformance to specification);
5. value-based (satisfaction relative to price).

According to Garvin it is necessary to change the approach from user-based to product-based as products move through market research to design and then from product-based to manufacturing-based as they go from design into manufacture. Hence the definition of quality will change in each approach and can coexist. He also suggested that the definition of quality will also change from industry to industry.

According to some authors, the definition 'quality is the capacity of a commodity or service to satisfy human wants' and the human 'wants' are complex and may not always be satisfied in a particular way. Users of products make a personal assessment of quality. Each case will be influenced by how well numerous aspects of performance are able to provide satisfaction of multiple wants and further distinguished by the subjective importance attached by the individual.

In recent years, like Garvin, Harvey and Green (1993) have suggested five discrete and interrelated definitions of quality. They are:

1. exceptional
2. perfection
3. fitness for purpose
4. value for money
5. transformative.

Further explanation of the above quality grouping can be seen as follows.

3.1 EXCEPTIONAL

There are three variations of this 'exceptional' concept. These are:

1. traditional
2. excellence
3. standards.

TRADITIONAL

This can be expressed as the distinctiveness, something special or high class. It confers status on the owner or users and implies exclusivity. This definition of quality promotes the elitist's view of the high quality.

EXCELLENCE

There are two schools of thought about this definition of quality. First of all it relates to high standards and secondly it describes the 'zero defects'. Here, 'excellence' is similar to the 'traditional' definition and identifies the component of excellence which is also unattainable. It is also an elitist concept and sees quality to be only attainable in limited circumstances. The best is required in order to achieve excellence.

STANDARDS

A quality idea in this case is one that has passed a set of quality checks, where the checks are based on certain criteria in order to eliminate defective items. Here quality is measured by the items which fulfil the minimum standards prescribed by the producer and can be described as 'conformance to standards'.

3.2 PERFECTION OR CONSISTENCY

Perfection definition concentrates on process and with the help of proper specification it transforms the 'traditional' idea of quality into something which can be achieved by everybody. It can also be redefined in terms of conformance to specification rather than high standards. However, one must realize that there is a difference between quality and standard because quality here simply conforms to a certain specification and the specification in general cannot be expressed as a standard. Under this definition, conformance to specification takes the role of achieving benchmark standard. Here the complete perfection means making sure that everything is perfect and there are no defects. Furthermore, no defects or zero defects demands that the perfection of product or services is delivered consistently. Therefore the idea of reliability in terms of 'exceptional' becomes the perfection view of quality.

Here, quality is one which conforms exactly to specification and whose output is free of defects at all times. Further, perfection here is not only the conformance to specification, it also acts as a philosophy of prevention. The idea is to make sure that a fault does not occur in the various stages of the process that is helping to create a quality culture.

For an organization, a quality culture is one in which everybody is responsible for quality improvement. With the help of this quality culture each organization develops a system of interrelated 'teams' which provide inputs and outputs. Hence the team plays a dual role (i.e. a customer and a supplier) and takes the responsibility of ensuring that its output matches the required input. So the idea of perfection as a definition of quality suggests that it has a philosophy of prevention which is an essential part of quality culture. Here the definition of quality focuses on everybody's involvements in quality improvement for achieving quality goals at each stage of the process.

3.3 FITNESS FOR PURPOSE

This definition focuses on the relationship between the purpose of the product or services and its quality. It examines each in terms of the product or services in order to compare whether it fits its purpose. This definition is a functional one and is different from the earlier 'exceptional' definition

Here, fitness of purpose is used in order to propagate and measure the perfection. If it does not fit its purpose then this definition of quality may run a risk of being totally useless. Although it is a simple idea, nevertheless, it raises some questions such as whose purpose and how is the fitness assessed?

3.4 VALUE FOR MONEY

Under this definition quality is described as the price you can afford to pay for your requirements at a reasonable cost, which means quality is compared with the level of specification and is directly related to cost. However, it ignores the effect of competitiveness which is based on the assumptions of quality improvement.

Here quality is equated with value for money and is assessed against such criteria as standards and reliability. The value for money definition therefore suggests the idea of accountability (e.g. public services are accountable to the Government). In general, market forces and competition help to develop the links between the value for money and quality.

3.5 TRANSFORMATIVE

Harvey and Green suggested the transformative view of quality as follows:

> The transformative view of quality is rooted in the notion of 'qualitative change', a fundamental change of form. Ice is transformed into water and eventually steam if it experiences an increase of temperature. Whilst the increase in temperature can be measured the transformation involves a qualitative change.

Ice has different qualities to that of steam or water. Transformation is not restricted to apparent or physical transformation but also includes cognitive transcendence. This transformative notion of quality is well established in Western philosophy and can be found in the discussion of dialectical transforms in the works of Aristotle, Kant, Hegel and Marx. It is also at the heart of transcendental philosophies around the world, such as Buddhism and Jainism. More recently it has been entertainingly explored in Pirsig's (1976) *Zen and the Art of Motorcycle Maintenance*. This notion of quality such as transformative raises issues about the relevance of a product-centred notion of quality such as fitness for purpose.

The measurement of value added, for example of input and output qualifications, provides a quantifiable indicator of 'added value' but conceals the nature of the qualitative transformation. Arguing against a fitness for purpose approach Müller and Funnell (1992) suggested that quality should be explored in terms of a wide range of factors leading to a notion of 'Value Addedness'.

The second element of transformative quality is empowerment (Harvey and Barrows, 1992). This involves giving power to participants to influence their own transformation. This is much more than the accountability to the consumer which is found in customer charters. Consumerist charters essentially keep producers and providers on their toes, but rarely affect the decision-making process or policy. The control remains with the producer or provider. Empowering the employee in order to capitalize on their knowledge and skill is a well established strategy in the business world (Stratton, 1988).

3.6 Conclusion

Quality has different meanings for different people (Ishikawa (1976), Taguchi (1986), Deming (1982), Kano (1984), Scherkenback (1988), Juran and Gryna (1980)). It is a philosophy with dimensions and can be summed up as 'doing things properly' for competitiveness and profitability.

It is a holistic concept and includes two different ideas of quality, i.e. quality as 'consistency' and quality as 'fitness for purpose'. The above two ideas are brought together to create quality as perfection within the context of quality culture.

Quality philosophy reflects various perspectives of individuals, groups of people and society. In a modern business world people are allowed to hold various views regarding quality which of course can change with time and situations. Many people, instead of getting involved with different definitions of quality, have developed some underlying principles and concepts of Total Quality Management.

In general we will follow the definition of TQM by Kanji (1990). According to him 'TQM is the way of life of an organization committed to customer satisfaction through continuous improvement. This way of life varies from organization to organization and from one country to another but has certain essential principles which can be implemented to secure greater market share, increase profits and reduce cost'.

We will be discussing principles, concepts and definitions of Total Quality Management in the next chapter.

REFERENCES

Deming, W.E. (1982) *Quality, Productivity and Competitive Position*, MIT, USA.
Garvin, D.A. (1984, 1988) *Managing Quality Edge*, Free Press, New York, USA.
Harvey, L. and Barrows, A. (1992) Empowering students. *New Academic*, 1(3), 1–4.
Harvey, L. and Green, D. (1993) Defining quality. *Assessment and Evaluation in Higher Education*, **18**(1), 9–34.
Ishikawa, K. (1976) *Guide to Quality Control*, Asian Productivity Organization, Tokyo, Japan.
Juran, J.M. and Gryna, F.M. (1980) *Quality Planning and Analysis – From Product Development through Use*, McGraw-Hill, New York, USA.
Kano, N. (1984) Attractive quality and must be quality. *Quality*, **14**(2).
Müller, D. and Funnell, P. (1992) *Exploring Learners' Perception of Quality*. Paper presented at the AETT Conference on Quality in Education, April 6–8, 1992, University of York.
Pirsig, R.M. (1976) *Zen and the Art of Motor Cycle Maintenance*, Copenhagen, Denmark.
Scherkenback, W.W. (1988) *The Deming Route to Quality and Productivity*, CEE Press Books Washington, DC, USA.

Stratton, A.D. (1988) *An Approach to Quality Improvement that Works with an Emphasis on the White-collar Area*, American Society for Quality Control, Milwaukee, USA.

Taguchi, G. (1986) *Introduction to Quality Engineering*, American Supplier Institute, Dearborn, Michigan, USA.

Philosophy, principles and concepts of TQM 4

TQM is a vision which the firm can only achieve through long-term planning, by drawing up and implementing annual quality plans which gradually lead the firm towards the fulfilment of the vision, i.e. to the point where the following definition of TQM becomes a reality:

> A corporate culture characterized by increased customer satisfaction through continuous improvements, in which all employees in the firm actively participate.

Quality is a part of this definition in that TQM can be said to be the culmination of a hierarchy of quality definitions:

1. Quality – is to continuously satisfy customers' expectations.
2. Total quality – is to achieve quality at low cost.
3. Total Quality Management – is to achieve total quality through everybody's participation.

TQM is no inconsequential vision. At a time when most domestic and overseas markets are characterized by 'cutthroat competition', more and more firms are coming to realize that TQM is necessary just to survive. Today, consumers can pick and choose between a mass of competing products – and they do. Consumers choose the products that give the 'highest value for money', i.e. those products and services which give the highest degree of customer satisfaction in relation to price.

A verse from the Book of Proverbs reads: 'A people without visions will perish.' Likewise, firms without visions will also perish, or, as Professor Yoshio Kondo, of Kyoto University, Japan, put it at one of his visiting lectures at the Århus School of Business in Spring, 1992: Companies without CWQC will sooner or later disappear from the telephone directory.

The concept of company-wide quality control (CWQC) has been described in more detail in Dahlgaard, Kristensen and Kanji (1994), from which the following quote has been taken:

The concept of TQM is a logical development of Total Quality Control (TQC), a concept first introduced by A.V. Feigenbaum in 1960 in a book of the same name. Though Feigenbaum had other things in mind with TQC, it only really caught on in engineering circles, and thus never achieved the total acceptance in western companies intended. TQC was a 'hit' in Japan, on the other hand, where the first quality circles were set up in 1962, and which later developed into what the Japanese themselves call CWQC, Company-Wide Quality Control. This is identical with what we in the West today call TQM.

In his book *Total Quality Control*, Feigenbaum (1960) states that TQC is an effective system for integrating the various initiatives in the field of quality to enable production and services to be carried out as cheaply as possible consistent with customer satisfaction.

This definition contains the very root of the problem. The reason why TQC was not a success in Western forms is especially due to the fact that Western management was misled by Feigenbaum's reference to an effective system into thinking that TQC could be left to a central quality department. As a result, management failed to realize that an essential ingredient of TQC is management's unequivocal commitment to quality improvements. Effective systems are a necessary but by no means sufficient condition for TQC.

The aim of the new concept of TQM is, by deliberately including management in the concept's definition, to ensure that history does not repeat itself. It makes it impossible for management to disclaim its responsibility and sends a clear message through the 'corridors of power' that this is a task for top management and thus also for the board of directors.

There is more to it than just substituting an M for a C, of course. Visions and definitions have to be operationalized before they can be applied in everyday life. We attempt to do this below through the construction of the so-called TQM pyramid.

4.1 THE FOUNDATION AND THE FOUR SIDES OF THE TQM PYRAMID

'The Quality Journey' firmly believes in tearing down outdated management pyramids, arguing instead for the need to build a whole new management pyramid – one which can live up to the vision and challenges inherent in the definition of TQM. An apt name for this pyramid would be the TQM pyramid (Figure 4.1).

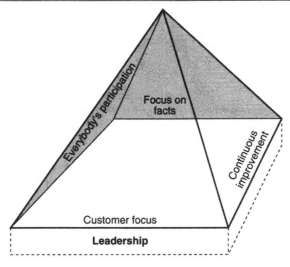

Fig. 4.1 The TQM pyramid.

As can be seen from Figure 4.1, the TQM pyramid (an adaptation of the Kanji and Asher pyramid model) is a proper pyramid, with a foundation and four sides.

TQM is characterized by five principles:

1. management's commitment (leadership);
2. focus on the customer and the employee;
3. focus on facts;
4. continuous improvements (KAIZEN);
5. everybody's participation.

These five principles will be discussed in greater detail below.

4.1.1 MANAGEMENT'S COMMITMENT (LEADERSHIP)

As mentioned earlier, TQM is the West's answer to Japan's company-wide quality control (CWQC). TQM's forerunner, TQC, had never been seen as anything other than the special responsibility of the quality department. Management at all levels and in all departments just could not see that 'total quality' can only be achieved with the active participation of management.

A vital task for any management is to outline quality goals, quality policies and quality plans in accordance with the four sides of the TQM pyramid. This is extremely important – so important in fact that, in many firms, top management (the board of directors) ought to review the firm's quality goals and policies and if necessary reformulate them so that they conform to the four sides of the TQM pyramid. Just as important, these goals and policies should be clear and meaningful to all employees in the firm. It is extremely important, for example, that the firm's **quality goals** signal to employees that the firm's principal task is to satisfy its external customers and that this can only be achieved if the firm is able to exceed customers' expectations. This is discussed in greater depth below.

The firm's quality goals give all employees a clear indication of what is going to be achieved concerning quality. The firm's **quality policies**, on the other hand, describe in more detail how employees are to achieve that goal. The firm's quality policies must also conform to the four sides of the TQM pyramid. One example of how a firm (ISS) had formulated its quality goals and quality policies can be found in section 2.3.

Quality goals and quality policies must be followed by meaningful **action plans**. Experience from firms which have understood and realized the TQM vision shows that firms ought to concentrate on short-term plans (one-year plans) and long-term plans, the latter often being three-year plans which are revised annually in connection with an annual **quality audit**.

The annual quality audit is an essential part of the TQM vision and is much too important to be left to a central quality department. Only through active participation in the quality audit can top management acquire the necessary insight into the problems the firm has had in realizing the quality plan. The annual quality audit gives top management the opportunity to put a number of important questions to departmental managers. Apart from the usual questions about quality problems and defects, they should include the following four questions:

1. How have 'customers' been identified (both internal and external customers)?
2. How have customers' requirements and expectations been identified?
3. How have managers and employees tried to satisfy customers?
4. What do customers think of our products and services and how has this information been collected?

These questions allow top management to check whether employees are in fact seriously trying to fulfil the firm's quality goals. By actively participating in the annual quality audit, top management shows that it has understood the TQM message, which is an essential condition for making and realizing new, meaningful quality plans. Such active partici-pation by top management also makes its commitment highly visible, which will have an extremely important effect throughout the organiza-tion when new action plans are drawn up – among other things, em-ployees will be reminded that the customer, not the product, is top priority.

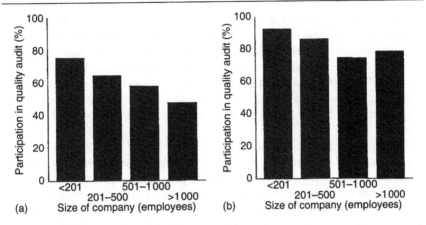

Fig. 4.2 Top management participation in quality audit. (a) West developed; (b) East developed. (Source: The QED Research Project.)

Unfortunately, as Figure 4.2 shows, top Western managers of especially bigger companies do not seem to have understood the necessity of participating in the annual quality audit as well as many of their international competitors. Today it is widely recognized that 'the art of TQM' when we talk about leadership is an attempt to bring the qualities of the small company into the large company. Figure 4.2 gives empirical evidence that this is exactly what has been understood in the East contrary to what we observe in the West. The bigger the company in the West the smaller the participation in the vital quality audit. On the other hand even if the Eastern companies are very large they have succeeded in creating a quality culture which resembles that of smaller companies.

In the run-up to the action plan, management must answer the following questions:

1. Where are we now? (the present situation).
2. Where do we want to be? (vision).
3. How do we get there? (action plans).

To do this requires knowledge of a number of management methods that have been specially developed within the field of quality. The question 'where are we now' is answered increasingly by means of self-assessment, based on the criteria of internationally-recognized quality awards. At present, there are four such awards:

1. The Deming Prize, founded in Japan in 1951.
2. The Malcolm Baldridge Quality Award, founded in the USA in 1988.
3. The European Quality Award, founded in 1992.
4. The Australian Quality Award, founded in 1988.

The American quality award in particular has been a great success in connection with self-evaluation, with several thousand firms sending off for information on self-evaluation every year (e.g. more than 250 000 in 1991). We hope that similar success awaits the European Quality Award (founded in 1992) and that the criteria of the award will, as in Japan and the USA, be used as a management tool in identifying 'opportunities for improvement'. See section 4.3 for further details on the European Quality Award.

Questions 2 and 3 – 'where do we want to be' and 'how do we get there' – can be answered by means of the benchmarking method. Benchmarking can be defined as a continuous process, the purpose of which is to measure services, products and procedures against the toughest competitors or leading procedures in a given market, the idea being to procure the information necessary for a firm to become the best of the best (Chapter 15).

The basic philosophy behind benchmarking can be traced back to the Chinese philosopher Sun Tzu (500 BC) and the Japanese art of warfare and can be summarized in the following points:

• know your own strengths and weaknesses;
• know your competitors (opponents) and the best in the field;
• learn from the best;
• achieve leadership.

It is important to realize that benchmarking is not just a question of comparing yourself with your competitors. Basically, there are four main types of benchmarking that can be used: internal benchmarking, competitor-based benchmarking, functional benchmarking and generic benchmarking.

Internal benchmarking means comparing yourself with departments and divisions in the same organization. This is normally the simplest form of benchmarking because data will always be available for the comparison. The most difficult form of benchmarking will normally be **competitor-based benchmarking**, where the firm compares itself with its direct competitors. In this case, data can be difficult to come by and must often be acquired by indirect means. This is not a problem in functional or generic benchmarking. **Functional benchmarking** is based on the functions which the firm concerned is especially noted for, the idea being that the firm compares itself with the leading firm in these functions (e.g. the use of robots, automization of the assembly lines, etc.). These firms can be direct competitors of the company concerned but will often not be. Finally, **generic benchmarking** includes procedures which are common on all types of companies, such as order-taking, the payment of wages, word processing and the like.

Benchmarking is a useful management tool in that the gap it reveals between internal and external practice in itself creates the need for change. In addition, an understanding of the 'best practice' has the virtue of identifying areas in need of change and gives an idea of what the department or company will look like after the change.

There is widespread consensus today that it is possible to produce goods and services with higher quality at lower costs. The best evidence for this has been collected in the book *The Machine that Changed the World* (Womack, Jones and Roos, 1990), which compares car assembly plants from all over the world. Benchmarking is a natural consequence of the results presented in this book.

The decision to use benchmarking is, of course, solely a management decision. The same is true of the decision to allow the firm to be assessed through comparison with the criteria for internationally-recognized quality prizes. Such evaluations can be acutely embarrassing for a company, since some of the criteria involve the evaluation of management's commitment – or lack of it. Fear of what such evaluations might reveal could therefore mean that the method is not used in the first place. It is thus crucial to point out from the start that the purpose of such evaluations is not to find sufficient grounds to fire a weak management but only to identify weak areas in the company. Such comparisons are, of course, only relevant to the extent that the company's owners and top management want to change its quality culture. The decision to change is entirely voluntary but if the TQM vision is to be realized, management's commitment is not. The realization of TQM requires both a profound knowledge of TQM and the active participation of top management.

This brings us to a very crucial point – it is easy enough to say that TQM requires management's commitment but it is much harder to explain how management should tackle the further implementation of TQM. This is essential.

Deming (1982) has formulated what management ought to do in his renowned 14 points (Dahlgaard, Kristensen and Kanji, 1994) and in point 14 presents seven points for implementing TQM which are often overseen. In shortened form, these seven points are:

1. Management must agree about goals, conditions and obstacles to the introduction of TQM.
2. Management must have the courage to break with tradition.
3. In building up a new 'quality organization', management must appoint a manager for quality improvements who has direct access to top management.
4. Management must, as quickly as possible, build up an organization to advise on the carrying out of continuous improvements throughout the firm.

5. Management must explain to employees why changes are necessary and that they will involve everybody in the company.
6. Management must explain that every activity and every job has its own customers and suppliers.
7. Management must ensure that every employee in the company participates actively in a team (work team, quality circle).

The above points implicitly include all four sides of the TQM pyramid to which we now turn in the following sections.

4.2 FOCUS ON THE CUSTOMER AND THE EMPLOYEE

Focusing on the customer and the customer's requirements and expectations is neither new nor revolutionary. This is precisely what the Service Management movement of the 1980s was about. The new message in TQM is:

1. In addition to focusing on external customers and their expectations and demands, it is necessary to focus on so-called internal customer and supplier relations.
2. To create customer satisfaction, it is not enough just to live up to the customer's expectations.

These points require some elaboration.

The first point is meant to show that employees are part of the firm's processes and that improving quality at lower and lower costs can only be achieved if a company has good, committed and satisfied employees. Before you can satisfy external customers, however, you must first eliminate some of the obstacles to the internal customers (i.e. the employees) and create the conditions necessary for them to produce and deliver quality. One such obstacle that must be eliminated in an organization is fear, while an example of the latter is education and training. Deming's 14 points contain the most important obstacles to eliminate and conditions to institute in order to improve quality at lower and lower costs.

At the same time, improvements ought to be process-oriented. A firm can be defined as a series of connected processes, of which employees are a part, so any management interested in quality must start by looking at the firm's processes. This is one of the reasons why the foundation of the TQM pyramid is called 'management's commitment'. The processes are established and function 'on the shop floor'. Quality improvements can only be achieved where things happen, which the Japanese express as 'Genba to QC', which means 'improve quality where things happen'.

In order to produce and deliver quality, employees need to know what both internal and external customers want/expect of them. Only when employees have this information will they be able to start improving the processes which is a first step towards becoming a 'TQM firm'.

The second point is attributed to Professor Noriaki Kano of Tokyo Science University, whose expanded concept of quality, formulated in 1984, contains the following five types of quality:

1. Expected quality, or must-be quality.
2. Proportional quality.
3. Value-added quality ('exciting/charming quality').
4. Indifferent quality.
5. Reverse quality.

In order to deliver the expected quality, firms have to know what the customers expect. When/if firms have this knowledge, they must then try to live up these expectations – this is so obvious that the Japanese also call this type of quality 'must-be quality'.

For many customers it is not enough, however, just to live up to their expectations. This in itself does not create satisfaction, it 'only' removes dissatisfactions. Creating satisfaction demands more. This 'more' is what Kano calls 'exciting quality'. We have chosen to call it 'value-added' quality because this describes more directly that the producer has added one or more qualities to the product or service in addition to those the customer expects and that these extra qualities give the customer extra value. These extra qualities will, so to speak, surprise the customer and make him/her happy, satisfied, or excited with the product. This is why Kano calls it 'exciting quality'. A closer study of the Japanese language reveals another name for this type of quality, however, namely 'charming quality', which is actually quite a good name for it.

Many firms seem to have had a great deal of difficulty in understanding and thus also accepting the relevance of 'value-added' quality. We will therefore try to explain this and the other types of quality with the help of an example which most of us are familiar with – hotel service.

Most people have a clear idea of the kind of service they expect at a hotel. Among other things, we expect the room to be clean and tidy when we arrive, we expect it to be cleaned every day and we expect there to be hot water in the taps, shower etc. We do not react much if these expectations are fulfilled – it is no more than we expected. We would not start singing the praises of a hotel that only lived up to these expectations. If, on the other hand, our expectations are not fulfilled, we immediately become dissatisfied and will often tell our friends and acquaintances about it. This is yet another explanation for the term 'must-be quality'. In order to survive, firms have to at least live up to customers' expectations.

When it comes to 'value-added qualities' in the hotel business, however, things may look complicated. Value-added qualities can be many things, limited only by our creativity and imagination. The main thing is to think about the customer's requirements and not one's own product.

Examples of typical value-added qualities are personal welcome cards in the hotel room, the morning paper every day, fruit, chocolates etc. although these do tend to be taken for granted these days. Another example is that the hotel provides a service which has nothing to do with the hotel's main business of providing accommodation, e.g. advising about traffic conditions, entertainment requirements (e.g. always being able to get hold of theatre tickets) and the creation of a home-like atmosphere (e.g. the possibility to cook your own meals). In most cases, 'value-added quality' has an enormous effect on customer satisfaction, while costs are often minimal. It is therefore foolish not to try to give the customer more than he/she expects. At the same time, however, one must remember that 'value-added quality' is not a static concept – after a while, 'value-added qualities' become expected qualities. Customers always expect more and only those firms which understand this dynamism will survive in the longer term.

'Proportional quality' or 'one-dimensional quality' is more straight-forward. If the product or service – or an attribute of a product or service – lives up to some agreed physical condition then satisfaction for some people will be the result and if not, dissatisfaction will become the consequence. Taking the hotel business once again, the variety of the breakfast may be an example of proportional quality. It should be noticed, however, that what is proportional quality to one customer may be regarded as expected or value-added quality by another customer.

Previously this 'one-dimensional quality view' was the most dominat-ing and this is the reason why quality management was also more simple than it is today. Today the customers are more complicated and this is one of the reasons why quality and TQM have become so important.

The last two types of quality – 'indifferent quality' and 'reverse quality' – are also straightforward and easy to understand in theory. As both types of quality may be important to identify in practice we will discuss them below.

Any product or service consists of a large number of quality attributes and some of the customers will always be indifferent if a specific attribute is or is not inherent in the product. This is the characteristic of 'indifferent quality'.

For some specific quality attributes we sometimes experience that customers become dissatisfied if the attribute is inherent in the product/service and the customers become satisfied if it is not. It is seen that these attributes have a reverse effect on customer satisfaction. This is the reason why Kano calls this type of 'quality' attribute 'reverse quality'.

Walt Disney Corporation is one of the firms to have incorporated some of the new concepts of quality in its definition of 'quality service'

(Dahlgaard, Kristensen and Kanji, 1994, p. 5): 'Attention to detail and exceeding our guests' expectations'.

Disney gives the following explanation of the importance of this definition:

- Our guests are considered to be VIPs – very important people and very individual people, too. What contributes to Disney's success is people serving people. It is up to us to make things easier for our guests.
- Each time our guests return, they expect more. That is why attention to detail and VIP guest treatment is extremely important to the success of the Disney Corporation.

These definitions and explanations are not only relevant for the Disney Corporation. They are as relevant for any firm, whether they are production firms or service firms. The customers, including the internal customers, are the starting point of all quality efforts.

However, while internal customers and internal processes are very important, one must never lose sight of the fact that, in the final analysis, the main purpose of focusing on internal customers is to create satisfied external customers.

Unfortunately, in their eagerness to improve the processes, many firms totally forget their external customers, which a 1989 Gallup Survey of American corporate leaders, undertaken for the American Society for Quality Control, clearly shows. The main results of the survey, which reports on the best methods of improving quality, are shown in Table 4.1 below.

Astonishingly, all the most important methods focus on internal processes. Not one of the methods concern relations to the external customers. This carries the considerable risk that despite vastly improving its internal quality, the firm will still lose market position. If the

Table 4.1 Quality improvement methods of American corporate managers (1989)

Area	%
1. Motivation	86
2. Leadership	85
3. Education	84
4. Process control	59
5. Improvement teams	55
6. Technology	44
7. Supplier control	41
8. Administrative support	34
9. Inspection	29

Source: American Society for Quality Control.

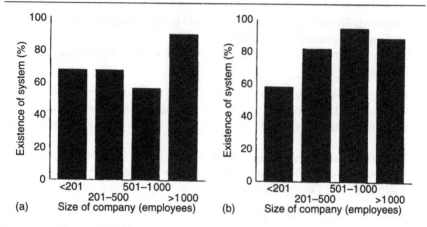

Fig. 4.3 System to check customer satisfaction. (a) West developed; (b) East developed.

company wants to survive in the longer term, improved internal quality must be accompanied by improved external quality. Internal and external quality will be discussed further in section 4.4.

The overall conclusion of this section is that one must always ensure the customer's satisfaction. Satisfied customers today are a condition for a satisfactory business result tomorrow. It is therefore imperative that firms establish the means to check customer satisfaction. On this score, Western firms leave a lot to be desired. This can be seen from the international survey on the use of TQM (the QED project), from which the above figures on the existence of systems for continuous monitoring of customer satisfaction are taken (Figure 4.3).

From Figure 4.3 it is seen that in general the level in the East is higher than the level in the West apart from small companies. No less than 86% of the large companies in the East report to have a system for monitoring customer satisfaction. In the West the figure is 73% and we find corresponding differences for the other sizes of groups except for the small companies. The results in the samples have not been weighted with the number of manufacturing companies in the different countries. Had this been the case we would have seen even larger differences than the ones reported in Figure 4.3.

4.3 FOCUS ON FACTS

Knowledge of customers' experiences of products and services is essential before the processes necessary for creating customer satisfaction can be improved. More and more firms are therefore coming to the conclusion that, to realize the TQM vision, they must first set up a system for the continuous measurement, collection and reporting of quality facts.

Milliken has written the following about the importance of quality measurements (Dahlgaard, Kristensen and Kanji, 1994):

Before you start to change anything, find out where you are now! Or, put another way:

The quality process starts with measurements

What the Danish Milliken organization was being told, in fact, was that the firm's future operations should be based on facts, not beliefs and opinions. This was echoed by Peter Hørsman, managing director, who declared that, from now on, guesswork was out, adding that 1 measurement was better than 10 opinions.

What kind of measurements are needed then? In this book we will deal briefly with three main groups:

1. External customers' satisfaction (CSI = Customer Satisfaction Index).
2. Internal customers' satisfaction (ESI = Employee Satisfaction Index).
3. Other quality measurements of the firm's internal processes, often called 'quality checkpoints' and 'quality control points'.

These three main groups are taken from the following proposal for a new classification of quality measurements. This proposal is a logical outcome of the expanded concept of quality implicit in TQM and is also an element of the European Quality Award.

As Table 4.2 shows, the measurements are divided according to both the party concerned and whether the measurement concerns the process or the final result. This is because, on the one hand, TQM is basically process-oriented while, on the other hand, the processes and results depend on the party concerned.

Traditionally, managers have mainly measured the firm's business result. The problem with this, however, is that it is retrospective, since the business result only gives a picture of past events. What is needed is a number of forward-looking measurements connected with the business result.

Focus on the customer and the employee is the cornerstone of TQM. It is only natural, therefore, that both employee and customer satisfaction

Table 4.2 Quality measurements: the expanded concept

	Firm	Customer	Society
Process	Employee satisfaction	Control and checkpoints	External checkpoints (environmental, political, social)
Result	Business result	Customer satisfaction	Ethical/social accounting

are included as quality goals. Satisfied customers and satisfied employees are prerequisites for a good business result, as are, of course, solid and dependable products and services. There is therefore a need for control and checkpoints in the processes the firm is built around. Finally, the firm's result will be a function of its general reputation in society. This is reported in both the ethical/social accounting and in relevant external checkpoints in, e.g. the environmental and social areas.

Many corporate managers are sceptical about the need for measurements. They find them unnecessary, time-consuming and bureaucratic, relying instead on the STINGER principle:

$$
\begin{aligned}
\text{ST} &= \text{STrength} \\
\text{IN} &= \text{INtuition} \\
\text{G} &= \text{Guts} \\
\text{E} &= \text{Experience} \\
\text{R} &= \text{Reason}
\end{aligned}
$$

While STINGER is undoubtedly useful to any manager, the complexity and dynamics of today's markets make it necessary to supplement STINGER with other skills than those which were sufficient only a decade ago. Furthermore, measurements are, in themselves, both a challenge and a motivation to achieve quality. Who could imagine playing a football match without goals?

In short we recommend below the combination of STINGER, Data and Methods:

STINGER + Data + Methods = MBF (Management By Facts)

As we see it, success with TQM implementation depends on all elements of this equation.

4.3.1 MEASUREMENT OF CUSTOMER SATISFACTION

Total quality, as experienced by the customer, consists of a large number of different elements, one example of which is shown in Figure 4.4 below.

It can be seen from the above that the customer's experience of the quality of a product or service is the result of a large number of stimuli relating to both the product itself, the services and the circumstances under which it is delivered to the customer. The customer's satisfaction must therefore be measured in many different dimensions (quality parameters) if it is to form the basis of quality improvements.

When measuring customers' satisfaction it is important to realize that the importance of the different quality parameters varies. We assume, therefore, that the customers evaluate the firm on n different dimensions or sub-areas, both as regards the quality of individual areas and the

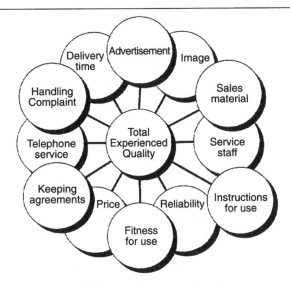

Fig. 4.4 Total experienced quality.

importance of these areas. We let the resulting evaluation for the ith sub-area be C_i and the associated importance W_i. Overall customer satisfaction – the Customer Satisfaction Index, or CSI – can then be calculated as a simple weighted average:

$$\text{CSI} = W_1 C_1 + W_2 C_2 + \cdots + W_n C_n \qquad (4.1)$$

The main use of this index is to provide the company with an instrument to choose the vital dimensions of customer satisfaction and to allocate resources to these areas. More on this subject in Chapter 10.

4.3.2 MEASURING EMPLOYEE SATISFACTION

The internal customer/supplier relationship is all-important in TQM. Being able to satisfy external customers depends on having satisfied internal customers or, as Imai (1986) puts it:

> When you talk about quality, you immediately tend to think about product quality. Nothing could be further from the truth. In TQM, the main interest is in 'human quality'. To instil quality into people has always been fundamental to TQM. A firm that manages to build quality into its employees is already half way towards the goal of making quality products. The three building blocks of any business are hardware, software, and 'humanware'. TQM starts with 'humanware'. Only when the human aspects have been taken care of can the firm start to consider the hardware and software

aspects. To build quality into people is synonymous with helping them to become KAIZEN-conscious.

One of the main control points of 'human quality' is employee satisfaction, which should be measured and balanced in the same way as customer satisfaction. The details on measuring employee satisfaction will be explained in Chapter 11.

4.3.3 QUALITY CONTROL POINTS AND QUALITY CHECKPOINTS

Any firm can be described as a collection of connected processes producing some 'result' or other – either input to subsequent processes (the internal customers) or output to external customers. We can measure the quality of the result of any process, i.e. ascertain whether we are satisfied with a particular result. When measuring the quality of a process result, we say that we have established a '**quality control point**'.

Examples of important quality control points vary with the type of company concerned and thus also with the process or function concerned. Furthermore, the processes can be described and thus considered, in more or less detail. A firm can be seen as a process which, on the basis of input from suppliers, produces one type of output (the finished products) for external customers. This output thus becomes the only potential quality control point in the firm.

This way of looking at things is insufficient in connection with TQM, however. TQM, as mentioned above, is process-oriented, which means that management and employees must be aware of, and deal with, the many defects/problems in the internal processes and, in particular, with their causes. The most common internal quality measurement that can be used as a control point in most processes is:

> Total defects per unit
> = number of defects/number of units produced or tested

This internal quality measurement, which can be used in most firms and processes, has been used with great success at Motorola, as the following quote from *Motorola: Six Sigma Quality – TQC American Style* (1990, p. 12) shows:

> The most difficult problem which faced Motorola during this period (1981–86) was the fact that each organizational unit was free to define its own quality metrics. Within Motorola, a very decentralized company of many different businesses, it was a generally held belief

that each business was truly different, so it made sense that each knew the best way to measure quality for its business.

Because of the different way each business measured its quality level, it was nearly impossible for top management, in the normal course of conducting periodic operations reviews, to assess whether the improvement made by one division was equivalent to the improvement made by another. In fact, it was difficult for the manager of an operation to rate his quality level compared to that of another operation, because the measurements were in different terms. However, significant improvements were made regardless of the metric used.

During the second half of 1985 ... the Communications Sector established a single metric for quality, Total Defects per Unit. This dramatically changed the ease with which management could measure and compare the quality improvement rates of all divisions. For the first time it was easy for the general manager of one division to gauge his performance relative to the other divisions. They all spoke the same language.

The use of the common metric, Defects per Unit, at last provided a common denominator in all quality discussions. It provided a common terminology and methodology in driving the quality improvement process. The definition was the same throughout the company. A defect was anything which caused customer dissatisfaction, whether specified or not. A unit was any unit of work. A unit was an equipment, a circuit board assemble, a page of technical manual, a line of software code, an hour of labor, a wire transfer of funds, or whatever output your organization produced.

In his famous book *Kaizen*, Imai (1986) recommends supplementing quality control points with so-called *'quality check points'*. Imai also calls quality control points 'R criteria' (= result criteria), while he calls quality checkpoints 'P criteria' (= process criteria). These alternative names clearly describe the difference between quality control points and quality checkpoints.

While a quality control point measures a given process result, a quality checkpoint measures the state of the process. Of the many different states that can be measured, it is important to choose one, or a few, which can be expected to have an effect on the result. Process characteristics, which must be expected to cause the results of the process, are good potential quality checkpoints. Clearly, a quality control point for one process can also be seen as a quality checkpoint for another. Deciding which is which therefore depends on how one defines the concept of process. For example, employee satisfaction is a quality control point for the firm's human resource process, but a quality checkpoint for others.

Examples of quality measures other than employee satisfaction and customer satisfaction that can be used as quality control points or quality checkpoints are given in Chapter 12.

4.3.4 QUALITY COSTS

Traditionally, so-called quality costs have been divided into the following four main groups:

1. preventive costs;
2. inspection/appraisal costs;
3. internal failure costs;
4. external failure costs.

In the quality literature, it is often claimed that total quality costs are very considerable, typically between 10–40% of turnover. This is why these costs are also called 'the hidden factory' or 'the gold in the mine'. We believe these figures can be much higher, especially if invisible costs are taken into account.

Invisible costs are everywhere. This can easily be seen by looking at developments in quality cost theory from before 'the TQM age' to the present.

(a) Before TQM

Quality costs consisted of the costs of the quality department (including the inspection department), costs of scrapping, repairs and rework and cost of complaints.

Firms were aware of the above division of quality costs and understood that prevention was better than inspection and that an increase in preventive costs was the means of reducing total quality costs. Most firms, however, did not deal either systematically or totally (i.e. in all the processes in the firm) with these costs.

(b) 'The TQM age'

Total quality costs are defined as the difference between the firm's costs of development, production, marketing and supply of products and services and what the (reduced) costs would be in the absence of defects or inefficiencies in these activities. Put another way, total costs can be found by comparing the firm with 'the perfect firm' or 'the perfect processes'. In this sense, there is a close connection between the concept of quality cost and benchmarking.

There is also a close connection between quality control points and quality costs. In the previous section, a quality control point was defined as a result (output) of a process which management has decided to control and therefore measure. The result of any process is thus a potential quality control point. Since all firms consist of a large number of processes, there will be a similarly large number of potential control points. Each of the firm's processes can be compared with 'the perfect process' and all the potential control points can therefore be compared with the result of 'the perfect process'. If the difference between the result of the perfect process and the firm's present process result is valued in money, we get the process's contribution to the total quality costs. We can also call this the process's OFI (Opportunity For Improvement) measured in money. The OFIs of individual processes can best be determined either at the time of the annual quality audit or during the year when the quality improvement teams choose new quality problems to solve. This will be discussed further in section 14.4.

It can easily be seen from the above that a large part of the total quality costs is invisible. Only a small part appears in the firm's accounting systems. This is the reason why 'The Quality Journey' calls for a new classification of quality costs. The division, which takes account of 'the invisible cost', is shown in Table 4.3.

Table 4.3 shows that total costs can be classified according to internal and external costs on the one hand and visible and invisible quality costs on the other. In Table 4.3, we have classified total costs into six groups. The question marks indicate that apart from the visible costs (1 + 2), the size of the individual cost totals is unknown.

Visible costs are costs which the firm has decided to record. In both theory and practice, the criterion for whether a cost should be recorded or not is that the benefit of doing so is greater than the costs involved. In this connection, the processes' estimated contribution to the total quality costs is a good starting point in deciding whether it is worthwhile measuring and recording a potential control point.

Table 4.3 A new classification of the firm's quality costs

	Internal costs	External costs	Total
Visible costs	1a. Scrap/repair costs 1b. Preventive/ appraisal costs	2. Guarantee/ *ex gratia* costs (complaints)	1 + 2
Invisible costs	3a. Loss of efficiency due to poor quality/ bad management 3b. Preventive/ appraisal costs	4. Loss of goodwill due to poor quality/ bad management	3 + 4 (?)
Total	1 + 3 (?)	2 + 4 (?)	1 + 2 + 3 + 4 (?)

In contrast to opinions from many writers, our view is that it is neither possible nor economically justifiable to determine total quality costs by expanding the recordings. There is therefore a need for other methods. One method is to compare oneself with one's most profitable competitor. This is a form of benchmarking, where the ratio 'ordinary financial result' is used in the comparison. This and other methods will be explained in Chapter 14.

4.4 CONTINUOUS IMPROVEMENTS

The importance of continuous improvements has by now been amply illustrated. Masaaki Imai's world-famous book *Kaizen*, written in 1986, focused precisely on this aspect of TQM. In this book, Imai presented an interesting, but also singular, definition of quality. He simply defined quality as 'everything which can be improved '. From a Western point of view, this sounds a bit extreme.

The interesting thing is, however, that the Japanese (or, at any rate, Imai) apparently see a very close connection between quality and the concept of improvement which is, in fact, an important message in TQM (Dahlgaard, Kristensen and Kanji, 1994, p. 45): 'A way can always be found to achieve higher quality at lower cost.'

Higher quality both should and can be achieved through:

1. internal quality improvements
2. external quality improvements.

The main aim of internal quality improvements is to make the internal processes 'leaner', i.e. to prevent defects and problems in the internal processes which will lead to lower costs.

As their name suggests, external quality improvements are aimed at the external customer, the aim being to increase customer satisfaction and thereby achieve a bigger market share and with it, higher earnings.

Both types of improvements are closely connected with the questions top management asks at the annual quality audit. These questions, together with the answers, are not only important in connection with the quality audit. The whole exercise should gradually develop to become an integral part of the company's quality culture, with the questions being regularly asked by all employees in all departments and all employees actively participating in answering them by suggesting quality improvements. The two types of quality improvements are shown in Figure 4.5. As the figure shows, both types of quality improvements – which should not be seen independently of each other – result in higher profits. This fact led to Phil Crosby's (1982) famous observation that 'quality is free'. Only poor quality is expensive.

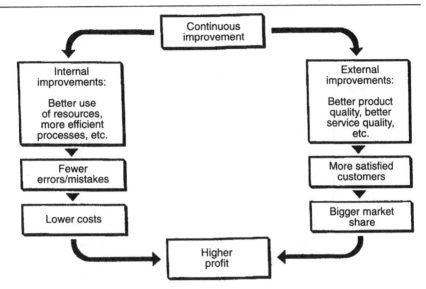

Fig. 4.5 Continuous improvements and their consequences.

Developing ideas for quality improvements is one of the approaches which gives the biggest return on investment. If the firm approaches the quality improvement process in the right way, a return of several hundred per cent would not be unusual.

Fukuda (1983, p. 133) has shown that the number of quality improvement suggestions from employees should be a very important quality measure in all firms. In 1978, Ryuji Fukuda received the prestigious Deming Award for his contributions to the improvement of quality and productivity. In the 1970s, Fukuda analysed the huge variation in productivity between the plants which together made up Sumitomo Electric Co. By collecting and analysing more than 30 variables which could possibly explain the variation in productivity growth, Fukuda was able to show that the most explanatory ones were:

1. Number of suggestions for improvements per employee per year.
2. Investment in machines, tools etc. per employee-year.

The results were presented in the model shown in Figure 4.6 below, with the number of improvement proposals per employee on the x axis and investments in machines, tools etc. on the y axis. The curve shows the possible combinations which, according to the empirical model, achieve a given productivity growth.

As an example the model shows that a particular plant has had a 20% growth in productivity and that this growth was achieved by means of an average of 3.2 employee suggestions per year and an investment of

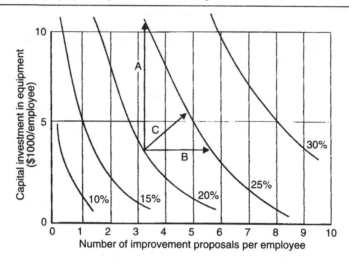

Fig. 4.6 A model to explain the productivity growth.

$3500 per employee-year. The model also shows that, if the firm wants to increase productivity by, e.g. 25%, there are various ways of achieving it. The figure shows three ways: A (increase capital investment per employee-year by about $7500), B (increase the number of suggestions per employee-year by about 2.5) and C (increase the number of suggestions by about 1.7 and capital investment by about $2500). The best way is normally a balanced compromise (e.g. C) between the two extreme points A and B.

It can also be seen from the model that, for the firm in question, the effect of increasing the number of suggestions per employee-year by one is the same as an increase in capital investment of $3000. The effect of both the suggested improvements and the capital injection depends, of course, on the starting point, i.e. the level of technology and management in the firm concerned. The number of suggested improvements per employee-year is in itself a reflection of the managerial level in the firm. This is why the number of suggested quality improvements is increasingly being used as an indicator of management quality.

While the model in Figure 4.6 should be seen as a general model, the message is still absolutely valid. This is that firms wanting to increase productivity growth have a very important alternative to the traditional approach of investing in new technology. This alternative is that firms increase their investments in education and training, so that all employees are motivated to make suggestions for improvements. Some Danish companies have already started along this path, e.g. Milliken, which has a target of 26 suggestions for improvement per employee in 1996 (see Chapter 19).

Education and training are only two, albeit necessary, conditions for the involvement of the firm's employees. They are far from sufficient. However, continuous improvements also require 'leadership', which was also part of the TQM pyramid. Without this solid foundation, the four sides of the 'pyramid' will never be built.

4.5 EVERYBODY'S PARTICIPATION

As previously mentioned, TQM is process-oriented. Customers, including internal customers (i.e. the firm's employees), are part of the firm's processes. These customers, together with their requirements and expectations, must be identified in all the processes. The next step is to plan how these requirements and expectations can be fulfilled. This requires feedback from the customers, so that their experiences and problems become known in all processes. This feedback is a condition for the continuous improvement of both products and processes. For this to be effective, it seems only common sense that everybody should participate.

However, things are not this simple. To get everybody to participate demands the education and motivation of both management and employees. The firm's management must get involved in as many education and training activities as possible. In our view, the active participation of top management in the annual quality audit is an important part of these activities, the effect of which will quickly filter down throughout the organization. Department managers will make demands on middle managers, who will make demands on their subordinates and so on down the hierarchy. Deming's seventh point of his plan to implement TQM (section 2.1) will be a natural consequence of the diffusion of the quality message: 'Management must ensure that every employee in the company participates actively in a team (work team, quality circle).'

These work teams are an important and indispensable part of the firm's quality organization and Japanese experiences (Lillrank, 1988) show that, to make sure that work teams start making improvements as quickly as possible, it may be necessary to establish a parallel quality organization (Deming, 1982, point 4): 'Management must, as quickly as possible, build up an organization to advise on the carrying out of continuous improvements throughout the firm.'

Through its active and committed participation in the quality audit and by making the necessary organizational changes, management has thus shown a leadership wholly in keeping with the Japanese definition of leadership, which is shown in Figure 4.7 below.

To sum up, leadership in Japanese means 'guidance by powerful education and training'.

SHI	DOU	RYOKU
Guidance	Guidance	Strength
Finger	Education	Power
	Training	

Fig. 4.7 Leadership in Japanese.

To realize the TQM vision, management must believe 'that it will help' to involve all employees. The next condition is that management also invests in the education and training of all employees at all levels in:

1. Identifying defects and problems.
2. Finding the causes of defects and problems.
3. Prevention, i.e. preventing the causes of defects and problems. A condition for effective prevention is that employees have completed points 1 and 2 and that, on the basis of a causal analysis, they make suggestions for and implement quality improvements.
4. Start again.

The thing that often prevents employees from participating in even a simple quality improvement process, such as the one outlined above, is that most employees in Western firms, including management, lack both knowledge of and training in the use of quality tools. There is a crying need for massive educational and training programmes to equip management and employees with both the knowledge and the motivation to want to go through the above quality improvement process again and again.

The above-mentioned parallel organization calls for additional comments. Figure 4.8 shows a general model for this parallel organization.

It can be seen from the figure that the parallel organization is extremely well organized but not as a part of the formal organizational structure. At the top of the parallel organization is the firm's overall steering committee for TQM and under this, the quality improvement teams. If the firm is divided up into divisions, then the next level would be a divisional steering committee. Under this, a department co-ordinator for quality improvement is appointed for each department. It will often be a good idea for each department to train a number of

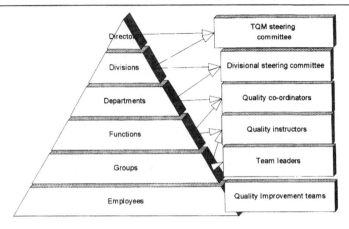

Fig. 4.8 The parallel quality organization.

quality instructors whom succeeding levels can draw on. Employees in the individual departments are organized in quality improvement teams or quality circles, each team having a team leader either chosen by the team or appointed by management.

The powers and responsibilities of the quality organization are as follows:

1. To set meaningful and ambitious quality goals for the individual team/employees. This is done is close co-operation with the teams/ employees who fulfil the goals.
2. To ensure that quality improvements are started and implemented in all parts of the organization, both by top-down and bottom-up initiatives. Quality improvement suggestions can come both from quality improvement teams and individual employees. The annual and three-year plans ensure that the improvements do not peter out.

In order to fulfil this responsibility, all tasks, schedules etc. for individual employees and co-ordinators must be described in detail.

All of the firm's managers and employees have a role in the new quality organization. The only problem is who to appoint to the various steering committees and who to appoint as department co-ordinators.

The managing director ought to be the leader of the overall steering committee. The other members can be the leaders of the various divisional steering committees, plus the firm's quality manager if it has one. The leaders of the divisional steering committees can be the divisional managing directors but they can also be one of the other managers. The reason for this is simple – the divisional managing directors often have not got the time. This is actually one of the reasons why it is necessary to build up a parallel quality organization. However, divisional managing directors ought to be members of the steering committee. On account of the time problem, departmental managers should not also be departmental co-ordinators. These co-ordinators can also be part of the divisional steering committee. It is up to the departmental co-ordinator to ensure that all employees in the various departments belong to a quality improvement team.

When the various positions in the quality organization have been filled, the quality journey, i.e. fulfilment of the TQM vision, can begin. The organization consists of small, permanent quality improvement teams in each department, together with cross-organizational and/or cross-hierarchical 'task forces', which can either be permanent or *ad hoc*. The quality improvement teams report to the overall quality co-ordinator, who in turn reports to the quality committee.

Both managing directors, departmental managers and ordinary employees work on equal terms in the quality improvement teams and they all strive to find common solutions to quality improvement problems. The construction of the quality organization resembles Likert and Seashore's (1962) 'team-oriented organization plan', shown in the form of a general model in Figure 4.9.

Likert's idea was that the formal organization should be built up after the team-oriented organization plan. The parallel quality organization, on the other hand, as the name suggests, does not change the formal organization plan. This is one of several advantages of this organizational form. It can be difficult to make changes in the formal organization and above all it takes time. The parallel organization, which often operates on its own conditions, solves this problem. The parallel organization is a mixture between a formal and an informal organizational form.

The smallest units of the quality organization are the permanent quality improvement teams. These teams have a great deal of freedom to choose the problems, or OFIs (Opportunities For Improvements), they want and even have the freedom to suggest solutions. It is up to the

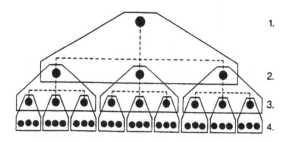

Fig. 4.9 The team-orientated organization plan. 1 = top manager; 2 = department managers; 3 = middle managers; 4 = operators, supervisors and other employees.

overall quality organization to make sure that the teams are working effectively and to ensure that they receive the necessary education and training in such elementary quality methods as:

- brainstorming
- cause-and-effect diagrams
- pareto diagrams
- affinity diagrams
- flow charts.

After they have received the necessary education, employees can begin training. The best form of training is to use the techniques on the problems the teams want to solve, i.e. training is job-oriented. This is the best guarantee that the quality journey will be embarked on. There will be more about education for quality in Chapter 18.

To close this section, we present some results from the QED survey. This focuses on various methods of ensuring that quality improvement suggestions are followed up and developed in the firm.

One of the aims of the afore-mentioned QED project is to understand the different methods used in different cultures to motivate employees to make suggestions for improving quality. We therefore put the following question to the participating companies: How do you ensure that your employees actively contribute with suggestions?

There were six main groups of answers:

- monetary rewards
- standards for number of suggestions
- prizes
- competitions
- education/training
- bonus systems.

The results appear in Figure 4.10.

Figure 4.10 shows that there are considerable differences between East and West. In the first four groups, Eastern firms have a much higher percentage of answers than Western firms, while in group 5 (education) and group 6 (bonus systems) the Eastern companies only have a slightly higher percentage of answers. The most noteworthy difference is in group 2 (standards), group 1 (monetary rewards) and group 3 (prizes).

Using standards for handling suggestions and for the number of suggestions per employee is practically non-existent in the West and using prizes to motivate employees is also relatively rare in these countries. An important observation, which cannot be seen from the figure, is that all Japanese companies reported that they used prizes as a motivator to ensure that the employees actively contribute with making suggestions.

The differences shown in Figure 4.10 are partly a result of cultural differences and partly a result of differences in management philosophies. Many employees in Eastern countries work in quality circles which is not the case in Western countries. With the use of quality circles, it is only natural to use the four methods which have the greatest differences. Interestingly, the least developed country (Estonia), which is not included in Figure 4.10, has the highest percentage in group 6 (bonus systems), while Japan has the lowest percentage in this group. Our explanation for this is that the more developed a country becomes and the more it uses quality management methods and principles, the less important bonus systems are as motivators.

Another observation is that there is, in most cases, a clear relationship between the use of motivators and the size of the company. It appears that the use of standards in the East becomes more and more necessary as the size of the company increases. This relationship is, of course, not surprising since the need for systems grows as a company becomes bigger. What is surprising, however, is that we do not observe such a relationship in the West.

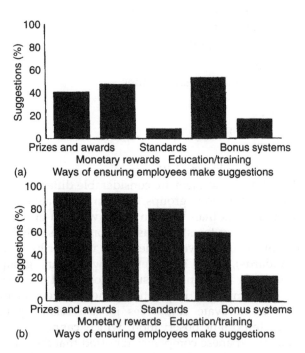

Fig. 4.10 Quality suggestions in East and West. (a) West developed; (b) East developed.

REFERENCES

Crosby, P.B. (1982) *Quality is Free*, The New American Library Inc., New York, USA.

Dahlgaard, J., Kristensen, K. and Kanji, G.K. (1995) *The Quality Journey – A Journey Without An End*, Productivity Press (India) Pvt. Ltd, Madras, India.

Deming, W.E. (1982) *Quality, Productivity and Competitive Position*, MIT, USA.

Feigenbaum, A.V. (1960) *Total Quality Control*, McGraw-Hill, New York, USA.

Fukuda, R. (1983) *Managerial Engineering*, Productivity Inc., Stanford, USA.

Imai, M. (1986) *KAIZEN – The Key to Japan's Competitive Success*, The Kaizen Institute Ltd, London.

Kano, N. (1984) Attractive quality and must be quality. *Quality,* **14**(2), 10–17.

Kondo, Y. (1991) *Human Motivation: A Key Factor for Management*, 3A Corporation, Tokyo, Japan.

Likert, R. and Seashore, S.E. (1962) Making Cost Control Work. *Harvard Business Review,* Nov./Dec., 10–14..

Lillrank, P.M. (1988) *Organization for Continuous Improvement – Quality Control Circle Activities in Japanese Industry* (PhD thesis), Helsingfors, Finland.

Motorola (1990) *Six Sigma Quality – TQC American Style*, Motorola, USA.

Womack, J.P., Jones, D. and Roos, D. (1990) *The Machine that Changed the World*, MIT, USA.

Quality management systems and standardization

5

5.1 THE CONCEPT OF SYSTEM

In recent years the term 'system' in TQM has become closely associated with documenting internal organizational processes which are repeatedly performed in such a way as to gain certification from an external validating body. Here we refer to such 'systems' as ISO 9000 and BS 5750. But the term 'system' has another broader connotation, a connotation which found favour during the development of TQM. It is upon 'system' in this wider, original meaning that emphasis is now placed.

Kanji *et al.* (1993) suggested that the origin of a system approach can be traced to the analogy drawn between the human body and simple, human society. The initial use made of the concept of system in social anthropology was further developed in sociology by such writers as Talcott Parsons before making its appearance in management writings. In its most basic form, a system can be portrayed thus:

Input – Throughput – Output
(transformation)

To add complexity, a feedback loop can be added to link output to input and thus to reactivate the system into another cycle.

It is important to note that a system approach contains a set of assumptions which are inherent within the model. The message is simple: use the model, accept the assumptions. The assumptions can be stated as follows:

- a number of more or less interrelated elements each of which contributes to the maintenance of the total system;
- synergy, in that the totality of the system is greater than the sum of its component elements;

- a boundary, which delineated the system and which may be open, partially open or closed in relation to exchanges between the system and its environment;
- sub-systems, comprising interrelations between particular elements within the total system and which themselves have the characteristics of a system;
- a flow or process throughout the system;
- feedback, which serves to keep the system in a state of dynamic equilibrium with respect to its environment.

The system approach in this wider, original sense and its application to the productive process can, e.g. be seen in Deming's work (1986) (Figure 5.1).

Indeed, it is feasible to contend that it was through the utilization of a system model that Deming's contribution to the development of TQM was born and permitted the delineation of the Deming Cycle of 'PLAN, DO, CHECK, ACT'.

5.2 QUALITY MANAGEMENT SYSTEMS

If a synthesis is attempted of the philosophical and system components of TQM with a view to the development of a model of implementation which encapsulates both of those key aspects, then, the following is offered as one way in which that might be brought to fruition (Figure 5.2).

Some explanation is required of the terms used in the above model.

Vision: refers to the future desired state, the situation which is being sought, to which the organization and its personnel are committed. It provides a central focus against which the managerial process of planning, leading, organizing and controlling can be co-ordinated. Its

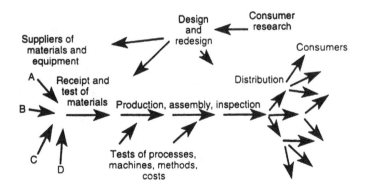

Fig. 5.1 System approach to the productive process.

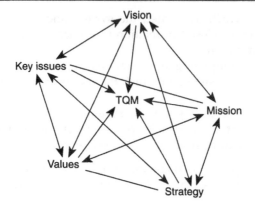

Fig. 5.2 Philosophy and system components of TQM. (Source: Kanji, Morris and Haigh, 1993.)

acceptance serves to give purpose day-to-day actions and activities at all organizational levels and to all organizational functions.

Mission: represents a series of statements of discrete objectives, allied to vision, the attainment of all of which will ensure the attainment of the future desired state which is itself the vision.

Strategy: comprises the sequencing and added specificity of the mission statements to provide a set of objectives which the organization has pledged itself to attain.

Values: serve as a source of unity and cohesion between the members of the organization and also serve to ensure congruence between organizational actions and external customer demands and expectations. Without such congruence no organization can expect to attain efficiency, effectiveness and economy let alone ensure its long-term survival.

Key issues: these are issues which must be addressed in pursuit of the quality which is demanded by customers to meet their needs and expectations.

The understanding of quality systems depends on two areas of thinking. Firstly, the understanding of Total Quality Management and secondly, the general understanding of system.

In his recent works (1986, 1993) Dr Deming was advocating very strongly the concept of 'profound knowledge' which shared the vision of system concept. In 1991, Senge advocated the development of learning organizations. According to him, system thinking plays a very important role in creating a learning organization. Here systems is a network of interrelated factors that work together to achieve the goal of the system.

According to us, an organization is a system, the goal of which is to create value-added activities for both internal and external customers.

Sometimes value chains have been used to obtain the borderlines of the local system (sub-system) but it can be seen that the local system is merely part of a larger system consisting of customers, suppliers, competitors and other aspects of the market and the society. In order to be successful it is therefore necessary to understand both the local system and a much bigger system. Senge (1991) has discussed a number of systems in order to help the readers understand the complexity of the system that exists in real life. According to Senge, developing a learning organization requires not only human mastery, teamwork, shared vision and image building, but also system thinking.

System thinking is also an important aspect of 'profound knowledge' and profound knowledge further incorporates theory of knowledge, theory of psychology and statistical thinking.

To sum up, the quality system can be looked at as a system which provides a high quality of activities incorporating TQM philosophy, principles and concepts and which creates added value to every aspect of an organization.

5.3 JOHARRY'S NEW WINDOW ON STANDARDIZATION AND CAUSES OF QUALITY FAILURES

Joharry's 'new window' is a diagram for classification of failures and causes of failures. The diagram was developed in a manufacturing company in Japan but the conclusions and the experience gained in this company are valid to both service companies and manufacturing companies. The conclusions were as follows:

1. Standardization is the basis of continuous improvements.
2. Standardization only is not sufficient. It may take a while before the standard methods for control and prevention of defects are in fact practised by everybody they concern.
3. Communication and motivation is the basis for everybody to practise the standardized methods and is also the basis for everybody trying continuously to improve existing standards.
4. There is no reason to try to find better methods before the existing know-how is being used by everybody it concerns.

The title of this section implies that Joharry had several windows. Who is Joharry and how do these 'windows' look? According to Fukuda (1983, p. 47) the name Joharry is an acronym made from the two names Joseph and Harry and Joharry's 'window' (the old window) was applied by Joseph Ruft and Harry Ingram to describe the communication between two persons (you and I). Joharry's window can be seen in Table 5.1.

Table 5.1 Joharry's window

You \ I	Know	Do not know
Know	I	II
Do not know	III	IV

We see that, in fact, Joharry's window consists of four small windows:

1. The first 'window' (category I) refers to what both you and I know.
2. The second 'window' (category II) refers to what I know and you do not know.
3. The third 'window' (category III) refers to what you know and I do not know.
4. The fourth 'window' (category IV) refers to that which neither knows.

Ruft and Ingram used this model to explain the internal conditions of the mind and it is not difficult to apply the model for describing the communication problems which may occur between two persons who are successively classified in the above four categories.

In Sumitomo Electric Industries, the Japanese company, Fukuda worked with quality and quality improvements in the late 1970s and for many years it was a major problem for Fukuda and many others to find the general causes of poor quality. Joharry's 'window' gave Fukuda 'the key' to find some important general causes of poor quality and at the same time it became 'the key' to understanding why a relatively simple quality management tool called 'CEDAC' showed to be so efficient, which in fact it was. Before 'CEDAC' can be described, Joharry's 'new window' must be dealt with briefly (Figure 5.2).

We see that Joharry's 'new window' is a further development of the 'old window' as the model now contains nine 'windows' or categories in total.

The following explanation of the model is given by Fukuda (1983, p. 48):

1. The different categories represent interrelationship of the counterparts Section A and Section B. These terms can be used to refer to individuals, groups, teams, sections within the organization etc.
2. In the 'known-practised' column, the respective party already knows the right methods to prevent defects and also executes them correctly.
3. In the 'known-unpractised' column, the respective party knows the right methods but executes them insufficiently or not at all.

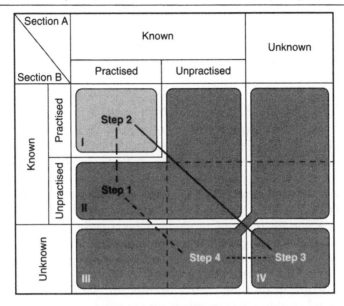

Fig. 5.3 Joharry's 'new window'. Step 1 = define the standard operation clearly and communicate it to all concerned; Step 2 = put into correct practice the established standard operation; Step 3 = improve the manufacturing method if a satisfactory quality level is not yet achieved; Step 4 = revise the standard operations.

4. In the 'unknown' column, the respective party does not yet know the right methods to prevent defects.
5. In category I, everyone in both parties knows and correctly practises the best and most effective operation known at any given time. All standard operations must be included in this category.
6. In category II, everyone in both parties is informed of the standard operations but there is someone who does not practise them correctly. This includes the case where someone fails to adhere to standard operations out of carelessness.
7. In category III, one party knows but the other party does not know the right operations for preventing defects.
8. In category IV, no one in either party knows the right techniques yet. The technical problems which cause defects remain unsolved in this category.

Through the development and use of Joharry's 'new window' it was realized that all previous measures for preventing failures could be explained as measures for transferring the categories II, III and IV to category I. This transfer can be made through the application of a basic quality improvement method consisting of four steps as shown in Figure 5.3. The importance of this method will be illustrated below.

In manufacturing companies as well as in service companies, you often hear the following excuses for failures and poor quality:

1. We have done our best but it is not possible to improve the quality further.
2. You cannot make an omelette without breaking eggs.
3. We must live with a certain number of failures.

When you start looking for the causes of defects in a serious way, it almost always turns out that the human factor is the main causal factor. This 'discovery' was also made by Fukuda in Sumitomo Electric Industries.

In order to understand the importance of this 'discovery', it was decided to use Joharry's 'new window' for the classification of all failures found in a certain plant of production for a certain period (January–February 1978). During the stated period, 165 failures were found, all produced in the plant in question. In order to make the classification of failures which best suited the problem, it was realized that the most reasonable 'group division' was a division in quality circle leaders on one side and quality circle members on the other.

The reason for this was that the employees in the specific production plant had created the so-called 'quality circles' (four in all), which had each appointed a 'quality circle leader'. The quality circles consisted of 6–8 employees within the same working area. The communication between the quality circle leader and the quality circle members had a crucial importance for the quality level of the processes for which the quality circles had responsibility and which the quality circles had taken on to improve.

For every failure found it was discussed whether both the quality circle leader as well as the quality circle members knew the cause of defect and in doing so, knew the method or methods which could be applied (practised) in order to prevent the failure found. Furthermore, it was discussed whether the methods were in fact practised by both quality circle leader and quality circle members. The result of this attempt to classify all failures found can be sen in Figure 5.4.

It appears that in the majority of cases, both the causes of failures and the preventing methods (the countermeasures) were known by a part of the employees. The number was exactly as shown in Table 5.2.

For the quality circle leaders a total number of 20 failures were classified under unknown causes/methods, whereas for the quality circle members a total of 81 failures were classified under unknown causes/ methods. It also appears that, to a large extent, neither the quality circle leaders nor the quality circle members practised the well-known methods for preventing failures. A total of 76 out of the 165 failures were classified in this 'class' (II).

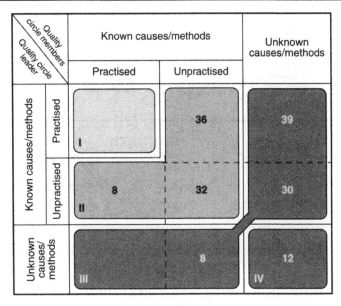

Fig. 5.4 Classification of failures made during the period January to February 1978.

Looking at this number of failures found, the importance of the four-step method for quality improvements indicated in Figure 5.3 was obvious to everybody. The problem was now to implement the method. For this purpose it turned out that the so-called 'CEDAC diagram' was very efficient.

CEDAC is an abbreviation of the 'Cause-and-Effect Diagram with Addition of Cards'. The diagram is a further development of the 'cause and effect diagram' typically used in quality improvements. An example of a cause and effect diagram can be seen in Figure 5.5.

The idea of this cause-and-effect diagram is that the 'causes' stated point at the 'effect' which means the quality problem, which you want to solve. In Figure 5.5 are indicated four main causes why the car will not start (man, materials, machine, method). These main causes must now be divided up into more specific sub-causes, e.g. a possible sub-cause may be a fault in the gas supply. Sub-causes are indicated as arrows pointing

Table 5.2 Number of causes of failures and the preventing methods

Category II	8 + 32 + 36	=	76
Category III	8 + 39 + 30	=	77
Total II + III		=	153

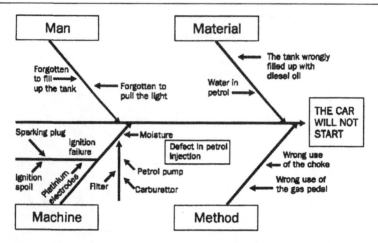

Fig. 5.5 An example of a cause-and-effect diagram (quality problem: the car will not start).

at the arrows from the main causes. The sub-causes may possibly be divided up further which is shown in the diagram by arrows pointing at the arrows from the main causes, e.g. the gas supply error is divided up in to three possible causes of defects (a defect at the filter, carburettor or gas pump).

The cause-and-effect diagram can be applied for analysing and thus for finding causes of quality defects or possible causes of other incidents than quality failures. In connection with brainstorming the diagram has proved to be a very efficient tool for teams (quality circles). In teamwork the problems are usually enlightened in several ways and in this way more ideas come up than one individual only may bring up, as a team has a larger experience pool than the single individual and team members can inspire one another to show more creativity.

Through the construction of the cause-and-effect diagram team members gain a deeper understanding of the causes creating poor quality. The idea is, of course, that team members become more motivated to control the causes stated in the diagram. In fact, the diagram 'invites' the team members to be creative as far as development of methods for controlling the specific causes are concerned.

However, there are more problems when the diagram is going to be used practically. Two of the main problems are:

1. Which causes are the main causes of failures and which control methods (prevention methods) are the most efficient?
2. The diagram does not contain any direct information about the methods to be applied for controlling each single cause of error.

The first problem is big enough as it is and shall be dealt with in Chapters 7 and 8. Suffice it to say that often people have a tendency of neglecting or refusing known methods because of the idea that a better method may be in existence. If we can find this 'better method' our quality problem will be solved. Therefore, much effort is used to find new and better methods, whereas quality problems may be better solved if the existing know-how was applied instead.

This was, in fact, one of the major problems in Sumitomo Electric Industries. The problem was that known methods were not efficiently communicated to the 'sections' who needed them. The method of communication was the well-known big manuals made for the various production processes in which the standard methods (production and control methods) were described. The problem with this communication method was, *inter alia*, that people forgot what was in the manual, or thought that each employee was perhaps 'wiser' than the manual and therefore developed their own home-made methods which may be better than the ones described in the manual. There are two main problems concerning such home-made methods:

1. The constructor believes that the method is at least just as good as the standard method although it may in fact be worse. The consequences of using the home-made method is that the quality gets poorer. This can get worse if other employees become 'infected', meaning that the home-made method turns into being the general method.
2. The home-made method is in fact better than the one described in the manual but the method is being used only by a limited number of people, possibly only by the person who has developed the method. Of course this is a waste of resources.

The second problem can be solved with the cause-and-effect diagram.

The solution in Sumitomo Electric Industries was that the individual quality circles were encouraged to add small cards to the causes in the diagram on which were written, in simple words, what the single quality circles or the single members considered was the best method for controlling the individual cause. When the cause-and-effect diagram was hung up in the various production processes, this method, which on the surface seemed rather common, acted as a very efficient communication tool. The employees working in production got a daily reminder about the causes of failures and which methods were most effective for controlling the causes of failures considering the knowledge they had. The effect of this new tool (the CEDAC diagram) was, *inter alia*, that in fact the employees started using the known knowledge. Besides CEDAC, another method also was introduced to improve quality, namely the so-called OET method. OET is an abbreviation of 'On the Error Training' and the idea of the method is that all shall learn from the failures which are made.

The joint effect of the CEDAC and OET methods measured on the number of failures found, appears by comparing Figure 5.6 with Figure 5.4. It can be seen that the number of failures found has dropped from 165 to 17. The production technology and the production level had remained practically unchanged!

In order to get a more general explanation of the success of the CEDAC diagram, 86 were selected at random from about the 300 CEDAC diagrams drawn until April 1978. The selected diagrams, and thus the selected quality circles, were divided into two groups. Group A consisted of the quality circles which did not find new methods during the use of CEDAC. Despite the fact that no new methods for improving the quality were found, the typical quality improvement was a 40–70% decrease of the percentage of failures (Figure 5.7a).

The explanation for this result was the one previously mentioned that, through the drawing of CEDAC and by looking daily at the CEDAC diagram, all quality circle members had the causes of failures and the already existing methods (standards) for controlling causes of failures repeated all over again. The result of this application of CEDAC was that the quality circle members started to use the existing but, for some

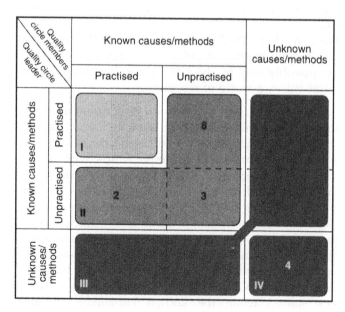

Fig. 5.6 Classification of failures made during the period January to February 1979.

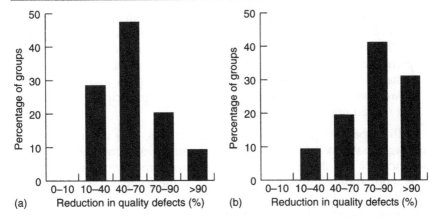

Fig. 5.7 Quality results by means of CEDAC (86 working groups selected at random). a = groups which focused their efforts only on adhering to established standards; b = groups which succeeded in finding new operation (production) methods. (Source: Fukuda, 1983.)

members, unknown methods. The use of CEDAC implied that the existing standards were communicated out to all quality circle members and they were – only by means of this communication – also motivated to observe the existing standards. The effect of this communication and motivation process can be seen in Figure 5.7a.

Group B consisted of the quality circles which first applied CEDAC as described above, meaning as the quality circles in Group A. The existing standards being communicated out and also adhered to in a satisfactory way, group A succeeded in finding improved methods for the control of the causes of failures through the use of CEDAC. The effect of these new methods and the effect of communication concerning CEDAC can be seen in Figure 5.7(b).

By comparing Figure 5.7b and Figure 5.7a, it can be seen that the joint effect in Figure 5.7b is of course the largest but the most important conclusion is that you must not think of developing new methods before you have succeeded in communicating and applying the known methods. This philosophy is the 'basic method for the improvement of quality' which appeared from Figure 5.2.

As indicated in the preface, the shown methods and results are not only of interest for quality management in manufacturing companies. The shown methods and results have equal importance in service companies and the results are not interesting only to the area of quality. Fukuda (1983, p. 51) says it indirectly in the following way:

Our method for transferring conditions in categories II, III, and IV to category I could have important implications for fields other than quality control. In a communications/information-oriented society, where knowledge and information play a key role, effective methods for perfecting channels of communication will be at a premium. Management in this society will have to provide a system in which all employees concerned with a given problem share necessary information and voluntarily participate in achieving shared objectives.

With respect to quality management systems, it is a very important message that a vital method of improving every company's quality, productivity and thus competitiveness is to improve communication and thus motivation within all departments of the company. The content of communication to each individual employee of the company is of course not unimportant. What every manager should be sure of is that every employee knows:

1. His or her own quality goals.
2. The causes of quality problems.
3. The necessary 'countermeasures', meaning the most efficient prevention.

The methods in item 3 above are the ones to be standardized and these are the methods which should form the backbone of the quality system in the company. These methods must not be static but should be continuously improved as soon as they are communicated out and practised by everybody they concern. Only if these conditions are fulfilled are the necessary conditions of quality production fulfilled.

When analysing the use of standardization in different countries we see that there is a big difference between East and West. In the West, many companies are sceptical towards the concept and hence they reject the concept as a management parameter. In the East, on the other hand, standardization is regarded as the entrance to quality improvement and hence the use of standardization is widespread in this area. The difference appears very clearly from Figure 5.8 below.

The use of standardization on the factory floor is almost twice as high in the East as in the West. When analysing the data more closely we find that this holds good whether the company is large or small or whether the country is developing or developed. One reason that standardization very often is rejected in the West is that it is believed to kill creativity. This assumption will be discussed more closely below.

5.4 STANDARDIZATION AND CREATIVITY

In section 5.3 we have presented strong arguments for standardization of work, i.e. standardization of operations (key procedures and methods) to follow until better methods have been developed. Even if we feel that the

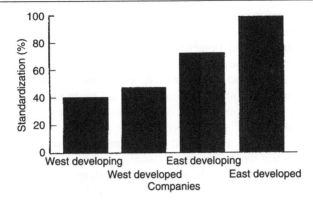

Fig. 5.8 The use of standards on the factory floor. (Source: QED study.)

arguments and results shown are strong enough to convince any manager, experience shows us that we should also analyse more deeply what standardization really is and what the relationship is between standardization and creativity. Standardization is misunderstood in many companies and because of that we too often meet objections towards it.

One of the objections is that standardization of work will kill creativity. Creative people in sales and product development especially use this argument. Another objection is that preparing standards is a complicated and difficult job and, at the end of the day, the standards are often not adhered to by the people concerned.

The problem of non-adherence is, in our view, caused by a lack of understanding of what work standards should include and what should not be included in the standards. The consequences may be that standards are made too complicated and hence are very difficult both to follow and to change. The standards act as barriers against continuous improvements instead of supporting improvements.

It is important to realize that standards may be set in various ways but it is also important – and may be more important – to realize that standards usually include the following three items (Kondo, 1991):

1. The objective of the work: taking a production process as an example, this includes the quality specifications or quality standards for the intermediate or final products which must be made in the process.
2. Constraints on carrying out the work: these consist of restrictions which must be adhered to in performing the work; items which ensure the safety of employees or assure product quality are the most important of these.
3. The means and methods to be employed in performing the work.

Item 1. above must always be achieved and therefore it is important to include this item in the work standard. Therefore it is also important to check and discuss the objectives of the many different processes – production as well as supporting processes – to secure that the objectives are existing, understood and accepted. In too many cases objectives are not existing, not understood and not accepted by the people responsible for the work or the people do not understand the objective and the relationship to items 2. and 3. above.

Item 2. must always be obeyed or adhered to by whoever is responsible for doing the work. There are usually no objections to including in the work standards items which ensure the safety of employees.

The objections may emerge on the items which have been included in order to assure product quality. The problem may be that too many of these items have been included in item 2. of the work standards and hence the workers feel that too many restrictions have been put on them. They do not feel responsibility because of the many restrictions and they feel that the work is not easy to do. It is therefore obvious that we should consider these constraints very carefully and we should strive to eliminate as many of them as possible. The fewer the restrictions listed under item 2. the greater the workers feel the degree of freedom and responsibility.

If we include restrictions in item 2. we must secure that they are well understood and accepted by everyone. The best guarantee for that is that the people concerned are involved in continuous quality improvements and hence the writing of the work standards. Then people know which restrictions are necessary to follow because they have understood the cause and effect relationships which must be controlled in order to assure quality. In other words they have realized which causes are crucial to control and which methods are crucial to follow.

Concerning item 3. there is a tendency to conclude that everybody must obey these standardization means and methods because they usually have been standardized after careful considerarion to quality and productivity. We often conclude that because they reflect existing know-how of the most effective means and methods everybody must adhere to these standards. But this is not necessarily true. We are convinced that no single standard method can be the most efficient for all people considering their different characteristics.

According to Kondo (1991) therefore the standardized means and methods in item 3. should be divided into two types or two manuals:

1. manual for beginners (novices);
2. manual for experienced workers.

The purpose of the manual for beginners is to help newcomers in their understanding and training. Newcomers have to understand and learn the basic rules and, if needed, the basic actions. Having understood, learned and practised the basic rules they are ready for experimentation, i.e. to find the best means and methods for themselves and they should be encouraged to do so.

The purpose of the manual for experienced workers is to have an updated collection of best practices in all areas of the company. Whenever an experienced worker finds a better way of performing a particular job this should be included in the work standards for experienced workers. It is extremely important that the management of the company establishes a system which secures that hints and ideas concerning new ways of doing things are collected and, if needed, included in the manual for experienced workers.

From this it is seen that this way of looking at standards will support creativity. It is of course necessary that management leads the process and encourages people to always be on the lookout for improvement of the standards. An existing standard should be a challenge for everybody.

In relation to ISO 9000 and other international standards it is apparent that items 1. and 2. mentioned above are well suited for certification while this is not necessarily true for all the elements mentioned under item 3.

5.5 ISO 9000 AND BS 5750 – A STEPPING STONE TO TQM?

5.5.1 ISO – A QUICK FIX

The ISO 9001 (BS 5750 part 1) requirements represent 20 qualified questions put to the company in order to determine the company's ability to control the specified quality agreed upon in a contract situation. Provided that the buyer is capable of expressing all his expectations for the delivery and putting them down in the contract, the 20 quality activities represented by ISO 9001 may create an excellent quality assurance for the buyer.

As a consequence of the importance of the basis on which a contract is made up and the faith in the quality assurance of the other 19 ISO 9001 requirements, the 'ISO people' are not necessarily interested in such vital areas as:

- vision and strategies;
- sales and marketing activities;
- customer satisfaction;
- management accounting;
- company culture and employee satisfaction;
- continuous improvement;
- technology;

- business ethics;
- impact on society.

If you build your quality management system narrow-mindedly on the ISO 9001, 9002 (BS 5750 part 2), or 9003 (BS 5750 part 3) standards, there is a big risk that the company will be divided up into two sections A and B. The 'A team' consists of the employees and activities influenced by 'ISO' and the 'B team' consists of the employees and the activities which are influenced by 'ISO' only to a limited degree. The sales and marketing function is often a significant example of one of the company's 'B teams' where quality management is concerned.

However, in many companies, to build a quality management system which alone is closely focusing on ISO 9001, 9002 or 9003 has turned out to be a barrier against subsequent quality development with everybody's participation.

ISO 9001, 9002 and 9003 represent a set of external standards for the assurance of the customer's interest (quality assurance). We have been familiar with such standards for decades, as a number of external quality standards flooded the international market in the time after the Second World War. The development of the standards had its root in the US military, space and atomic energy programmes but gradually any self-respecting country acquired its own standard.

The new and important characteristic about ISO 9000 has been the thought that the ISO series should represent the best among the numerous national, military and other standards used, which consisted either of one total standard (e.g. ANSI Z-1.15) or – as ISO 9000 – consisted of more standards divided up into levels (such as NATO's AQAP series and BS 5750). Canada was pretty much alone with its CSA Z299 standards in four levels but the Canadian quality standards, which were considered by many to be those most intensively prepared, were refused and instead BS 5750 was chosen as the foundation of ISO 9000 in 1987.

Whether the ISO 9000 series does represent the best from the previous standards is still a question to be answered as the first edition of the ISO 9000 from 1987 must in fact be seen as the 'compromise of the compromises', which had, as its superior goal, to create one series of standards which were internationally recognized. The international recognition of the ISO 9000 standards and the international co-operation between the certifying bodies of every country gives an ISO 9000 certification international importance.

An ISO 9000 certification is in the process of becoming a necessary driver's licence being internationally recognized. A driver's licence the credibility of which is dependent on at least three factors: the qualifications of those who give the certification, the check-list (the ISO standard) and the time reserved for the certification. The purpose of this section is to focus on the advantages and disadvantages of the spread of the ISO 9000 series seen in relation to the TQM strategy.

When we entitled this section 'ISO 9000 – a quick fix', it was not to detract from the long-standing efforts made by many companies to obtain an ISO 9000 certificate. The reason for the phrase 'a quick fix' has two elements. Firstly, it is possible to certify nearly every company within a few years once the money for it is granted. Secondly, there is a considerable risk – and we will go deeper into this later – that, once certified, the quality management system, which is orientated toward customers' demands, will be frozen and only improved concurrently with the improvements of the ISO 9000 standard.

However, we are of the opinion that an ISO certification used in a thoughtful way may be a useful step in a company's efforts 'to do things right' and thus contribute to the company's TQM development for which the goal is not only to do things right, but to do 'the right things'.

The ISO series is trying to quality assure the customer requirements specified in the contract. In other words, the company tries to do the things right which are specified in the contract. There are, however, two limitations in this 'philosophy'. One of them is that the customer is not always able to specify his real needs and the other is that customer requirements are dynamic and are therefore constantly developing. ISO 9000 does thus not necessarily assure that we do the right things.

The difference between an ISO 9000 certificate and the visionary TQM goal can be expressed in this way: 'Catch a fish for a man and he is fed for a day (a quick fix), teach him to fish (not a quick fix) and he is fed for life.'

5.5.2 ISO 9000 – A MEANS OF STANDARDIZATION?

We must admit that we profess the mere ISO certification process is recognized as a means of standardization and this opinion is based especially on the following two facts:

1. It is allowable to use the ISO 9000 and the result of a certification in the best possible way.
2. A certification can be an excellent starting point for the support of a disciplined effort to get the best practice standardized as the foundation and necessary condition for continuous improvements.

Besides this disciplined effort to attain the perhaps much-needed standards demanded by an ISO certification and which we consider the most important positive element of a certification, we should like also to emphasize other elements which are considered positive by many companies:

- Uniform criteria for external assessment of the quality management system of a company.
- A third party certification may often result in a heavy decrease of second party audit.
- A simplification and rationalization of new contract situations between customers and their suppliers.

A last element of an ISO 9000 certification, which is certainly not to be underestimated, is the fact that for many of the companies it is the first time that money is granted for a quality project.

5.5.3 ISO 9000 – A BARRIER TOWARDS NEW THINKING AND IMPROVEMENTS?

Since the ISO 9000 series first appeared in 1987, a rigid debate for and against ISO has been carried on.

Sympathizers of ISO are often people who have carried through a certification process and the opponents on the other side are people who have never been involved in a certification process. The opponents attack sympathizers as people who are in a tight corner. People in this category can be company owners who have spent a great deal of money on the project or perhaps certification bodies which have gained permanent income from the increasing number of certified companies or it can be ISO consultants.

Sympathizers attack opponents and accuse them of being people without any ISO experience. People in this category can be those company owners who prefer to go for the European Quality Award, it can be TQM experts, TQM consultants or just people who doubt the excellence of the ISO 9000.

The only issue upon which sympathizers and opponents seem to agree is that often an ISO certification requires a great deal of paperwork and money.

As this section will especially focus on the more critical sides of an ISO 9000 certification, we should like to include some statements from a newspaper article by Louis Printz, professor at the Aarhus School of Business, Denmark, in which he – under the headline 'Highly Dangerous Medicine' – expresses the following opinions:

- ISO is gradually developing to become patented medicine for leaders and specialists who do not know the real requirements of a company.
- Nobody has, for instance, criticized the concept for not taking into consideration the company's place in the right market.
- Today the concept is, as a rule, used uncritically without any explanation that it certainly also has its limitations.

- ISO is only a single medicine in the company's cabinet and it should be used together with other tools in the correct order and in the right dosage to have the maximum effect. Otherwise, the organization lacks what it needs to survive. The medicine may become highly dangerous.
- ISO is easily applied and managed to create discipline in the production process without any involvement by the management worth mentioning.
- At the same time an organization is created in which necessary alterations at a later stage will be both costly and difficult to make.
- It is not only a question of the quality of a product. Quality applies to the same extent to the management, the culture of the company, the marketing etc.

The essence of Professor Printz's message is, in our opinion, that the ISO 9000 is very appropriate for the standardization process but the company will not make any progress without relying on excellent leadership – that is what we have named Total Quality Management.

We see two problems in the current ISO debate. One of them is that no objective investigation based upon facts of what an ISO certification does actually mean for the company has ever been made. The other problem, which is often ignored, is that it is not the ISO 9000 standards – or their fathers, the technical committee behind the ISO standards – who claim that the standards are more than the documents of requirements. No, it is the sympathizers, opponents and doubters trying to overestimate, underestimate, or who do not care at all about the ISO 9000 standards who are the real problem.

We do not believe that the ISO crusade can be stopped and why indeed stop a reasonable work of standardization? The real issue is to ensure that standardization goes hand in hand with excellent management and creativity and, as we have seen from both Joharry's window and from Kondo, this is indeed possible.

REFERENCES

Deming, W.E. (1986, 1993) *Out of the Crisis*, MIT, USA.

Fukuda, R. (1983) *Managerial Engineering*, Productivity Inc., Stanford, USA.

Kanji, G.K., Morris, D. and Haigh, R. (1993) Philosophy and system dimension of T.Q.M.: a further education case study, in *Proceedings of the Advances in Quality Systems for TQM*, Taipei, Taiwan.

Kondo, Y. (1991) *Human Motivation: A Key Factor for Management*, 3A Corporation, Tokyo, Japan.

Senge, P.M. (1991) *The Fifth Discipline – The Art and Practice of the Learning Organization*. Doubleday Currency, New York, USA.

Printz, L. (1993) *Highly Dangerous Medicine*, Aarhus Stiftistidende, Aarhus, Denmark.

The European Quality Award 6

The aim of including a section about the European Quality Award is to give companies an operational tool. This tool can be applied in the education of internal management as well as in the internal auditing process.

Many companies, of course, already have a management education programme, but it is only rarely that such a programme builds on a joint description (model) of what signifies good management. Such a model is included in the assessment material for the European Quality Award which thus gives an obvious opportunity of creating an educational programme in a balanced way which is also internationally recognized.

This way of approaching education has gradually become more recognized, e.g. Renault, the large European car manufacturer, built its management education systematically upon the model of the American Quality Award (Malcolm Baldridge) and at the University of Kaiserslautern they have consistently built their two-year master programme in TQM upon the model for the European Quality Award.

It may seem strange to the reader that we advocate building an educational model on the basis of a quality award. Our comment on this is that the models behind the modern quality awards comprise many other areas than product quality, although this is, of course, also included. In reality these models are a description of the joint enablers and the joint results of the company, that means the total quality and they therefore comprise all aspects of management.

As previously indicated in section 4.1.1 the annual quality audit of the management is an important condition for the implementation of TQM. The effort made by European companies in this area ought to be improved in the light of the results found in the QED investigation. We realize that many European companies carry out auditing following their ISO 9000 certification but in our opinion this auditing is too narrow from a TQM point of view. The model for the European Quality Award comprises the whole company and all elements of the new management pyramid (the TQM pyramid) are included. This model opens up the possibility of a deeper and more varied auditing than that following the certification.

SIQ, the Swedish Institute for Quality, points out that all companies which carry out a self-assessment based upon the criteria of the Swedish Quality Award are winners whether they win the Award or not. They write:

> Through self-assessment the development of the company is stimulated. The organization gets knowledge of where it stands and what can be improved. Everybody who carries through such an assessment are winners as they have gained knowledge of their own strengths and weaknesses. Employees in the whole organization have obtained new knowledge and a natural motivation for working with improvements is created.

6.1 THE BACKGROUND TO THE EUROPEAN QUALITY AWARD

The European Foundation for Quality Management (EFQM) awards the European Quality Award to an applicant who:

> has demonstrated that their effort in the TQM area has contributed considerably to satisfy customers' and employees' expectations and also those of others with interest in the company in recent years. An award winner is a company who enlightens the European market place. It can be of any size or type, but its excellence through quality is a model to any other companies which can measure their own quality results and their own effort to obtain current improvements.

The initiator of this Award was EFQM which is an organization whose purpose is to promote quality as the fundamental process for continuous improvements within a company. EFQM was created in 1988 on the initiative of 14 leading European companies (*inter alia* Philips, L.M. Ericson, British Telecom and Volkswagen). EFQM today has around 600 members. The European Quality Award was awarded for the first time on 15 October 1992 to Rank Xerox Limited. This yearly award is recognized as the most successful exponent of TQM in Europe for that particular year. In 1993, the award was given to Milliken Europe, a company which was runner-up in 1992. Among the runners-up in 1993 was the British computer company ICL (i.e. D2D) which became the winner in the following year. The 1994 Award Winner was D2D, UK. The Award Winner in 1995 was Texas Instruments, Europe, and the Winner in 1996 was BRISA, Turkey.

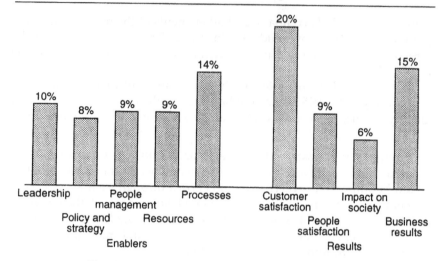

Fig. 6.1 The model for the European Quality Award.

6.2 THE MODEL

The model for the European Quality Award is given in Figure 6.1.

It appears that the model consists of nine elements grouped in two halves, one of which comprises the enablers of the company and the other the results.

The interesting thing about the model is the fact that it comprises both the enablers and the results. Through ISO 9000 many European companies have gradually become acquainted with the assessment of parts of the enablers of quality management and of course they are also familiar with the assessment of parts of the results (the business results). However, there is no tradition that the two areas are assessed as a whole and in the same detail as shown here. Furthermore, it is interesting that an exact weight is stated for each single element of the model. These weights can of course be discussed and may be changed as time goes by. The assessment reflects the general perception of what characterizes leading TQM companies. In the following section each single element of the model is explained including also the detailed areas of every element which will later form the basis of the actual assessment.

6.2.1 ENABLERS

Criterion 1: Leadership

How the behaviour and actions of the executive team and all other leaders inspire, support and promote a culture of Total Quality Management.

Criterion parts:

1a. How leaders visibly demonstrate their commitment to a culture of Total Quality Management.
1b. How leaders support improvement and involvement by providing appropriate resources and assistance.
1c. How leaders are involved with customers, suppliers and other external organizations.
1d. How leaders recognize and appreciate people's efforts and achievements.

Criterion 2: Policy and strategy

How the organization formulates, deploys, reviews and turns policy and strategy into plans and actions.

Criterion parts:

2a. How policy and strategy are based on information which is relevant and comprehensive.
2b. How policy and strategy are developed.
2c. How policy and strategy are communicated and implemented.
2d. How policy and strategy are regularly updated and improved.

Criterion 3: People management

How the organization releases the full potential of its people.

Criterion parts:

3a. How people resources are planned and improved.
3b. How people capabilities are sustained and developed.
3c. How people agree targets and continuously review performance.
3d. How people are involved, empowered and recognized.
3e. How people and the organization have an effective dialogue.
3f. How people are cared for.

Criterion 4: Resources

How the organization manages resources effectively and efficiently.

Criterion parts:

4a. How financial resources are managed.
4b. How information resources are managed.

4c. How supplier relationships and materials are managed.
4d. How buildings, equipment and other assets are managed.
4e. How technology and intellectual property are managed.

Criterion 5: Processes

How the organization identifies, manages, reviews and improves its processes.

Criterion parts:

5a. How processes key to the success of the business are identified.
5b. How processes are systematically managed.
5c. How processes are reviewed and targets are set for improvements.
5d. How processes are improved using innovation and creativity.
5e. How processes are changed and the benefits evaluated.

6.2.2 RESULTS

Criterion 6: Customer satisfaction

What the organization is achieving in relation to the satisfaction of its external customers.

Criterion parts:

6a. The customers' perception of the organization's products, services and customer relationships.
6b. Additional measurements relating to the satisfaction of the organisation's customers.

Criterion 7: People satisfaction

What the organization is achieving in relation to the satisfaction of its people.

Criterion parts:

7a. The people's perception of the organization.
7b. Additional measurements relating to people satisfaction.

Criterion 8: Impact on society

What the organization is achieving in satisfying the needs and the expectations of the local, national and international community at large (as appropriate). This includes the perception of the organization's approach to quality of life, the environment and the preservation of global resources, and the organization's own internal measures of effectiveness. It will include its relations with authorities and bodies which affect and regulate its business.

Criterion parts:

8a. Society's perception of the organization.
8b. Additional measurements of the organization's impact on society.

Criterion 9: Business results

What the organization is achieving in relation to its planned business objectives and in satisfying the needs and expectations of everyone with a financial interest or other stake in the organization.

Criterion parts:

9a. Financial measurements of the organization's performance.
9b. Additional measurements of the organization's performance.

6.3 ASSESSMENT CRITERIA

Generally speaking, assessment of the above elements is made in the same way as at a skating competition: scores are given both for artistic impression and for technical performance. The principle is illustrated in Figure 6.2.

The exact assessment is carried through as indicated below as the score given within each part area as an average of the artistic impression and the technical performance.

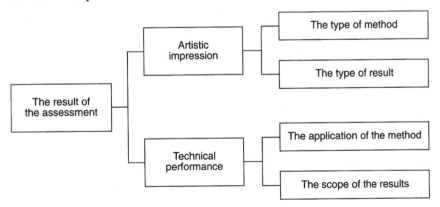

Fig. 6.2 Assessment according to principles at a skating competition.

6.3.1 ENABLERS

Scores are given in each part of the enablers criteria on the basis of a combination of two factors:

1. the approach chosen;
2. the deployment and extent of the approach.

Scores are given as a percentage of the maximum score obtainable according to Table 6.1 below. For both parts one of the five levels can be chosen or scores can be interpolated between the values.

6.3.2 RESULTS

Scores are given for each of the results criteria on the basis of the combination of two factors (Table 6.2):

1. the degree of excellence of the results;
2. the scope of the results.

Table 6.1 Scores for enablers

Approach	Score %	Deployment
Anecdotal or non-value adding	0	Little effective usage
Some evidence of soundly based approaches and prevention based systems. Subject to occasional review. Some areas of integration into normal operation	25	Applied to about one-quarter of the potential when considering all relevant areas and activities
Evidence of soundly based systematic approaches and prevention based systems. Subject to regular review with respect to business effectiveness. Integration into normal operations and planning well established	50	Applied to about half the potential when considering all relevant areas and activities
Clear evidence of soundly based systematic approaches and prevention based systems. Clear evidence of refinement and improved business effectiveness through review cycles. Good integration of approach into normal operations and planning	75	Applied to about three-quarters of the potential when considering all relevant areas and activities
Clear evidence of soundly based systematic approaches and prevention based systems. Clear evidence of refinement and improved business effectiveness through review cycles. Approach has become totally integrated into normal working patterns. Could be used as a role model for other organizations	100	Applied to full potential in all relevant areas and activities

Table 6.2 Scores for results

Degree of excellence	Score %	Scope
Anecdotal	0	Results address few relevant areas and activities
Some results show positive trends. Some favourable comparisons with own targets	25	Results address some relevant areas and activities
Many results show positive trends over at least three years. Some comparisons with external organizations. Some results are caused by approach	50	Results address many relevant areas and activities
Most results show strongly positive trends over at least three years. Favourable comparisons with own targets in many areas. Results address most relevant areas and activities. Favourable comparisons with external organizations in many areas. Many results are caused by approach	75	Results address all relevant areas and facets of the organization
Strongly positive trends in all areas over at least five years. Excellent comparisons with own targets and external organizations in most areas. 'Best in Class' in many areas of activity. Results are clearly caused by approach. Positive indication that leading position will be maintained	100	Results address all relevant areas and facets of the organization

Scores are given as a percentage of the maximum score obtainable as below. For both parts one of the five levels can be chosen or scores can be interpolated between the values.

The joint score for an area is then calculated as an average of the score of each sub-area. If a sub-area is not relevant to a certain company, it is acceptable to calculate the average on the basis of the sub-areas used. The joint score for the whole company is calculated by using the weights which each area has been given in the model. The joint score will be a number between 0 and 1000 (see Table 6.3).

6.4 EXPERIENCES OF THE EUROPEAN QUALITY AWARD

The European Quality Award was awarded for the first time in 1992 as mentioned above. The Award was applied for by approximately 150 companies which were evaluated by a specially trained assessement committee according to the above principles. The result of this assessment made as average scores for all applicants is shown in Figure 6.3.

It appears from Figure 6.3 that there are three areas which were assessed relatively high, namely people management, the management

Table 6.3 Chart for calculation of the joint score

Area	Score i (%)	Weight	Points
1. Leadership		× 1.0	
2. Policy and strategy		× 0.8	
3. People management		× 0.9	
4. Resources		× 0.9	
5. Processes		× 1.4	
6. Customer satisfaction		× 2.0	
7. People satisfaction		× 0.9	
8. Impact on society		× 0.6	
9. Business results		× 1.5	
Total score			

of resources and business results, while three other areas are assessed rather low, namely people satisfaction, customer satisfaction and impact on society. The average scores lie in the area from around 425 to 510. We do not have any information on the variation in each single area but it is of course obvious that the winner lies considerably above the average scores presented in the figure.

Whether the scores found are good or bad, we cannot say, as we have no basis for comparison. However, we can raise the question whether the companies have adapted themselves to the weights in the model. If an area of the model is considered to have a high weight, we must expect that high scores are also obtained in this area. To what degree this is the case is shown in Figure 6.4.

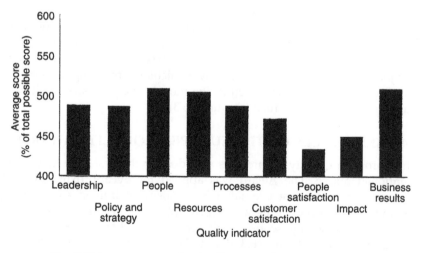

Fig. 6.3 Average scores for the European Quality Award 1992.

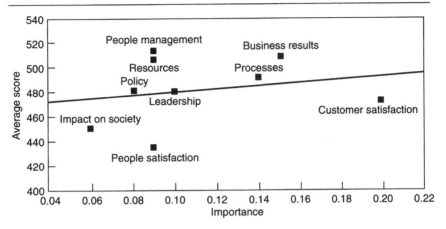

Fig. 6.4 Relation between importance (weights) and the scores obtained in European Quality Award 1992.

From Figure 6.4 it appears that by and large there is no relation between the scores obtained and the weights of the areas. This can be expounded in two ways. Either the companies disagree on the weights expressed by the model. In that case there will be some auditing work ahead. Another exposition is that the companies in Europe are very far from the ideal situation expressed by the model.

No matter whether one or the other of these expositions is correct, it gives food for thought that customer satisfaction, which is the area valued highest in the model, scores so relatively poorly as is the case here. No doubt this shows that European companies have a long way to go before the TQM vision becomes a reality.

PART TWO
Methods of
Total Quality Management

Tools for the quality journey

7

As was mentioned earlier in section 4.4, quality improvements can be divided into the following two categories:

1. internal quality improvements;
2. external quality improvements.

The aim of this part of the book is to present the reader with the methods (tools and techniques) which may be used in the quality improvement process.

As a carpenter needs tools, e.g. a saw, a hammer, a screwdriver etc. management and employees need tools in order to make effective quality improvements. The quality tools are valuable both when planning for quality improvements and when checking/studying the results after the implementation.

It is also important to understand that some of the tools which are presented in this part of the book may be used by top and middle management in their planning and checking activities while other tools have been developed in order to satisfy the needs of the masses (blue collar workers, supervisors, employees in administration etc.). To put it another way, the different tools have been developed to be used in different circumstances. Only when understanding both the circumstances and the tools to be used under these circumstances can the quality improvement process become effective.

7.1 THE QUALITY STORY

The main aim of internal quality improvements is to make the internal processes 'learner', i.e. to prevent defects and problems in the internal processes which will lead to lower costs.

At the start of the 1960s the Japanese discovered that if they were to continue their quality improvements it was indispensable that blue collar workers became involved in the quality improvement process. The

Japanese managers noticed that the workers were passive in the quality improvement process and they realized that something had to be changed. It is interesting in this context to make reference to the founder of the Japanese quality control (QCC) circles Kaoru Ishikawa (1985, p. 138):

> Since 1949, when we first established a basic course in quality control, we have endeavoured to promote QC education across the country. It began with the education of engineers, and then spread to top and middle managers and then to other groups. However, it became clear that we could not make good quality products by merely giving good education to top managers and engineers. We needed the full cooperation of the line workers actually making the products. This was the beginning of the journal *Gemba-to-QC* (or *QC for Foreman*), referred to as FQC, first issued in April 1962. With the publication of this journal, we began QC circle activities.

This is quality history and we know that QC circles have become an enormous success in Eastern countries and that Western countries have experienced a great deal of trouble when trying to implement them. There are many reasons for that which we will not discuss in this chapter. What we will discuss is the problem-solving process called 'the QC story', which has proven to be very valuable when working with quality improvements. We believe that a lack of knowledge or a general misunderstanding of the following quality improvement process may have been one of the reasons for the lack of success with QC circles in the West.

The problem-solving process called 'the QC story' results from the following 10 steps (a slight extension of Ishikawa's nine steps, 1985):

- Plan:
  1. deciding on a theme (establishing goals);
  2. clarifying the reasons this particular theme is chosen;
  3. assessing the present situation;
  4. analysis (probing into the causes);
  5. establishing corrective measures;
- Do:
  6. implementation;
- Check:
  7. evaluating the results;
- Action:
  8. standardization;
  9. after-thought and reflection, consideration of remaining problems;
  10. planning for the future.

The above 10 steps were initially designed to make the reporting of QC activities easier. From the beginning it was stressed that the QC problem-solving process was as important as the result. Hence it was natural that the reporting contained the whole process from deciding on the theme to evaluation, consideration of remaining problems and planning for the future.

Reporting 'the quality story' became an important training activity which we in the West did not understand. The companies had (and still have) their annual QC circle conferences where the best presentations were awarded and those QC circles participated in the regional QC circle conferences where the best presentations were awarded. The awarded QC circles participated in the national QC circle conference where the best presentations again were awarded (gold, silver and bronze medals) and were selected to participate in the international QC circle conference.

It soon became clear that the 10 steps of 'the quality story' were more than a good way to report (Ishikawa, 1985): 'If an individual circle follows these steps closely, problems can be solved; the nine steps are now used for the problem-solving process.'

The quality story solved the problem of standardizing the problem-solving process. If the problem-solving process is not standardized much experience tell us that the process of continuous improvements will only become a top-down activity which is not very effective. The QC circles must have a standard to follow otherwise they will not participate actively with continuous improvements. The start-up will simply become too difficult.

It can be seen from the 10 steps that 'the quality story' follows the quality improvement (PDCA) cycle or the Deming cycle and each step is written in a language which is easy to understand for the members of the QC circle.

It is important to realize that the PDCA cycle is the common work cycle to follow when working with quality improvements but it is also important to realize that it has many appearances depending on the purpose of the improvements and the participants in the improvement process. The 10 steps of 'the quality story' have proven to be successful in relation to QC circle activities while the PDCA cycle may appear quite different when focusing on top management's TQM-leadership cycle (Chapter 16).

The quality tools which are presented in this part of the book may be used in different steps of the PDCA cycle and some of the tools are especially designed to be used in relation to QC circle activities, i.e. in relation to the problem-solving process called 'the quality story'. These tools will be dealt with in the next section.

7.2 THE SEVEN + TOOLS FOR QUALITY CONTROL

In section 7.1 we discussed the so-called 'quality story' which today has become a standardized quality improvement process in which Japanese quality circles are trained to follow. As 'the seven tools of quality control' is a phrase which originated from Japan and which is inseparable from quality circles we will begin this section with a definition from the 'quality circle bible' (Japanese Union of Scientists and Engineers, 1970).

A quality circle is:

- a small group
- voluntarily carrying out quality control activities
- within its own work area.

This small group, where each member participates, carries out:

- continuously
- as part of the company's total quality control activities
- quality and improvement
- within its own work area
- using quality control techniques.

It is apparent from the definition that the use of quality control techniques in problem solving has been regarded as so important that it has been included in the definition of a quality circle.

One of the reasons for the success of the so-called quality circles in Japan is that in the 'Deming cycle' a substantial part of the activities – 'check', 'action' and 'planning' – have been transferred to the 'process level' (operator level). This 'transfer' of responsibility and competence is shown in Figure 7.1.

By training workers in a number of basic quality control tools including 'the quality story' it has been possible to create such a transfer of responsibility and competence. The result of this transfer has been more satisfied employees and, at the same time, the employees' creative abilities have been utilized much better than before which in turn has resulted in better quality, greater productivity and thus a better financial position in the company.

In order for the groups to qualify as 'quality circles' they 'must' use a suitable quality control technique (method or tool) in their work. This of course requires training.

How important the different quality control techniques are depends on the nature of the problem. In a comparative study between Denmark,

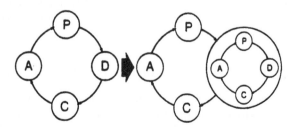

Fig. 7.1 Transfer of PDCA activities to the 'do' level.

Table 7.1 Average ranking values for 10 different quality techniques

Quality technique	Denmark	Japan	South Korea
1. Stratification	6.4 (8)	2.9 (3)	5.0 (7)
2. Pareto diagram	3.6 (5)	2.9 (2)	3.5 (3)
3. Check sheet	3.3 (2)	4.5 (4)	3.0 (1)
4. Histogram	3.5 (4)	4.5 (5)	3.9 (5)
5. Cause-and-effect diagram	5.0 (6)	2.9 (1)	3.6 (4)
6. Control chart	3.4 (3)	4.6 (6)	3.1 (2)
7. Scatter diagram	7.4 (9)	6.5 (8)	6.6 (8)
8. Sample plans	2.6 (1)	8.0 (10)	8.0 (9)
9. Analysis of variance	6.2 (7)	7.6 (9)	9.0 (10)
10. Regression analysis	7.7 (10)	5.8 (7)	4.0 (6)

Japan and South Korea (Dahlgaard, Kristensen and Kanji, 1990) there was an attempt to collect data clarifying the importance of the quality techniques most often 'mentioned' in literature, by asking the companies to rank the quality techniques shown in Table 7.1 in order of importance.

In Japan, the first seven quality control techniques in Table 7.1 are called 'The 7 basic tools for Quality Control'.

The table shows the average ranking values of these seven basic techniques plus three others in the three different countries.

The figures in parentheses indicate the ranks of the different techniques, as the ranking has been made on the basis of average ranking values.

It can be seen from Table 7.1 that the most important quality technique in Japan is the cause-and-effect diagram and as the Pareto diagram is often used in connection with the cause-and-effect diagram, it is not surprising that this quality technique in Japan is ranked as number 2.

In South Korea these two quality techniques are ranked as 4 and 3, whereas the techniques in Denmark are ranked as 6 and 5 respectively.

The cause-and-effect diagram and the Pareto diagram are examples of two relatively simple quality techniques the use of which does not require any special theoretical education in contrast to the quality technique of 'sample plans'. This is one reason why these two quality techniques are regarded as extremely effective in quality circle work. This is why these techniques are regarded as the most important in Japan.

By inspection and cause analyses it is important that lots from different processes, suppliers etc. are not mixed up. Stratification is the name of this philosophy or procedure. It is interesting that this quality technique in Japan is ranked as number 3 and with an average ranking value equal to the average ranking values of the cause-and-effect diagram and the Pareto diagram. In South Korea and in Denmark this quality technique is considered quite unimportant. The most important quality technique in Denmark is 'sample plans', typically used to check the failure proportion of purchased lots, own semi-manufactures or finished goods. This is called inspection. At this point, it is worth recalling the well-known sentence: 'Quality cannot be inspected into a product.'

The three most important quality techniques in Japan are typically used to find and remove the causes of poor quality. When these causes have been found and removed, the importance of the use of sample plans is reduced. This correlation explains why Japanese companies, in contrast to Danish companies, have given the lowest rank to 'sample plans'. Japanese companies are simply in the lead when it comes to finding and removing the causes of quality errors. This is an important reason why the quality of Japanese products is regarded as the best in the world.

All employees, including management, need training in the use of a number of the basic quality tools. Only through familiarity with these tools can give employees the deep understanding of the concept of variation necessary for total commitment to quality.

Management and employees in most Western firms have only a superficial knowledge of these tools. Some of them will be familiar from school and college (e.g. with stratification, check sheets, histograms and scatter diagrams) but it is not always fully appreciated that they can actually be used in combination to great effect in the quality improvement cycle (PDCA) in all the firm's functions and at all levels.

The basic principles underlying the methods also are not fully understood. In Japan, quality training courses for managers attach great importance to these basic principles. In the description of the various methods, we will therefore focus on these principles and in section 7.11 we will summarize where in the PDCA cycle the various methods can be used.

7.3 CHECK SHEETS

There are two different types of 'checks' in the quality improvement cycle (the PDCA cycle). For both types of checks a specifically designed sheet (form) may be very helpful.

In the 'do phase' of the PDCA cycle there are usually some standards (standard operations) which must be followed. Such 'must-be operations' were previously described in section 5.4 as 'constraints on carrying out the work'.

These constraints consist of restrictions which must be adhered to in performing the work; items which ensure the safety of employees or assure product quality are the most important of these.

To ensure adherence it is advisable to design a check-list check sheet with the constraints ('must-be operations') listed. During the process the operator has to document that all the must-be operations have been followed. The documentation may be the signature of the operator or an 'OK mark' for each operation listed and a signature at the end of the check-list.

It is a good idea that the operators are educated, trained and motivated to use such a check-list check sheet. In many cases it is possible and a good idea to involve the operators in the design or improvement (redesign) of check-lists. An example of a check-list check sheet is shown in Table 7.2.

The second type of 'check' during the PDCA cycle is done in 'the check phase'. Here the results are compared with the plan and the causes behind any significant gaps are identified and studied. The keywords here are study, learn and understand variations. If, and only if, the variations are understood it is possible to continue the rotation of the PDCA cycle in an efficient way. But profound understanding is only possible if meaningful data is available and meaningful data will only be available if it has been well planned.

In the plan phase of the PDCA cycle the necessary data collection must be planned so that the collection can be done in the do phase and so that the necessary data analysis can be done in the check phase.

Table 7.2 An example of a check-list check sheet

Prepare car for vacation	
1. Check parts important for safety	
Lights	( )
Tyre tread depth	( )
Bumpers	( )
Steering	( )
Brakes	( )
2. Clean car	
Interior	( )
Windshield	( )
Lights	( )
3. Check, fill	
Brake, fluid	( )
Battery water	( )
Coolant	( )
Windshield washer system	( )
Frost protection	( )
Fuel	( )
Tyre pressure	( )
Maps	( )
Music cassettes	( )

Table 7.3 An example of a
check sheet

Machine	Number of failures
1							
2												
3			

In order to carry out the data collection and analysis effectively it is a good idea to design a check sheet which simplifies the whole process. Such a check sheet must be specifically designed for each PDCA application because the need for data varies from application to application.

As a rule of thumb check sheets need both 'result data' and 'cause data'. Examples of result data are number of defects/failures, production size or inspection size. Examples of cause data come from 'the six Ms' (men, machines, materials, methods, management and mileu). An example of a check sheet is shown in Table 7.3.

7.4 THE PARETO DIAGRAM

The Pareto diagram is a graphic depiction showing both the relative distribution as well as the absolute distribution of types of errors, problems or causes of errors. It is generally known that in most cases a few types of errors (problems or causes) account for 80–90% of the total number of errors in the products and it is therefore important to identify these few major types of errors. This is what the Pareto diagram is used for. An example will show how the diagram is constructed.

Table 7.4 shows data collected from a given production process. The table shows that the process functions with a failure rate of about 19% and that almost half of the errors stem from error type 1, whereas error types 1 and 3 account for about 72% of all errors. The Pareto diagram is constructed on the basis of Table 7.4, ranking the error types according to

Table 7.4 Absolute distribution and relative distribution
of errors on different error types (number of
components inspected = 2165)

Error type	Number of errors	Failure percentage (%)	Relative failure percentage (%)
I	198	9.2	47.7
II	25	1.2	6.0
III	103	4.8	24.7
IV	18	0.8	4.3
V	72	3.3	17.3
Total	416	19.3	1000

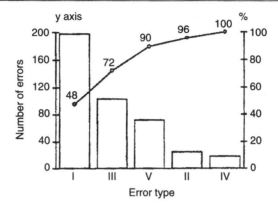

Fig. 7.2 The Pareto diagram.

their failure percentage, thus giving a better overview of the same distributions, cf. Figure 7.2.

It should be noted that the relative failure percentage expresses the failure percentage in proportion to the total failure percentage.

It can be seen from Figure 7.2 that the Pareto diagram consists of a bar chart showing the error distribution measured in absolute terms (left axis) as well as relative terms (right axis). Furthermore, the Pareto diagram consists of a broken curve showing the accumulated number of errors and the accumulated relative failure proportion.

The Pareto diagram indicates the type of error (problem) to be reduced first to improve the production process. Judging from Figure 7.2, one should concentrate on reducing error type I first, then error type III etc. If this procedure is to be economically optimal, the greatest reduction in quality costs is obtained by first concentrating on error type I, then error type III etc. The Pareto diagram is often used as the first step of a quality improvement programme. A precondition for using the Pareto diagram in the first steps of a quality improvement programme is of course that data has been collected, i.e. the PDCA cycle has rotated at least once. Otherwise more soft data must be used to identify 'the vital few' causes.

When quality improvement programmes are initiated, it is important that:

1. all those involved co-operate;
2. a concrete goal is chosen (the problem);
3. the programme has a great effect.

If all the persons involved try to bring about improvements individually, the result will often be that much energy is wasted and only modest results are achieved.

The Pareto diagram has proved to be useful for establishing co-operation around the solution of common problems as simply looking at the diagram tells the persons involved what the greatest problems are. When this is known to everybody, the next step is to find and remove the causes of these problems. The cause-and-effect diagram may be useful in further quality improvement work.

7.5 THE CAUSE-AND-EFFECT DIAGRAM AND THE CONNECTION WITH THE PARETO DIAGRAM AND STRATIFICATION

The cause-and-effect diagram is also called an Ishikawa diagram because the diagram was first introduced by Dr Kaoru Ishikawa in 1943 in connection with a quality programme at the Kawasaki Steel Works in Japan. Sometimes the diagram is also called a fishbone diagram.

Cause-and-effect diagrams can be extremely useful tools for hypothesizing about the causes of quality defects and problems. The diagram's strength is that it is both simple to use and understand and it can be used in all departments at all levels.

Returning to the underlying connection between quality tools, when the first cause-and-effect diagram has been drawn, it is necessary to identify the most important causes, including the eventual testing of some of them. It is not always easy to identify the most important causes of a given quality problem. If it were, poor quality would be a rare occurrence and this is far from being the case.

Most causes can be put down to men, materials, management, methods, machinery and milieu (the environment), cf. Figure 7.3.

The above diagram may be a good starting point for constructing the first cause-and-effect diagram for a given problem. Note that there are now six main causes in the diagram. Whether any of the six causes can be left out must be determined separately in each specific problem situation.

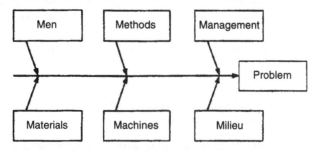

Fig. 7.3 A cause-and-effect diagram showing the most common main causes of a given problem.

Identification of the main causes is carried out through a series of data analyses in which the other quality tools (stratification, check sheets etc.) may be extremely useful when hard data are collected. Some situations call for the use of more advanced statistical methods, e.g. design of experiments or when soft data are used the so-called 'seven new management tools' which are presented in Chapter 8.

When hard data are not available you can only construct the cause-and-effect diagram by using soft data. One method is to use brainstorming and constructing an affinity diagram (Chapter 8) which can be used as an input to a further brainstorming process or cause analysis where the participants try to describe the first identified causes from the affinity diagram in more detail.

This cause analysis consists of a series of why . . . ? questions, cf. Toyota's method, 'the five whys'. The answer to the first 'why' will typically consist of a list of the problems which have prevented the results being as planned. It will normally be quite easy to collect data for a Pareto diagram at this level. The answer to the next 'why' will be an enumeration of the causes of one or more of the problems which were uncovered after the first 'why'. The third 'why' seeks to uncover causes of causes and the questions continue until the problems/causes have become so concrete that it is possible to start planning how to control them.

If the problems/causes are so abstract that planning a quality improvement programme to control them is too difficult, then the questions must continue. Thus it can be seen that the cause-and-effect diagram and the Pareto diagram can and in many cases ought to be used simultaneously.

The answers to the individual 'whys' can be directly plotted on the first constructed cause-and-effect diagram, making if gradually more and more detailed. The main trunk and branches of the diagram show the answers to the first 'why', while secondary branches show the answers to the next 'why', and so on, cf. Figure 7.4. Having been very careful in this process the cause-and-effect diagram may look like a fish where the causes resemble fishbones.

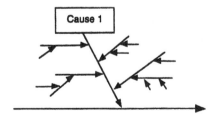

Fig. 7.4 Identifying root causes of a quality problem.

On completion of the data analyses and with the most important causes identified, quality planning can begin. Quality planning involves both determining which preventive methods to use in controlling identified causes and setting goals for 'planned action'.

Since it is not such a good idea to 'attack' all the causes at the same time, the Pareto diagram may be a valuable tool. An example of how the Pareto diagram can be used can be seen in Figure 7.5.

It can be seen from Figure 7.5 that problem A (= cause A) has consumed by far the most working time and more than the other three problems together. It is therefore decided to 'attack' this problem first and a method is found to control A. After one rotation of the Deming Circle (Plan-Do-Check-Act), a new Pareto diagram can be constructed. This can be seen in the right part of Figure 7.5 and it now shows that new quality improvement activities ought to be directed towards problems B and C which now constitute the 'vital few'. The Pareto diagram in Figure 7.5 shows that the quality improvement programme has been effective. If there is not any change in 'the vital few' after one rotation of the Deming Circle, it is a sign that the programme has not been effective.

In the above, we have equated problems with causes. This is perhaps a bit confusing but the explanation is really quite simple. If a problem has many causes, which is often the case, then it can be necessary to construct a cause-and-effect diagram to show in more detail exactly which causes underlie the given problem. If data on the individual causes are available, then the Pareto diagram can be used again afterwards, as shown in Figure 7.5. The Pareto diagram can therefore be used both at

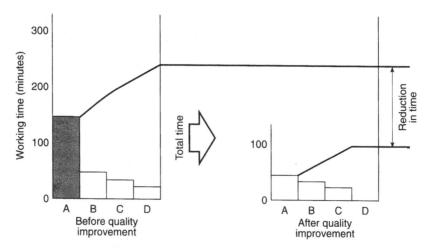

Fig. 7.5 An example of the use of a Pareto diagram before and after the implementation of a preventive method.

the problem level and the cause level. This can be extremely useful in connection with step 4 of the Deming Circle, i.e. in connection with the analysis of causes.

The Pareto diagram, which is used in connection with data analysis, can only be used to the extent that data exists on the problems or causes. Quality planning should therefore also take account of the data which are expected to be used in the subsequent data and causal analyses. Since, as previously mentioned, the cause-and-effect diagram is basically a hypothesis of the connection between the plotted causes and the stated problem, then it should also be used in the planning of which data to collect. If this is neglected, it can be very difficult to test the hypotheses of the cause-and-effect diagram and thus difficult to identify the most important causes.

This brings us to the important stratification principle which, in Japan, is regarded as the third most important quality tool, after the cause-and-effect and Pareto diagrams, cf. Table 7.1.

The principle of stratification is, simply, that consignments of goods must not be mixed up, so making effective data analysis impossible. Put another way, it should be possible to divide production results up into a sufficiently large number of subgroups (strata) to enable an effective causal analysis to be carried out. This is made easier if measurements of the production result are supplemented by data on the most important causes. Experience shows, e.g. that measurements of the production result in many manufacturing firms ought to be supplemented by data on people (which operator), materials (which supplier), machines (type, age, factory), time (time of day, day, season), environment (temperature, humidity) etc. Without such data, it can, e.g. be impossible to determine whether the cause of a particular quality problem can be narrowed down to a particular operator or whether it is due to something completely different.

In Denmark, stratification was ranked eighth out of ten quality tools, with the Pareto and cause-and-effect diagrams coming in at numbers 5 and 6 respectively. In Japan, these three were ranked as the three most important quality tools of the 10. This makes it easier to understand Deming's characterization of the Japanese: 'They don't work harder, just smarter.'

When constructing cause-and-effect diagrams it may sometimes be a good idea to equate the main causes in the diagram with the processes to follow when producing a product or service. The production process of preparing (boiling) rice can be used as an example.

The rice is the raw material which has to be washed first (process 1). Next, the rice is boiled (process 2) in a pot (means of production) and finally, the rice is 'steamed' at moderate heat for a suitable period of time (process 3).

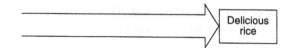

Fig. 7.6 The quality you wish to improve.

The following steps are used in the construction of the cause-and-effect diagram:

Step 1: Choose the quality you wish to improve or control.
In the 'rice example' it is the taste of rice. The effect most people wish to obtain is 'delicious rice'.

Step 2: Write the desired quality in the 'box' to the right and draw a fat arrow from the left towards the box on the right.

Step 3: Write down the most important factors (causes) that may be of importance to the quality considered. These possible causes are written in boxes and arrows are drawn from the boxes towards the fat arrow drawn in Figure 7.6.

Within quality control of industrial products, the 'six Ms' are often listed as the most important potential causes, i.e.

- manpower
- materials
- methods
- machines
- management
- milieu.

This division is only one out of many possible divisions, however and in the production process under review it may be relevant to disregard one or more of the above causes and another division may also be informative.

In the 'rice example' the main causes shown in Figure 7.7 have been chosen.

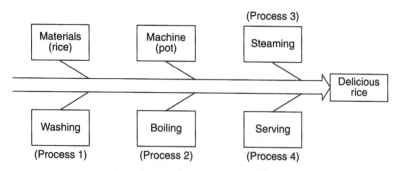

Fig. 7.7 The main causes for cooking delicious rice.

In Figure 7.7 the 'serving process' has been included, as that may be the reason why the rice is regarded as being delicious (or the opposite).

Step 4: New arrows or branches are now drawn on each of the side arrows in Figure 7.7 explaining in greater detail what may be the cause of the desired effect. New branches (= arrows) may be drawn on these branches, describing in even greater detail what the possible causes are. If this method is used in connection with group discussion or 'brainstorming', there is a greater chance that the causes will be uncovered. Often new causes, hitherto unknown, will 'pop up' as a result of a brainstorming and the construction of the 'cause and-effect diagram'.

Figure 7.8 shows the cause-and-effect diagram in the rice examples.

It should be pointed out that the 'cause-and-effect diagram' shown in Figure 7.8 is only one of several possible results. Some will be of the opinion that the causes shown are less important and can therefore be left out, while others will be of the opinion that the way the rice is served has nothing to do with 'delicious rice'. In that connection it is important,

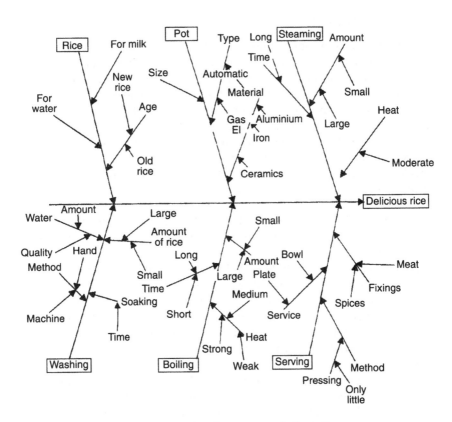

Fig. 7.8 An example of a cause-and-effect diagram.

of course, that you fully understand the event (here 'delicious rice'). To a Japanese, the importance of 'delicious rice' will be different from the importance of delicious rice to a Dane and the importance varies from person to person. What is needed, in fact, is a specification explaining in detail what exactly is meant by the event indicated.

In practical quality control the 'cause-and-effect diagram' is typically used in the production process partly as a means of finding the causes of the quality problems that may arise and partly as a daily reminder of the causes to be inspected if the production result is to be satisfactory. Together with the process control charts and the Pareto diagram the 'cause-and-effect diagram' is probably the most widely used quality control technique at the process level, i.e. thus also the technique most often used by quality circles.

The 'cause-and-effect diagram' can be used in all departments of a company, however, from product development to sales and, as mentioned before, on problems other than quality problems.

7.6 HISTOGRAMS

A histogram is a graphic summary (a bar chart) of variation in a specific set of data. The idea of the histogram is to present the data pictorially rather than as columns of numbers so that the readers can see 'the obvious conclusions' which are not always easy to see when looking more or less blindly at columns of numbers. This attribute (simplicity) is an important asset in QC circle activities.

The construction of the histogram may be done directly after the collection of data, i.e. in combination with the construction and use of a check sheet or the construction may be done independently of the use of check sheets, i.e. when analyzing data which have been collected by other ways.

The data which are presented in histograms are variables data, i.e. time, length, height, weight. An example will show how to construct a histogram.

A fictive company with 200 employees (the data has been constructed from several companies of that average size) has had some success with the involvement of the employees in continuous quality improvements. The employees have been educated in using the seven QC tools and a suggestion system has been set up to handle the suggestions which are expected to come up. During the first year the total number of suggestions was 235.

From the beginning it had been decided that the suggestion committee should have meetings once a week (every Monday morning) in order to make sure that suggestions were evaluated almost continuously so a quick feedback could be given to the individual or to the group which had written the suggestion. The members of the suggestion committee realized that the response time was an important 'checkpoint' for the number of suggestions and they realized that the higher the response time the fewer suggestions would be the result of the suggestion system.

A standard for the response time was discussed and a so-called 'loose standard' of 13 working days (= two weeks and three working days) was decided. The standard of the 13 working days was decided because it was expected that the complex and difficult questions would need detailed analysis and discussions at perhaps one to two meetings of the suggestion committee.

It was also decided that the response time for each suggestion should be measured and after a year the collected data from the first year should be analysed in order to better understand the system for suggestions and to decide on a fixed standard for the following year. Table 7.5 shows the collected data arranged in groups of five and in the order of suggestions.

From Table 7.5 it can be seen that the response time varies from seven days to 20 days. It is also apparent that 'the loose standard' of 13 working days has been difficult to meet.

To achieve a deeper understanding of the variation in the data it was decided to construct a histogram.

The following four steps are recommended when constructing a histogram.

Step 1: Plan and collect the data. The data has been collected and shown in Table 7.5.

Step 2: Calculate the range of the data. The range is equal to the difference between the highest and the smallest number in the data set. In the case example the range is equal to $(20 - 7)$ days = 13 days.

Step 3: Determine intervals and boundaries. The purpose of this step is to divide the range into a number of equal broad intervals in order to be able to calculate the frequencies in each interval. The number of intervals depends on the number of data but both too few intervals and too many intervals should be avoided. A number of intervals between eight and 12 is normally a good rule of thumb.

When you have determined the desired number of intervals then the width of each interval can be calculated by dividing the range by the desired number of intervals.

In the example it would be natural to construct a histogram with 13 intervals, so the width of each interval would be equal to one day. If the variation in the data had been higher the width of each interval would have been higher. For example if the range had been 24 days than each interval would have been equal to two days. The intervals are usually calculated by a computer program.

Table 7.5 Response time (days) of suggestions

Group	Response time
1	14, 14, 11, 13, 10
2	19, 10, 11, 11, 14
3	11, 11, 17, 10, 11
4	13, 10, 13, 10, 13
5	11, 13, 10, 13, 10
6	11, 16, 12, 10, 13
7	11, 16, 10, 10, 9
8	9, 14, 12, 10, 13
9	13, 14, 10, 10, 11
10	10, 13, 11, 9, 11
11	13, 9, 11, 10, 10
12	10, 9, 11, 11, 10
13	14, 11, 11, 9, 10
14	10, 11, 9, 14, 11
15	14, 11, 17, 10, 11
16	11, 11, 9, 16, 10
17	10, 11, 10, 10, 14
18	14, 13, 9, 11, 14
19	10, 10, 10, 14, 11
20	11, 14, 11, 10, 11
21	8, 11, 11, 11, 11
22	9, 11, 11, 10, 10
23	10, 11, 9, 10, 13
24	11, 11, 10, 20, 14
25	10, 10, 11, 10, 11
26	11, 9, 11, 14, 11
27	11, 14, 17, 14, 9
28	9, 12, 11, 11, 14
29	16, 16, 13, 11, 15
30	16, 14, 13, 9, 16
31	18, 16, 14, 9, 16
32	15, 13, 13, 10, 10
33	13, 13, 11, 18, 9
34	11, 10, 14, 7, 14
35	10, 14, 9, 9, 13
36	11, 10, 11, 10, 9
37	9, 9, 10, 14, 10
38	13, 14, 16, 17, 14
39	10, 16, 19, 11, 11
40	9, 12, 13, 14, 11
41	11, 10, 14, 11, 11
42	11, 10, 13, 16, 10
43	11, 11, 11, 11, 11
44	9, 14, 14, 13, 13
45	10, 13, 16, 11, 14
46	13, 9, 11, 14, 14
47	11, 13, 14, 14, 11

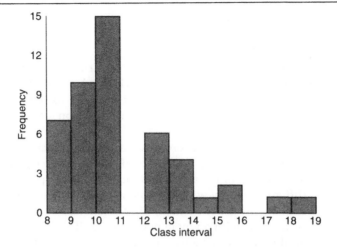

Fig. 7.9 Response time for suggestions (in days).

Step 4: Determine the frequencies and prepare the histogram. Now the data in each interval shall be tallied, i.e. the frequencies have to be calculated so that the histogram can be constructed. Today when data is usually stored in a computer this step is unnecessary. For most software packages steps 2 to 4 are done interactively with a computer program.

Figure 7.9 shows the histogram of the subgroup averages constructed on a computer package.

The following are easily concluded from the histogram:

1. The standard of 13 days was met only in approximately two out of three cases.
2. There   seem to be two different distributions mixed in the same histogram. Perhaps the left distribution is the result of simple suggestions and the right distribution is the result of more complex suggestions.

One weakness of the histogram is that you do not see a picture of the variation in time. For example the variation shown in a histogram may be the result of a combination of two or more different distributions. In Figure 7.9 the response time data may have come from a distribution with a higher mean in the first half-year than in the second half-year, or the data may have come from distributions where the means have changed following a decreasing trend. To analyse if that is the case you have to construct a control chart. This will be examined in section 7.7.2.

7.7 CONTROL CHARTS

7.7.1 THEORY

Control charts may be used partly to control variation and partly in the identification and control of the causes which give rise to these variations. To better understand this, we must go back to Shewhart's 1931 definition of a production process and his division of the causes of failures.

Shewhart defined a production process as, in principle, a specific mixture of causes. Changing just one of the causes, e.g. change of operator, results in a completely different production process. A new machine, a different tool, new management, a new training programme etc. are all changes in causes which, after Shewhart's reasoning, mean that we are now faced with a whole new process. It is vital for managers to understand this. Without such an understanding, it will be practically impossible for them to demonstrate leadership.

Shewhart divided the causes of quality variations into the following groups:

1. specific causes
2. 'random' causes (= system causes).

'Random' causes are characterized by the fact that there are many of them and that the effect of each of these causes is relatively small compared to the special causes. On the other hand, the total effect of random causes is usually quite considerable. If the aggregate effect of the many 'random' causes is unacceptable, then the process (production system) must be changed. Put another way, another set of causes must be found.

Shewhart's use of the word 'random' is somewhat unfortunate – we prefer system causes instead. Deming (1982) uses the designation 'common causes' and emphasizes that it is these causes which must be 'attacked' if the system is to be improved. This is our justification for calling them system causes. With this definition there is no doubt as to where responsibility for these causes lies.

As opposed to system causes, there are only a small number of specific causes and the effect of each specific cause may be considerable. This being so, it is possible to discover when such specific causes have been at work which, at the same time, allows us to locate and thus eliminate them. An example of a specific cause is when new employees are allowed to start work without the necessary education and training. This is management's responsibility. Another example could be an employee who arrives for work on Monday morning, exhausted after a strenuous weekend, with the result that the quality of the employee's work suffers as the day progresses. The employee is responsible here. It can be seen, therefore, that while responsibility for system causes can be wholly laid at management's door, responsibility for specific causes can be placed with both employees and management.

A process control chart is a graphic comparison of the results of one or more processes, with estimated control limits plotted onto the chart. Normally, process results consist of groups of measurements which are collected regularly and in the same sequence as the production the measurements are taken from. The main aim of control charts is to discover the specific causes of variation in the production results.

We can see from the control chart when specific causes are affecting the production result because the measurement of this result lies outside the control limits plotted onto the chart. The job of having to find the cause or causes of this brings us back to the data analysis, where the Pareto and cause-and-effect diagrams can be invaluable aids.

Figure 7.10 shows the basic construction of one of the most widely-used control charts. This chart shows the average measurements of a production process plotted in the same sequence as production has taken place, e.g. the five last-produced units of each hour's production could be measured. The average of these five measurements is then plotted on the control chart.

The control limits are known as UCL (Upper Control Limits) and LCL (Lower Control Limits), which are international designations. Exactly how these limits are calculated depends on the type of control chart used, many different kinds having been developed for use in different situations. As a rule, control limits are calculated as an average of the measurements plus/minus three standard deviations, where the standard deviation is a statistical measure of the variation in the measurements. The technicalities of these calculations lie outside the framework of this book.

As Figure 7.10 shows, there are two points outside the control limits. This is a sign that the process is out of statistical control. Each of these two points has had a special cause which must now be found. If a point

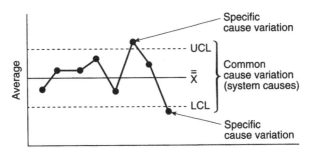

Fig. 7.10 The basic outline of a control chart for the control of average measurements.

outside the control limits represents an unsatisfactory result, then the cause must be controlled (eliminated). This of course does not apply if it represents a good result. In such a case, employees and management, working together, should try to use the new knowledge thrown up by the analysis to change the system, turning the sporadic, special cause into a permanent system cause, thus permanently altering the system's results in the direction indicated by the analysis.

As Figure 7.10 also shows, there is also a variation inside the control limits. This is due to the many system causes which can be more difficult to identify.

One aim of the control chart is to help in evaluating if the quality production process is in statistical control. In fact quality improvements should start with bringing the process in statistical control and then improving the system (re-engineering) if the quality is not satisfactory. Hence it is very important that any manager has a profound understanding of this concept.

A production process is in statistical control if the control chart's measurements vary randomly within the control limits.

It follows from this that a production process is out of statistical control if either the control chart's measurements lie outside the control limits, or if these measurements do not vary randomly within the control limits.

Concerning the variations within the control limits there are many rules to use when deciding if variations are random or not. One well-known rule is that seven points in succession either above or below the chart average indicates the presence of a special cause. This is due to the fact that there is a less than 1% probability of getting such a result if the process is in statistical control.

A production process in statistical control is said to be both stable and predictable. Unless new special causes turn up, we can predict that the future results of the process will lie within the central limits. Characteristic of a production process in statistical control is that all special causes so far detected have been removed, the only causes remaining being system causes.

We can derive two very important principles from the basic concepts mentioned above:

1. If we can accept the variation which results from system causes, then we should not tamper with the system. There is no point in reacting to individual measurements in the control chart. If we do react to individual measurements of a process in statistical control, the variations will increase and the quality will deteriorate.
2. If we are dissatisfied with the results of the process, despite the fact that it is in statistical control, then we must try to identify some of the

most important system causes and control them. The process must be changed so that it comes to function under another set of causes. The production system must be changed, and this is always management's responsibility.

We have previously mentioned the so-called CEDAC diagram. Introducing this diagram at Sumitomo Electric led to a fall in visible failure costs of 90% in only one year, due to the control of a number of causes. The problem was that existing knowledge about the causes of defects and existing knowledge of preventive methods was not always used in daily production. A study showed (Fukuda, 1983) that a relatively large number of production group members were ignorant of the existing knowledge about causes and methods which was written down in production or quality manuals and even when they had the requisite knowledge, a relatively large number of them did not always make use of it. There are many reasons for this, of course and we will not go into them here, except to repeat that the CEDAC diagram was able to control a number of these causes, so that visible failure costs fell by 90%. The production processes were in statistical control both before and after CEDAC was introduced but management (Fukuda, 1983) still was not satisfied, which resulted in the development and implementation of CEDAC. If management still is not satisfied after such a 'quality lift', which Fukuda was not, then it has no option but to continue identifying new system causes and developing new methods to control them.

Using the theory we have just described, it is now possible to define the so-called capability. The capability of a production process which is in statistical control is equal to the acceptable spread of variation in the product specification divided by the variation due to system causes. Since the acceptable spread of variation in a production process can be expressed as the upper specification limit minus the lower specification limit, the capability can be calculated as:

$$\text{Capability} = \frac{(USL - LSL)}{(UCL - LCL)\sqrt{n}} = \frac{(USL - LSL)}{6\delta} \qquad (7.1)$$

where:

USL = Upper Specification Limit
LSL = Lower Specification Limit
UCL = Upper Control Limit
LCL = Lower Control Limit
n = Sample size
δ = the standard deviation of the individual measurements.

If the capability is less than 1.25, there is a real risk that the process will be unable to meet the quality expressed by the specification limits. The reason for setting the critical limit at 1.25 is that experience shows that there must be room for the process mean to shift both upwards and downwards. Motorola's quality goal was that, by 1992 at the latest, all their processes, both administrative and production, should have a capability of at least 2.0.

7.7.2 VARIABLES CONTROL CHART AND A CASE EXAMPLE

In section 7.6 a histogram was constructed by using the data from a case example. The data collected was the response times on each of 235 suggestions for improvements. The data was presented in the same order as the suggestions were received by the suggestion committee and the data was grouped with five measurements in each subgroup (Table 7.5).

The grouping of observations is done in order to calculate and analyse the variation between the mean response times and the variation within the groups measured by the range. The suggestion system may be out of statistical control either because of non-random patterns in the means or non-random patterns in the range. Table 7.6 shows the calculated means and ranges within each subgroup.

The number of observations within each subgroup determines the number of subgroups. The number may vary according to the total number of observations in the data set but five observations are usually recommended in each subgroup and for the first construction of the control chart which we deal with in this example, it is recommended that there are at least 80–100 observations (16–20 subgroups). For further explanations study the literature concerning control charts.

The steps to be followed when constructing the M–R control chart are the following.

Step 1: Plot the calculated means (M) and ranges (R) in two different charts (diagrams) where the abcissa is equal to subgroup number and the ordinate measure are the means and ranges respectively.

Step 2: Calculate the average range and the process average (= the average of the subgroup means):

$$\text{Average Range} = \bar{R} \tag{7.2}$$

$$\text{Process Average} = \bar{M} \tag{7.3}$$

Step 3: Calculate the control limits UCL (Upper Control Limit) and LCL (Lower Control Limit):

Control limits for the means (= M):

$$UCL(M) = \bar{M} + A2 \times \bar{R} \tag{7.4}$$

$$LCL(M) = \bar{M} - A2 \times \bar{R} \tag{7.5}$$

Table 7.6 Response times, means and ranges for quality suggestions

Subgroup	Response time (X)	Mean (M)	Range (R)
1	14, 14, 11, 13, 10	12.4	4
2	19, 10, 11, 11, 14	13.0	9
3	11, 11, 17, 10, 11	12.4	7
4	13, 10, 13, 10, 13	11.8	3
5	11, 13, 10, 13, 10	11.4	3
6	11, 16, 12, 10, 13	12.4	6
7	11, 16, 10, 10, 9	11.2	7
8	9, 14, 12, 10, 13	11.6	5
9	13, 14, 10, 10, 11	11.6	4
10	10, 13, 11, 9, 11	10.8	4
11	13, 9, 11, 10, 10	10.6	4
12	10, 9, 11, 11, 10	10.2	2
13	14, 11, 11, 9, 10	11.0	5
14	10, 11, 9, 14, 11	11.0	5
15	14, 11, 17, 10, 11	12.6	7
16	11, 11, 9, 16, 10	11.4	7
17	10, 11, 10, 10, 14	11.0	4
18	14, 13, 9, 11, 14	12.2	5
19	10, 10, 10, 14, 11	11.0	4
20	11, 14, 11, 10, 11	11.4	4
21	8, 11, 11, 11, 11	10.4	3
22	9, 11, 11, 10, 10	10.2	2
23	10, 11, 9, 10, 13	10.6	4
24	11, 11, 10, 20, 14	13.2	10
25	10, 10, 11, 10, 11	10.4	1
26	11, 9, 11, 14, 11	11.2	5
27	11, 14, 17, 14, 9	13.0	5
28	9, 12, 11, 11, 14	11.4	5
29	16, 16, 13, 11, 15	14.2	5
30	16, 14, 13, 9, 16	13.6	7
31	18, 16, 14, 9, 16	14.6	9
32	15, 13, 13, 10, 10	12.2	5
33	13, 13, 11, 18, 9	12.8	9
34	11, 10, 14, 7, 14	11.2	7
35	10, 14, 9, 9, 13	11.0	5
36	11, 10, 11, 10, 9	10.2	2
37	9, 9, 10, 14, 10	10.4	5
38	13, 14, 16, 17, 14	14.8	4
39	10, 16, 19, 11, 11	13.4	9
40	9, 12, 13, 14, 11	11.8	5
41	11, 10, 14, 11, 11	11.4	4
42	11, 10, 13, 16, 10	12.0	6
43	11, 11, 11, 11, 11	11.0	0
44	9, 14, 14, 13, 13	12.6	5
45	10, 13, 16, 11, 14	12.8	6
46	13, 9, 11, 14, 14	12.2	5
47	11, 13, 14, 14, 11	12.6	3

Table 7.7 Factors for M and R charts

Number of observations in each subgroup	A2	D3	D4
2	1.880	0	3.268
3	1.023	0	2.574
4	0.729	0	2.282
5	0.577	0	2.114
6	0.483	0	2.004
7	0.419	0.076	1.924
8	0.373	0.136	1.864
9	0.337	0.184	1.816
10	0.308	0.223	1.777

Control Limits for the ranges (= R):

$$UCL(R) = D4 \times \bar{R} \qquad (7.6)$$

$$LCL(R) = D3 \times \bar{R} \qquad (7.7)$$

The factors A2, D3 and D4 can be found in Table 7.7.

The factors in this table have been calculated in order to make the calculations of the control limits easier. The theory behind these factors is a known relationship between the standard deviation and the range when it can be assumed that the calculated means follow a normal distribution.

The following control limits can now be calculated:

Control limits for the means (= M):

$$UCL(M) = \bar{M} + 0.577 \times \bar{R} = 14.69 \qquad (7.8)$$

$$LCL(M) = \bar{M} - 0.577 \times \bar{R} = 8.94 \qquad (7.9)$$

Control limits for the ranges (= R):

$$UCL(R) = 2.114 \times \bar{R} = 10.53 \qquad (7.10)$$

$$LCL(R) = 0 \times \bar{R} = 0 \qquad (7.11)$$

Control charts constructed with a computer package are shown in Figure 7.11.

By analyzing the control charts the following can easily be concluded:

1. In the first chart one of the means is out of control and another mean is near to the upper control limit (UCL). A specific cause has to be found and removed.

   The point which is outside the control limit should be investigated. This is a signal that a specific cause has not been controlled. This specific cause should be identified and controlled so that the cause

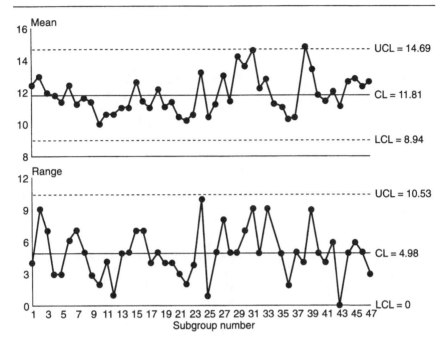

Fig. 7.11 Control charts (M and R) for the response time for suggestions.

will not impact variations in the future. This data should be taken out of the data set and a revised control chart for future use should be constructed.

2. In the second control chart (Figure 7.12(a)) it is assumed that the specific cause has been removed so that new control limits can be calculated without the out-of-control point. But still there is one point out of control. Having found the specific cause behind the out-of-control point a revised control chart can be calculated.

3. In the third control chart (Figure 7.12(b)) there are no points out of control limits. It looks as if the mean chart is in statistical control. In the R-chart there are nine points in a row above the centre line. This is a signal that there is a specific cause behind these points which should be found and controlled. Looking at the mean chart it can be seen that most of the means are above the centre line. So the specific cause may be that the stratification principle has not been used when constructing the control chart (refer to section 7.6). It may be the complex suggestions which dominate the observations in that period. If that is the case two control charts should be constructed to control the process – one for the simple suggestions and one for the complex suggestions. The two control charts will then each have smaller variations than the combined chart.

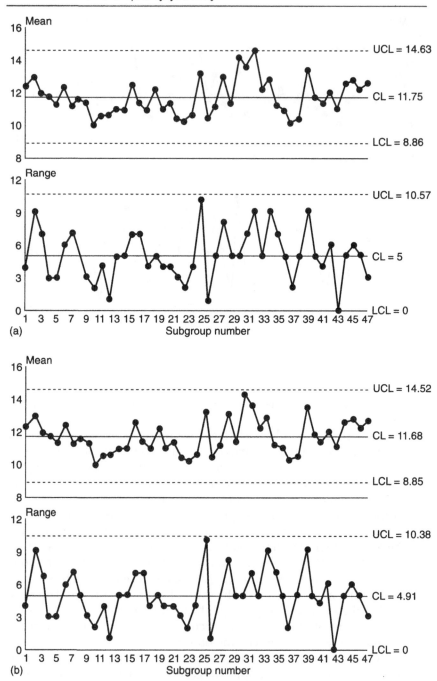

Fig. 7.12 Revised control charts (M and R) for the response time.

4. The revised control charts can then be used to control the process (the suggestion system) in the future. If the average response time in each chart is not satisfactory the suggestion system must be changed (change the system causes) and new control charts must be constructed for this new system.

7.7.3 ATTRIBUTE CONTROL CHARTS

In many cases the data are not a result of measuring a continuous variable, but are the result of counting how often a specific event or attribute, e.g. a failure has occurred. For these circumstances another type of control chart has been developed – the attribute control charts.

There are four types of attribute control chart as shown in Table 7.8.

As shown in Table 7.8 the attribute control charts are classified into the four groups depending on what kind of measurements are being used. The simplest control charts to use are the np chart and the c chart because the number of non-conforming units or non-comformities are charted. It is a drawback, however, that the sample size must be constant for these simple charts. The charts to measure and analyse proportions are a little bit more difficult to use but both can adjust for varying sample sizes. Some further explanations will be given below.

The p chart is a control chart to analyse and control the proportion of failures or defects in subgroups or samples of size n. This control chart, as well as the np chart, is based on assumptions such as the binomial distribution.

The attribute being looked at must have two mutually exclusive outcomes and must be independent from one sampled unit to another. For example the unit being looked at must either be good or bad according to some quality specification or standard. The unit may be a tangible product or it may be a non-tangible product (event). For example the suggestions analysed in section 7.7.2 could be analysed by a p chart because each response time either conformed to the standard (13 days) or not. Another assumption from the binomial distribution is that the probability for the specified event, e.g. defect, is constant from sample to sample, i.e. variation around the average is random. This and the other assumptions are analysed and tested by using the control chart.

The np chart is a control chart to analyse and control the number of failures or defects in subgroups or samples of size n. As mentioned

Table 7.8 The four types of attribute control chart

Data	Non-conforming units	Non-conformities
Numbers	np chart	c chart
Proportion	p chart	u chart

above the assumptions of the binomial distribution are the theoretical foundation of this chart.

The c chart is a control chart to analyse and control the number of non-conformities (defects, failures) with a constant sample size. The difference from the np chart is that for each unit inspected there are more than two mutually exclusive outcomes.

The sample space for the number of non-conformities for each inspected unit has no limits, i.e. the number of non-conformities (failures) may in theory vary from zero to infinity. The c chart as well as the u chart is based on the poisson distribution. As with the assumptions for the binomial distribution it is assumed that the probability for the specified event (e.g. defect) is constant, i.e. variation around the distribution average is random.

Complex products, e.g. cars, computers, TV sets etc., require the use of c charts or u charts. The same is the case with continuous products, e.g. cloth, paper, tubes etc. For random events occurring in fixed time intervals, e.g. the number of complaints within a month, the poisson distribution is also the correct distribution to apply and hence the control charts to apply should be the c chart or the u chart.

The u chart is a control chart to analyse and control the proportion of non-conformities (defects, failures) with a varying sample size. As with the c chart the theoretical foundation and hence the assumptions behind the u chart is the poisson distribution.

To construct the control charts use the following formulas:

(a) The p chart

For each sample (subgroup) the failure proportion (p) is calculated and charted in the control chart. The failure proportion is calculated as shown below:

$$p = \frac{NF}{n} \tag{7.12}$$

where:

NF = number of failures in the sample
n = sample size (number inspected in sub group)

Construction of control limits is done as follows:

$$UCL(p) = \bar{p} + 3\sqrt{\bar{p}\frac{(1-\bar{p})}{n}} \tag{7.13}$$

$$LCL(p) = \bar{p} - 3\sqrt{\bar{p}\frac{(1-\bar{p})}{n}} \tag{7.14}$$

where:

$$\bar{p} = \frac{TNF}{TNI} \qquad (7.15)$$

and:

TNF = Total Number of Failures in all the samples inspected
TNI = Total Number Inspected (the sum of all samples).

For varying sample sizes the control limits vary from sample to sample. If varying control limits may give problems to the users then plan for fixed sample sizes. For small variations ($\pm$ 20%) using the average sample size is recommended. The benefit of using the average sample size is that the control limits are constant from sample to sample.

(b) The np chart

For each sample the number of failures (np = the number of non-conforming units) is counted and charted in the control chart. Construction of the control limits is done as follows:

$$UCL(n \times p) = n \times \bar{p} + 3\sqrt{n \times \bar{p}(1 - \bar{p})} \qquad (7.16)$$
$$LCL(n \times p) = n \times \bar{p} - 3\sqrt{n \times \bar{p}(1 - \bar{p})} \qquad (7.17)$$

(c) The c chart

For each sample (subgroup) the number of non-conformities (c) is counted and charted on the c chart.
   Construction of the control limits is done as follows:

$$UCL(c) = \bar{c} + 3\sqrt{c} \qquad (7.18)$$
$$LCL(c) = \bar{c} - 3\sqrt{c} \qquad (7.19)$$

where:

$$\bar{p} = \frac{TNF}{TNI}$$

(d) The u chart

For each sample the number of non-conformities (failures) is counted and measured relatively (u) to the number of units inspected and chartered in the control chart.
   The average number of non-conformities per inspected unit is calculated as follows:

$$\bar{p} = \frac{TNc}{TNI} \qquad (7.20)$$

where:

    TNc = total number of non-conformities (c) in all samples
    TNI = total number of units inspected

Construction of the **control limits** is done as follows:

As with the p chart the control limits vary if the sample size ($= n$) varies.

$$UCL(u) = \bar{u} + 3\sqrt{\frac{\bar{u}}{n}} \tag{7.21}$$

$$LCL(u) = \bar{u} - 3\sqrt{\frac{\bar{u}}{n}} \tag{7.22}$$

(e) A case example

A company decided to choose the number of credit notes per week as a checkpoint because they realized that credit notes were a good indicator for customer dissatisfaction. The historical data for the last 20 weeks were collected and the data are shown in Table 7.9. The number of sales invoices per week was relatively constant in this period.

Table 7.9 The number of credit notes per week in 20 weeks

Week	Number
1	2
2	0
3	11
4	5
5	3
6	4
7	4
8	1
9	3
10	7
11	1
12	1
13	3
14	0
15	2
16	10
17	3
18	5
19	3
20	4

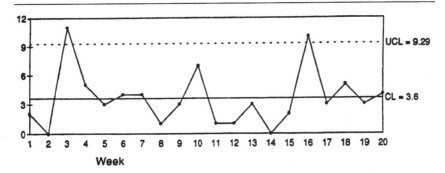

Fig. 7.13 Control chart (c chart) for the number of credit notes per week.

Using the c chart the following control limits can be computed.

$$\bar{c} = \frac{72}{20} = 3.6 \tag{7.23}$$

$$UCL(c) = \bar{c} + 3\sqrt{\bar{c}} = 3.6 + 3\sqrt{3.6} = 9.3 \tag{7.24}$$

$$LCL(c) = \bar{c} - 3\sqrt{\bar{c}} = 0 \tag{7.25}$$

The control chart is shown in Figure 7.13.

From Figure 7.13 we can see that the process is not in statistical control. The specific causes behind the out of control data in weeks 3 and 16 should be identified and controlled. Under these assumptions the control chart should be revised by deleting the data from these two weeks.

The revised control chart is shown in Figure 7.14 and as we see the process is now in statistical control. The control chart can now be used to control future credit note data.

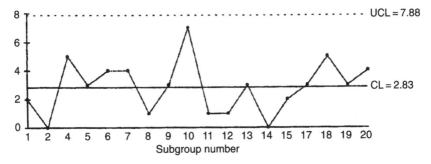

Fig. 7.14 Revised control chart for the number of credit notes per week.

7.7.4 RECOMMENDATIONS FOR APPLICATION

We have described above the fundamental and extremely important theory underlying the use of control charts in controlling average measurements (*M–R* charts, p charts and the u chart) together with the charts to control absolute measurements (the np chart and the c chart). There are many other types of control charts which, however, lie outside the framework of this book but the fundamental theory is the same for all. It is essential that all managers understand this theory, irrespective of whether control charts are used explicitly in the firm's administrative and production processes or not. We are convinced, however, that control charts both can and ought to be used far more than is the case in Western firms today. Together with the other quality tools, control charts can, as mentioned above, be used in many of the traditional functions of the firm, whether they be actual production functions or other functions such as administration, sales and services. The basic theory underlying control charts is still the same as described here. Some examples of such uses follow.

(a) Traditional production

1. Number of defects per manufactured unit, both overall and for individual processes.
2. Visible failure costs as a percentage of the production value for both internal and external failure costs.
3. CSI (consumer satisfaction index) for internal customer relations.
4. Average measures of individual production processes.
5. Number of quality improvement proposals per employee.
6. Number of defects per employee or production per employee. What is controlled here is whether some employees are 'special causes' who either need help themselves (negative deviation), or who can help other employees (positive deviation).

(b) Administration, sales and service

1. Number of defects per produced unit in the individual functions. The unit chosen can be an invoice, a sales order, an item in the accounts, an inventory order, a sales monetary unit, etc.
2. Sales costs as a percentage of the invoiced sale.
3. Production per employee.
4. Sales per employee.
5. CSI for the firm as a whole and possibly also for the more important products/services.

The first example in each category, number of defects per unit, is a general quality metric which can be used in all the functions of the firm.

Motorola has had great success with this, cf. Chapter 4. We will not comment further on the above examples other than to say that they are a good illustration of the many possible uses to which control charts can be put in a number of the firm's departments. That this tool is not used more in the West is because, in our opinion, firms have not done enough to train their employees in its use. These charts will not be successful until employees understand the basic theory behind them. This deep understanding can only come from education and training on the job.

7.8 SCATTER DIAGRAMS AND THE CONNECTION WITH THE STRATIFICATION PRINCIPLE

In section 7.5 the important stratification principle was discussed in relation to the cause-and-effect diagram and the Pareto diagrams. The basic reason for dealing with stratification is that it enables an effective causal analysis to be carried out and so improves the design of effective prevention methods.

An effective causal analysis will only be effective if measurements of production results are supplemented by data on the most important causes, e.g. by data on people (which operator), materials (which supplier), machines (type, age, factory), time (time of day, which day, season), environment (temperature, humidity) etc. Without such data, it can, e.g. be impossible to determine whether the cause of a particular quality problem can be narrowed down to a particular operator, or whether it is due to something completely different.

When planning the first data collection you usually have some weak hypotheses about the relation between 'results' and 'causes'. Budgets and other goals are in fact predictions of results based on incomplete knowledge about the set of causes (the cause system). The better the knowledge about the relationship between the cause system and the result the better the predictions will be.

In many situations we might have result data, e.g. data on the number of failures, failure proportions, number of complaints, productivity, quality costs etc. which may be continuous, related to some cause data. There may, e.g. be a linear relationship between the result data and the cause data which can be estimated by traditional regression analysis. The drawback to using this method is that employees at the shop floor level very seldom have the necessary background for using such an 'advanced method'. The method will not 'invite' employees at the shop floor level to participate in problem solving. Instead the method may act as a barrier against everybody's participation. More simple methods are needed. In these circumstances the scatter diagram may prove to be very powerful.

In the following section we will show a scatter diagram which has been constructed by a QC circle in Hamanako Denso, a company which belongs to the Toyota group. The QC circle at the coil-winding section, which consisted of a foreman and nine female workers, had problems with a high break rate for coils. The break rate was equal to 0.2% and the circle members decided on an aggressive goal which should decrease the break rate to 0.02% within six months.

By using flow charting, cause-and effect diagrams, data collection (check sheets), Pareto diagrams, histograms and scatter diagrams they succeeded in decreasing the break rate to 0.01% within the six months.

Another example of a scatter diagram is shown in Chapter 14 where the relationship between the ordinary profit and the company size measured by the number of full-time employees in the Danish printing industry is presented. This is an example of where there is no direct causal relationship between the two variables. It was not possible to construct and measure a causal variable in this example and hence it was decided to use a simple variable instead which correlated with the cause system (see section 14.2).

7.9 CASE EXAMPLE: PROBLEM SOLVING IN A QC CIRCLE USING SOME OF THE SEVEN TOOLS (HAMANAKO DENSO)

The following case study has been included by permission from the Asian Productivity Organization, Tokyo, Japan. The case was published in 1984 in *Quality Control Circles at Work – cases from Japan's manufacturing and service sectors*. Even though we are aware that production technology has changed since the case was written we have chosen to include the case as it was written in 1979.

7.9.1 PREVENTING BREAKAGE IN V COILS

Full participation as the first step in reducing defects
Takeshi Kawai
Parts Manager, 1st Production Section
Hamanako Denso
(March 1979)

Editor's introduction: this QC circle is made up primarily of housewives who approach their circle activities in the spirit of brightening and enlivening their work, an important factor when one must manage both a home and a job. The company is sited near the birthplace of Sakichi Toyoda. In fact, the circle meetings are held in the house where he was born and to pay respect to his dying exhortation to 'strive to learn and create and stay ahead of the times'. The three lines of their QC circle motto start with the three syllables of his given name:

SAra ni hatten (further development)
KItaeyo tagai ni (mutual improvement)
CHIe to doryoku de (with wisdom and effort)

The following account of their activities concerns the use of special equipment for winding automobile regular coils. Responding to a zero-defects policy at the company, the entire group set out to reduce the rate of defects from 0.2% to 0.02%. To see this difficult project through to completion, the leader applied the whole range of QC techniques and obtained co-operation from the company staff as well as the full QC circle. Patient data collection and analysis bore fruit and after six months, the target was more than achieved.

The report below covers all the necessary information about reducing defects in a machine processing step but, doubtless due to space limitations, it is less detailed than one would like in describing the housewife-dominated membership of the circle and explaining how the improvements were carried out.

(a) Introduction

Our QC circle is engaged in making one of the important parts of an automobile: we wind regulator coils. Stimulated by the catch-phrase 'zero major defects,' we decided to tackle the problem of breaks in these V coils.

(b) Process and our circle

Our process consists of machine-winding the coil, wrapping the lead wire around the terminal, soldering it to the terminal, checking the resistance and visual appearance and delivering the coil to the next process (Figure 7.15). I am the only male in this 12-member circle. Nine

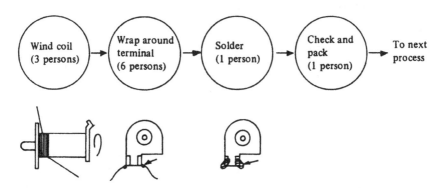

Fig. 7.15 Regular coil winding. (Source: Asian Productivity Organization, 1984.)

of the women are housewives. The housewives' average age is 38 and they have an average of two children each.

The QC circle got off to a difficult start, with only 50% attendance at the weekly after work meetings. The low attendance was discussed during the noon breaks and members gave such reasons as, 'It makes people late in fixing meals for their families' and 'Transportation home afterwards is a problem.' As a result, we decided to:

1. Hold the meetings on Mondays, so that members could make their dinner preparations the day before (Sunday).
2. Give everybody a lift home afterwards.

We also decided to put craft materials and other diversions in the rest area at the factory and to take other steps to create a pleasant atmosphere, as well as to supply members who could not attend meetings with notepaper on which they could submit their suggestions so that everyone could participate in some way.

(c) Reason for starting the project

The company had begun a zero-defect campaign. Since breaks were the most serious defect in the regulator coils for which we were responsible, we chose this as our project.

(d) Goal setting

We set a target of reducing the break rate from its current (June 1977) value of 0.2% to 0.02% by the end of December.

(e) Understanding the present situation

I looked over 500 defective coils manufactured during June to see where the breaks had occurred and showed 206 of them to the entire circle. Together, we summarized the general results of this study in a Pareto diagram (Figure 7.16).

(f) Study of causes

We decided to focus on breaks at the beginning of the winding and had each member suggest three reasons why breaks might occur there. We then arranged these suggestions in a cause-and-effect diagram (Figure 7.17).

(g) Factorial analysis

1. Individual differences: to see how different workers performed, we had three people wind coils on the same machine (No. 1). These turned out to be no great difference in the rate of defects.
2. Material differences: three gauges of copper wire are used. All of the breaks occurred with the thinnest gauge (diameter 0.14 mm).
3. Machine differences: breaks occurred on all the machines but we found that the rate increased with the tension load.
4. Correlation between tension load and rate of breaks was determined from a study of 3000 coils produced at each workstation (Figure 7.18). I did this analysis myself and presented the results to the circle members.

Our QC circle then made another cause-and-effect diagram to try to find the reason for the variation in tension. We investigated and planned studies of the spring pressure, the felts and rollers A and B (Figure 7.19). A special instrument was needed to measure spring pressure, so we asked the production engineering section to make that measurement.

I appointed three assistants for the felts and rollers and they willingly took on this responsibility. As a result of these investigations, we found

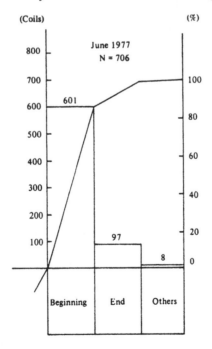

Fig. 7.16 Pareto diagram showing locations of breaks. (Source: Asian Productivity Organization, 1984.)

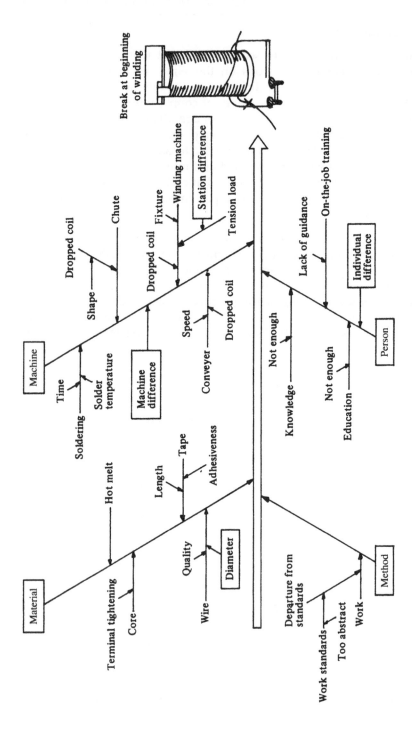

Fig. 7.17 Cause-and-effect-diagram for suggestions why breaks occur. (Source: Asian Productivity Organization, 1984.)

no problems with the spring pressure or distorted felts but we found uneven revolution in the rollers.

(h) Actions and results

By putting sealed bearings on both rollers A and B, we got the variation in tension load within the designated limits and the defect rate, which

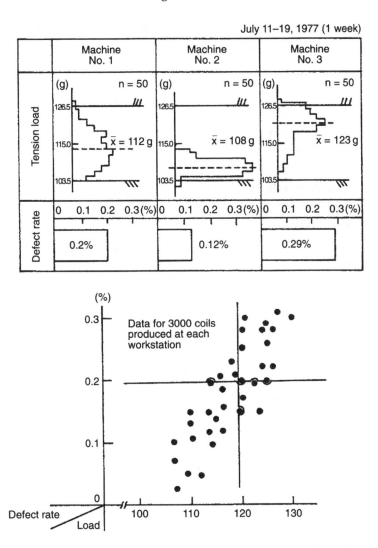

Fig. 7.18 Correlation between tension load and rate of breaks. (Source: Asian Productivity Organization, 1984.)

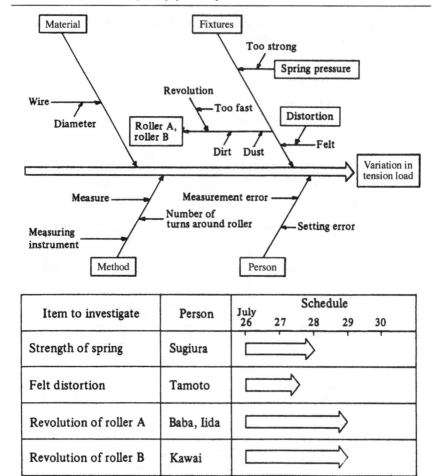

Fig. 7.19 Investigation plan. (Source: Asian Productivity Organization, 1984.)

had been 0.2% in June, fell to 0.09% in September (Figure 7.20). But this was still short of our target of 0.02%. Our circle therefore made yet another factorial analysis to search for other causes that might be keeping the defect rate high (Figure 7.21).

In regard to action 3, slackening the lead wire, I showed the members how to put light thumb pressure on the wire when wrapping it around the terminal. As a result, breaks at the beginning of the winding disappeared.

(i) Results and institutionalization

By actions 1 to 4, we were able to get the rate of breaks down from 0.2% in June 1977 to the 0.02% target level in November (Figure 7.22).

To institutionalize this result, we had the following four items added to the check sheet and work instructions:

1. Check tension load.
2. Check tension, roller A and roller B.
3. Clean rollers.
4. Handle coils correctly.

(j) Conclusion

Through the co-operation of the QC circle members, the causes of the breaks were found, corrective actions were taken and the target was achieved by the end of the year. There was a time along the way when the circle's efforts did not seem to be having results and members began to lose heart but, thanks in part to advice from management, we were able to complete our project and enjoy a sense of collective satisfaction.

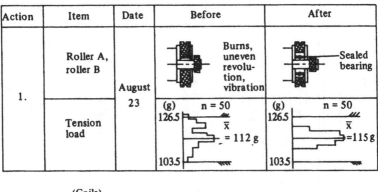

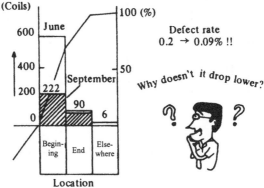

Fig. 7.20 Results of actions. (Source: Asian Productivity Organization, 1984.)

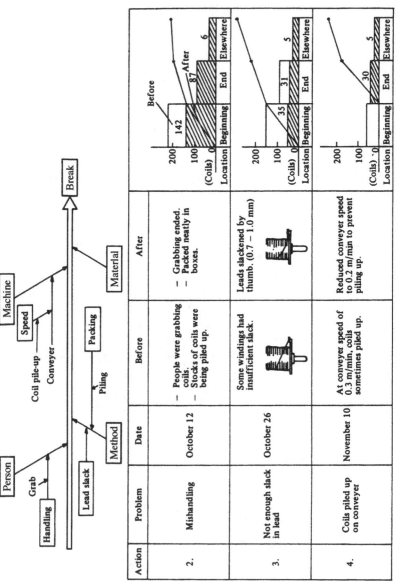

Fig. 7.21 Further factorial analysis and actions. (Source: Asian Productivity Organization, 1984.)

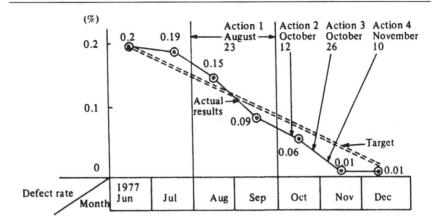

Fig. 7.22 Results achieved. (Source: Asian Productivity Organization, 1984.)

(k) Future plans

1. Having achieved our year-end target of 0.02% break defects, we plan to revise our goal and go for zero.
2. By stimulating QC circle activities and getting everybody to work on the problem, we hope to reduce the break rate in other steps in the production process.

7.10 FLOW CHARTS

With this last tool we have 'passed the seven basic tools for quality control'. That is the reason why we use the phrase in section 7.2 'the seven + tools for quality control'. But as the bible says – the last shall be the first – so is it often with the flow chart technique. John T. Burr (Costin, 1994) said it in this way:

- Before you try to solve a problem, define it.
- Before you try to control a process, understand it.
- Before trying to control everything, find out what is important.
- Start by picturing the process.

We also agree 100% with his following comments:

Making and using flow charts are among the most important actions in bringing process control to both administrative and manufacturing processes. While it is obvious that to control a process one must first understand that process, many companies are still trying to solve problems and improve processes without realizing how important flow charts are as a first step.

The easiest and best way to understand a process is to draw a picture of it – that's basically what flow charting is.

In the early days of ISO 9000 many companies made many mistakes on the recommendation of consultants who neither understood the basics of standardization (see section 5.5.1) nor the key points which we quoted at the beginning of this section.

The typical advice was: 'You just have to document what you are doing in your key processes – then we will check if there are gaps compared with the ISO requirements.' With such a 'low quality' advice it is not surprising that many companies later realized that ISO 9000 did not live up to their expectations. The opportunity for improvements of the production processes as well as the administrative processes were lost. Perhaps this is the root cause for the dramatic increase in the interest for Business Process Re-engineering (BPR). The processes were not well engineered from the start.

Another typical mistake was that the employees were not involved very much in documenting the processes using flow charts. Many companies still had the belief that involvement of the employees in the certification process would delay the certification because the employees did not have the necessary profound knowledge of ISO 9000 and they did not have sufficient overview of the processes. They did not realize that involvement of their people in the documentation was a necessary first step and the entrance to continuous improvements.

Milliken Denmark is one of the companies which has learned this lesson. We quote from Dahlgaard, Kristensen and Kanji (1994):

The last months of 1988 were a milestone in the history of the company. This was when our quality control system finally obtained ISO 9001 certification. Twenty office staff had spent 4000 working hours over 10 months in documenting the system.

The documentation process was extremely important, since it gave us the opportunity of looking into every nook and cranny in the firm. There were overlapping areas of responsibility in several parts of the firm and, what was perhaps worse, other areas where there was no precisely defined responsibility at all. Co-ordination at management level during this phase undoubtedly speeded the quality process along.

We thought we would end up with quality management, but we found that an ISO certification is more about the quality of management. We must demand integrity and responsibility from our managers if the certification is to be more than just a pretty diploma on a wall.

We underestimated the interest and involvement of shopfloor workers in the documentation phase. We were so caught up in things that there wasn't time to tell them what sort of certificate we were trying to get, what lay behind such a certificate, or how they would be affected by it. Employees were fobbed off with assurances that, as far as they were concerned, it would be 'business as usual', the only difference being that now it would be in the name of a formal quality control system.

Once the press conferences and receptions were over, management was accused by employees of having pulled a fast one. We were put in the same category as the Emperor's New Clothes.

We have included these quotations at the beginning of this section in order to explain to the reader that quality tools are only effective if they are used in the right way and the basic rules to follow are:

1. Educate your people in understanding the aims and principles of the different tools.
2. Train your people in applying the tools.
3. The best training is 'on the job training'.

These rules are also good rules to follow when constructing flow charts.

When constructing a flow chart we recommend you follow the following nine steps.

7.10.1 AGREE UPON THE FLOW CHART SYMBOLS TO BE USED

There is not a single standard for construction of a flow chart.

The most simple flow charts use only four symbols which are shown in Figure 7.23 (Robert Bosch, 1994).

We have just one comment to add to these symbols. The connect symbol is used when there is no more space on the page for continuation of the flow chart. The figure in the connect symbol tells you which connection you should look for on the following page(s).

It is important to realize that any symbols can be used for flow charts but their meaning must be clear for all the people involved in the construction and use of the flow chart. We recommend the above four symbols to be used but we also realize that varying symbols are used today in the different QC tools software packages (Tool Kit, SAS QC, etc.).

7.10.2 DEFINE THE PROCESS

Here it is important to define the boundaries of the process, i.e. the first activity which you want to include as well as the last activity. The

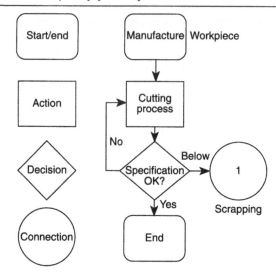

Fig. 7.23 Symbols for use in a flow chart. (Source: Robert Bosch, 1994.)

detailed activities between these boundaries will be described in the next step.

7.10.3 IDENTIFY THE STEPS IN THE PROCESS

The output of this step is a list of the detailed process steps. A good way to construct such a list is to follow normal transactions through the process and write down on a piece of paper what is happening. When a 'new activity' is carried out on the transaction you have a new step. It is usually necessary to make observations and inquiries where the activities are happening. In this way you will also be able to identify abnormal transactions.

7.10.4 CONSTRUCT THE FLOW CHART

Here the correct symbols are used to draw the flow chart. In a QC circle it is normally a good way to construct the flow chart on large pieces of paper (flip chart paper) which are put sequentially side by side on the wall, so that each participant can overview the whole process during the construction. With the latest computer packages (Tool Kit, SAS QC etc.), which are very easy to operate, new ways of constructing the flow chart are emerging.

The text on the flow chart should be short and clear for the people involved in the process. For each step describe what, who and where.

The people involved in the construction should include those who carry out the work of the process, the internal suppliers and customers, the supervisor of the process and a facilitator.

The facilitator is a person specifically trained in construction of flow charts. Besides drawing the flow chart the facilitator's job is to secure that all the participants are active in discussing the flow. An important issue to discuss during the construction is the measurement issue. Discuss what is important for the internal suppliers, the process and the customers (internal as well as external customers) and what is possible to measure. But remember:

• Before trying to control everything, find out what is important.

Allot enough time to the construction of the flow chart. It may be advisable to meet at more than one session in order to have time for further data collection.

7.10.5 DETERMINE THE TIME FOR EACH STEP

Time is both a measure of the resources used and a dimension of quality. Customers' perception of a product or service are usually high correlated with time. Therefore it is recommended that the estimated average time to complete each step in the flow chart is discussed and estimated. It is especially important to estimate the time for delays because the total process time may consist of 90% delays (waiting time, storage etc.) and 10% activity. All the estimated times should be written on the flow chart beneath each step.

7.10.6 CHECK THE FLOW CHART

Having completed the previous steps it is now time to check and analyse the constructed flow chart. Is it really a good flow? Where are the weak points in the process? What are the internal customer-supplier requirements of each step? What are their experiences? What are the external customer–supplier expectations, needs and requirements? How did we live up to these needs, expectations and requirements? How can we improve the process in order to improve customer satisfaction? How can we reduce waste?

The facilitator's job is to secure that the vital questions as above are discussed. It is important that the participants both are objective (facts) as well as creative in this step. There are good opportunities here to apply the seven basic tools for quality control as well as some of the seven new management tools (e.g. affinity diagram).

The output of this step should be a list of 'OFIs' (Opportunities For Improvements). Some of the suggestions may be complex and difficult to implement immediately so a plan for evaluation and implementation may be needed.

7.10.7 IMPROVE THE FLOW CHART (IMPROVE THE PROCESS)

The output of the previous step is a list of improvements to be implemented immediately. The flow chart has to be revised according to this list and the process has to be changed accordingly (education, training, communication, etc.). The quality measures and goals as well as a plan for data collection should be decided.

7.10.8 CHECK THE RESULT

This step follows the rules of the check activity in the PDCA cycle.

7.10.9 STANDARDIZE THE FLOW CHART (STANDARDIZE THE PROCESS)

If the results are satisfactory the process can be standardized. The process flow chart is a vital part of the documented standard.

7.11 RELATIONSHIP BETWEEN THE TOOLS AND THE PDCA CYCLE

As a conclusion to this chapter we present Table 7.10 which gives the reader an overview of the seven + tools for quality control and their potential application in the PDCA cycle.

As can be seen from the Table 7.10 the seven + tools for quality control can be applied in different parts of the PDCA cycle. Three of the methods may be applied in the planning phase (P), all of them may be applied in the Do and Check phases while three of the methods may be applied in the Action phase. Only one of the methods – flow charts – may be applied in all the phases of the PDCA cycle. In Chapter 8 we will improve this table in order to show the importance of applying the various methods in the different phases of the PDCA cycle. For further information about various methods for TQM, see Kanji and Asher (1996).

Table 7.10 The relationship between the PDCA cycle and the seven + tools for quality control

Tool	P	D	C	A
Check sheet		X	X	
Pareto diagram		X	X	X
Cause-and-effect diagram		X	X	X
Stratification	X	X	X	
Histogram	X	X	X	
Control charts		X	X	
Scatter diagram		X	X	
Flow charts	X	X	X	X

REFERENCES

Asian Productivity Organization (1984) *Quality Control Circles at Work*, Tokyo, Japan.

Burr, T., in *Readings in Total Quality Management* (ed. H. Costin), The Dryden Press, Harcourt Brace College Publishers, New York, USA.

Dahlgaard, J.J., Kanji, G.K. and Kristensen, K. (1990) A comparative study of quality control methods and principles in Japan, Korea and Denmark. *Journal of Total Quality Management*, **1**(1), 115–132.

Dahlgaard, J.J., Kristensen, K. and Kanji, G.K. (1994) *The Quality Journey – A Journey Without An End*, Advances in Total Quality Management, Total Quality Management, Carfax Publishing Company, London.

Deming, W.E. (1986) *Out of the Crisis*, MIT, USA.

Fukude, R. (1983) *Managerial Engineering*, Productivity Inc., Stanford, USA.

Ishikawa, K. (1985) *What is Total Quality Control? – The Japanese Way*, Prentice Hall, Englewood Cliffs, USA.

Japanese Union of Scientists and Engineers (1970) *QC Circle Koryo – General Principles of the QC Circle*, Tokyo, Japan.

Kanji, G.K. and Asher, M. *100 Methods for Total Quality Management*, SAGE, London.

Robert Bosch (1994) *Elementary Quality Assurance Tools*, Robert Bosch, Denmark.

Shewhart, W.A. (1931) *Economic Control of Quality and Manufactured Products*, D. van Nostrand & Co., Inc., New York. USA.

Some new management techniques

8

As Senge (1991) points out, the evolution of quality management may best be understood as a series of waves. In the first wave the focus was on the front-line worker and the idea was to improve the work process. To this end the seven old QC tools played and still play a very important role. In the second wave focus is on the manager and the idea is to improve how the work is done. This calls for a new set of techniques which specifically focus on the way that managers work and co-operate. Contrary to the seven old techniques these new techniques are mainly qualitative with a purpose to help the manager, among other things, to organize large amounts of non-quantitative data, create hypotheses, clarify interrelationships and establish priorities.

The techniques, although for the most part not invented by the Japanese, were first presented as a collection in 1979 in a Japanese publication edited by Shigeru Mizuno. In 1988, the publication was translated into English and since then the seven new management techniques have come to play an important role in the education of Western managers. This is especially true after an adaption of the techniques to the Western way of teaching and thinking made by Michal Brassard in 1989. His publication is called *The Memory Jogger Plus* and it features six of the original techniques plus a further one.

In his introduction of the techniques, Professor Mizuno analyses the necessary prerequisites for a continuation of the quality journey and comes up with the following seven capabilities that should be present in any company:

1. Capability of processing verbal information.
2. Capability of generating ideas.
3. Capability of providing a means of completing tasks.
4. Capability of eliminating failures.

5. Capability of assisting the exchange of information.
6. Capability of disseminating information to concerned parties.
7. Capability of 'unfiltered expression'.

After studying these demands a collection of techniques was suggested. Most of the techniques had their origin in the West and were well-known to Western researchers. They came from various areas of management science, among others, operations research and multivariate statistics. The only original technique among the seven was the so-called affinity diagram method which was invented by a Japanese anthropologist for use within his own area.

In what follows we examine some of the seven techniques and supplement them with the technique that was included by Bassard as mentioned above. Hence our seven new management techniques will in fact be eight and to be in line with the *Memory Jogger* philosophy we might call them 'The Seven New Management Techniques PLUS'. Further management techniques can be found in Kanji and Asher (1966).

The placing of the eight techniques in relation to other quality management techniques can be demonstrated in Figure 8.1 below. In this the techniques are classified according to whether they are quantitative or qualitative, whether or not they are advanced and whether they belong to the old or the new group of techniques.

The seven old techniques have already been described in the previous chapter. Design of experiments will not be dealt with in detail in this book but an example will be given when we describe measurement of quality in relation to product development in Chapter 15. In what follows we examine a couple of the new techniques. In our opinion the most powerful of the new techniques are matrix data analysis, affinity analysis, matrix diagrams, relations diagrams, tree diagrams and analytical hierarchies and hence these are the ones that we will be discussing in detail with in this chapter. However, the tree diagram is a very well-known and very easy to use method of breaking down a problem or a phenomenon into details (a tree like the one given in Figure 8.1) and likewise the relationship diagram is a very easy graphical method of showing the links between the elements of a given problem by simple putting the elements down on a piece of paper and then drawing the relevant arrows between them. None of these elements involves special techniques and hence we will not discuss here.

The remaining techniques, the PDPC and the arrow diagram (equal to PERT), are, to our experience, seldom used by mainstream managers and hence we will not provide any information on them here. Instead we ask the reader to consult Kanji and Asher (1996).

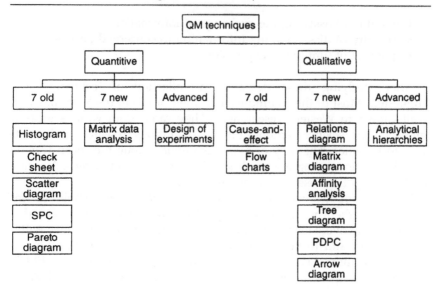

Fig. 8.1 A classification of quality management techniques (tree diagram).

8.1 MATRIX DATA ANALYSIS

As shown in Figure 8.1 above, matrix data analysis is the only real quantitative technique among the seven new techniques. The objective of the technique is data reduction and identification of the hidden structure behind an observed data set. The name matrix data analysis refers to the data input to the technique which is a matrix of data consisting of a number of observations on a number of different variables. This is demonstrated in Table 8.1 in which we have a matrix of n observations on p different variables. A typical data set of this type will be when the observations are different products and the variables are different characteristics of the products or when the observations are customers and the variables represent customer satisfaction measured in different areas.

When you have a data set like this it is very difficult to get a clear picture of the meaning of the data. Here are the variables interrelated

Table 8.1 A matrix of data

	Variable 1	Variable 2	Variable 3	$\cdots$	Variable p
Observation 1	x_{11}	x_{12}	x_{13}		x_{1p}
Observation 2	x_{21}	x_{22}	x_{23}		x_{2p}
Observation 3	x_{31}	x_{32}	x_{33}		x_{3p}
Observation 4	x_{41}	x_{42}	x_{43}		x_{4p}
$\cdots$					
Observation n	x_{n1}	x_{n2}	x_{n3}		x_{np}

and what does the interrelation mean? What we need is some kind of visualization of the data set and especially a reduction of the dimensionality from p or n to two or three which, to most people, are the maximum that the human brain can deal with.

The procedure is as follows:

1. Arrange your data in an $n \times p$ matrix as shown in Table 8.1. Call this matrix X.
2. Compute the matrix of squares and cross-products, $X'X$. Alternatively compute the matrix of variances and covariances or the correlation matrix.
3. Compute the principal components of the matrix given in 2.
4 Compute the correlations between the original variables and the principal components, the so-called loadings.
5. Use the first two principal components to give a graphical presentation of the loadings computed in 4. This presentation gives the best possible description of the original data set using only two dimensions.

As appears from the description above the backbone of matrix data analysis is the technique called principal components. It is a multivariate statistical technique which originates back to the 1930s and which originally was used especially by psychologists to discover latent phenomena behind the observed data.

The calculation of the principal components of a data set is done by solving the following equations:

$$(X'X - \lambda_j I)v_j = 0 \qquad j = 1, \dots p. \tag{8.1}$$

where λ_j is the jth characteristic root and v_j is the corresponding characteristic vector. The jth principal component (y_j) which is uncorrelated with all other principal components is calculated as a linear combination of the original observations as follows:

$$y_j = v_j' x \tag{8.2}$$

The principal components are characterized by the fact that the first principal component explains most of the variance in the original observations. The second principal component explains second most of the variance and so forth. It is outside the scope of this book to go more into detail with the technique of principal components but a thorough presentation of the technique may be found in the excellent book by Johnson and Wichern (1993).

Calculation of the principal components and loadings and the corresponding graphics is easily done by using one of the major statistical software packages, e.g. SPSS, SAS or SYSTAT.

As a demonstration of matrix data analysis consider the following example. A major company producing and selling different kinds of electric equipment decided to carry out a customer satisfaction survey. In the survey approximately 200 customers were asked about the importance of and their satisfaction with the following dimensions:

1. assortment;
2. support to the customer's own sales and marketing effort;
3. delivery;
4. technical support;
5. technical quality of products;
6. catalogues;
7. close relationship to people working in the sales department;
8. speed of introduction of new products and new ideas;
9. close contact to the company in general;
10. prices.

Each of these areas was evaluated by the customer both concerning importance and concerning the performance of the company. In order to simplify actions to be taken later on it was decided to analyse the importance scores in more detail to see how the areas were interrelated and to find out the simplest way to describe the 10 dimensions. A matrix data analysis was carried out which resulted in the mapping given below in Figure 8.2.

Based on the placing of the points in the diagram it was decided to group the customer satisfaction parameters in two groups. These were:

1. contact parameters;
2. product parameters.

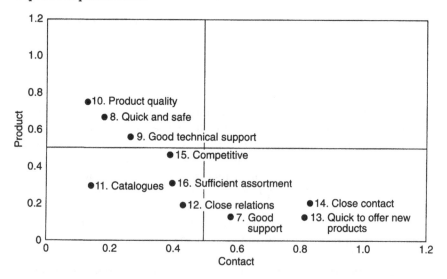

Fig. 8.2 Matrix data analysis of customer satisfaction parameters.

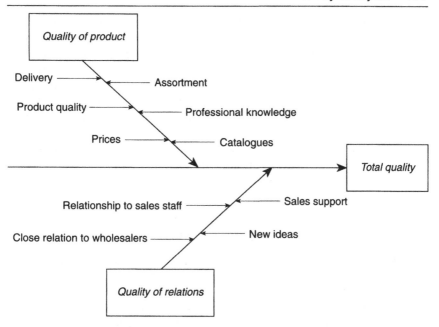

Fig. 8.3 Cause-and-effect diagram of customer satisfaction parameters.

The grouping appears from the cause and effect diagram given in Figure 8.3.

These two groups have a high correlation within the groups and a smaller correlation between the groups. This means, e.g. that customers giving high importance to assortment also tend to give high importance to technical support. From a quality point of view it follows from this that when action is going to be taken it will be wise to treat the elements belonging to a group as a whole.

Matrix data analysis is a very effective technique to help you to discover the structure of large data sets. The technique is a bit complicated from a technical point of view but fortunately very easy to use software packages are on the market. In order to use the technique you need to know what it does and how the output is interpreted. You need to know all the mathematical details of the technique and hence we believe that in spite of the technicalities there is no reason why the method should not become a standard technique for the modern manager.

8.2 AFFINITY ANALYSIS

A technique called affinity analysis was developed in the 1960s by Japanese anthropologist Kawakita Jiro. When he was working in the field he made detailed notes of all his observations for later study. But this meant that he would be faced with large amounts of information in the future. In order to simplify the process he developed a new method for handling the information which he called the KJ method. The idea behind the method was to be able to go through large amounts of information in an efficient way and, at the same time, to establish groupings of the information. The method was later generalized and called the affinity method.

For the modern business person the affinity analysis is an efficient and creative way to gather and organize large amounts of qualitative information for the solution of a given problem. The procedure is described in Figure 8.4 below.

8.2.1 STAGES 1, 2, 3 AND 4 (IDEA GENERATION)

As mentioned above the idea of affinity analysis is to gather and combine large amounts of verbal information in order to find solutions to a specific problem. Hence the first two stages of the process will be to define the problem and to generate ideas. When defining the problem it is very important to reach consensus about the words that you are going to use. There must be absolutely no doubt about the issue under discussion because if this is the case it may later on be very difficult to use the results. The generation of ideas will follows the traditional guidelines of brainstorming, structured or unstructured, with no criticism of ideas whatsoever.

Each idea is written down on a small card or a Post-it note and placed randomly on the centre of the table where everybody can see it.

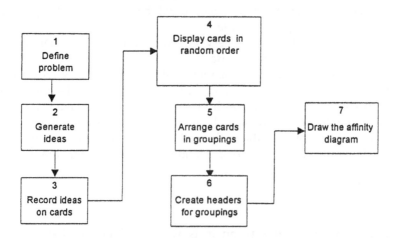

Fig. 8.4 Procedure for affinity diagram.

8.2.2 STAGES 5, 6 AND 7 (IDEA GROUPING AND PRESENTATION)

After generation of the ideas the grouping session starts. The idea is to arrange the cards in related groupings. This grouping is done by the entire team and it takes place in silence. In practice the team members start the grouping by picking out cards that they think are closely related and then placing these at one side of the table or wall, wherever the session takes place. Eventually groups of cards appear and the grouping process continues until all team members are satisfied with the grouping. If a member is not satisfied he simply moves a card from an existing group to another which he finds more appropriate. Sometimes a card keeps moving from one group to another. In such a case it is a good idea to break the silence and discuss the actual meaning of the wording on the card. When a card keeps moving the usual reason is that the wording on the card is unclear or equivocable.

After the grouping has come to an end it is time to break the silence. Now the team discusses the groups and they decide upon headings for the groups. Finally an affinity diagram showing the entire grouping is drawn.

In our opinion this technique is very efficient in connection with problem solving. It may seem very simple and unsophisticated but experience shows that it may be of great help at all levels of management. Furthermore it is a very fast method due to the silence. Time is not spent in argument, instead you go directly to the point and solve the problem!

As an example we report the results of a study made by a large supplier of food. He was interested in getting an idea of what the ordinary female consumer thought characterized the ordinary daily meal. He started the study by setting up two focus groups each consisting of eight persons. The first group consisted of females below the age of 35 and the latter of females above 35. Within the groups the members were distributed according to occupation, education and family situation.

One of the exercises that the groups did was to use the affinity technique (after proper introduction to the technique) to define and group elements that they thought characterized the daily meal. They followed the procedure given above and one of the results was the affinity diagram given in Figure 8.5 below.

The two groups came up with almost identical groupings which in itself is very interesting. The grouping given here is for the 35 + team and the only difference between this one and the one given by the other team was that for the younger females the fatty content was moved from the healthy group to the quality group. For this team less fat meant higher quality. We believe that if the affinity technique had not been used we would never have discovered the difference – a difference which is actually very important that you communicate to your customers.

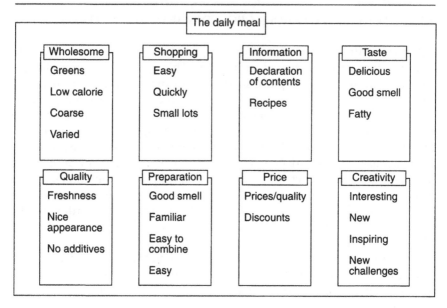

Fig. 8.5 Affinity diagram describing the daily meal.

8.3 MATRIX DIAGRAMS

The matrix diagram is a technique which is used for displaying the relationship between two or more qualitative variables. It is the direct counterpart of graphs in two or more dimensions showing the relationship between quantitative variables.

There are many uses of matrix diagrams in daily business life. Below are shown some of the more typical:

- ORGANIZATIONAL
  initiative diagrams
  responsibility diagrams
  educational planning
- PRODUCT DEVELOPMENT
  quality function deployment
- MARKETING
  media planning
  planning of a parameter mix

There are a number of different forms of matrix diagram. The most common and useful forms are the ones given in Table 8.2 above where the so-called L-, T- and X-shaped matrices are described.

The contents of the matrices are symbols describing the strength of the relationship between the variables. A blank cell means no relationship,

Table 8.2 Matrix forms

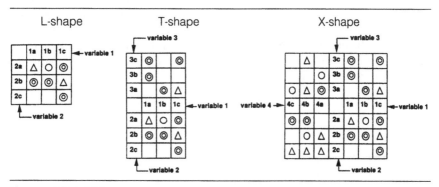

(Source: GOAL/QPC 1989)

while a triangle means a weak relationship, a circle a medium relationship and a double circle a strong relationship.

The L-shaped matrix is the most common. It shows the relationship between two variables and is the direct basis for, e.g. the well-known house of quality from Quality Function Deployment. The T-shaped matrix is just two L-shaped matrices on top of each other. The idea of stacking the matrices follows from the fact that, in this way, it will be possible to make inductions between two of the variables via the third. This is also the idea of the X-shaped matrix. In this matrix the relationship between three variables is directly described and the relationship to the fourth is then found by induction.

The procedure for constructing a matrix may be as follows:

1. Define the problem and choose the team to solve it.
2. Choose the variables to enter the solution.
3. Decide upon the relevant matrix format (L, T, X).
4. Choose symbols for the relationships.
5. Fill in the matrix.

In what follows we describe part of the planning process for a bakery producing and selling butter cookies. The problem described was concerning the distribution of the budget for consultancy at different markets but in order to find a solution it was necessary to break down the problem into relationships that were known and then try to use inference to establish the unknown relationships.

As a starting point the relationship between the motive for buying butter cookies and production parameters was considered and a matrix diagram was built up. On top of this another matrix was built describing the relationship between production parameters and the necessary help at different markets. The result was now a T-shaped matrix but the problem was not yet solved. Hence it was continued with another known relationship which was built into the diagram: the relationship between countries and motives. By adding this to the T-shaped matrix it was possible to infer the relationship between markets and the help needed at different markets. The final result is shown in Figure 8.6 below. The symbols in the upper-left matrix have been calculated by using the algorithm given below the matrix.

Spain	Germany	Japan		Wrapping	Taste	Nourishment	Marketing
○	○	●	Advertising agency	○			○
○	▲	▲	Food specialist			○	▲
○	●	▲	Sensoric experimentation		○	▲	▲
▲	▲	○	Designer decorator	○			
Spain	Germany	Japan	✕	Wrapping	Taste	Nourishment	Marketing
▲	▲	○	Present	○			○
●	○	▲	Snacks	▲	○		○
▲	○		Coffee		●		▲
○			Morning		●	○	▲
●	▲	▲	Sweets	▲	○		○

Algorithm:

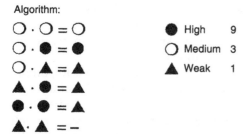

$$\bigcirc \cdot \bigcirc = \bigcirc$$
$$\bigcirc \cdot \bullet = \bullet$$
$$\bigcirc \cdot \blacktriangle = \blacktriangle$$
$$\blacktriangle \cdot \bullet = \blacktriangle$$
$$\bullet \cdot \bullet = \blacktriangle$$
$$\blacktriangle \cdot \blacktriangle = -$$

● High 9
○ Medium 3
▲ Weak 1

Fig. 8.6 Matrix diagram showing the plan matrix for a bakery.

8.4 PRIORITIZATION MATRICES AND ANALYTICAL HIERARCHIES

We all know that in very many cases it will be necessary to choose between alternatives, e.g. for the solution of a problem. When the number of alternatives is large the process of choosing between them becomes increasingly complicated and we need a methodology to help us.

In America there is a methodology called the analytical hierarchy process which breaks down the decision into hierarchies and into simple two-dimensional comparisons which may be understood by anybody. This type of methodology is, in our opinion, extremely important and may be of very great help to managers dealing with quality improvements.

To describe the idea of prioritization let us assume that for the solution of a given problem we have identified four different alternatives A, B, C and D. What we need is the relative importance of these alternatives but we cannot establish this directly. What we then do is to set up a matrix where the alternatives are written both as rows and columns. This is shown in Table 8.3.

Now the prioritization starts by comparing each row with the columns and asking the question: How important is the row alternative compared to the column alternative? The answer to the question is a number describing the relative importance. When the total matrix has been filled in we have the final prioritization matrix from which the idea is that it should be possible to calculate an estimate of the relative importance of the individual alternatives. Before we can do that, however, we must consider some theoretical aspects of the prioritization matrix.

8.4.1 THEORETICAL OUTLINE

Let the i,j entry of the matrix be a_{ij}. We then immediately know that the following must hold good of the entries:

$$a_{ii} = 1 \tag{8.3}$$

i.e. the diagonal elements must be equal to unity and the matrix will be reciprocally symmetric.

$$\frac{1}{a_{ij}} = a_{ji} \tag{8.4}$$

Table 8.3 Prioritization matrix

	A	B	C	D
A				
B				
C				
D				

What we need from this prioritization is a weight describing the relative importance of the four alternatives. Let these weights be w_1 to w_4 (or in general w_n). From this follows that the relationship between the ws and the as must be as follows if the matrix is consistent:

$$a_{ij} = \frac{w_i}{w_j} \qquad (8.5)$$

This leads to the conclusion that

$$a_{ij}\frac{w_j}{w_i} = 1 \qquad (8.6)$$

and from which, by summation over all alternatives, we find that the following interesting relationship must hold:

$$\sum_{j=1}^{n} a_{ij}\frac{w_j}{w_i} = n \leftrightarrow \sum_{j=1}^{n} a_{ij} w_j = nw_i \qquad (8.7)$$

This tells us that a consistent matrix will have rank 1. Furthermore it will only have one eigenvalue different from zero and this eigenvalue will be equal to n, the number of alternatives. The eigenvector corresponding to the eigenvalue n will be equal to the relative weights of the alternatives.

Of course a matrix will in practice seldomly be consistent (apart from 2×2 matrices) but then we can still use the theoretical outline to get the best estimate of the relative weights and furthermore the theory also gives us an indication of the degree of consistency of a given matrix.

In practice we will define the vector of relative weights as the solution to the following matrix equation which is equal to the characteristic equation of the prioritization matrix A:

$$Aw = \lambda_{max} w \qquad (8.8)$$

where λ_{max} is the largest eigenvalue and w is the corresponding eigenvector. In addition we will define the inconsistency by measuring the degree to which the largest eigenvalue deviates from the theoretically largest eigenvalue, n. As suggested by Saathy (1980), the inconsistency index will be measured as follows:

$$ICI = \frac{\lambda_{max} - n}{n - 1} \qquad (8.9)$$

This number tells us how consistent the decision makers have been when they constructed the prioritization matrix. Saathy has suggested that if the ICI exceeds 0.10 the matrix should be rejected and the process should start over again.

This is, of course, a rather complicated theory and to many mainstream managers it may be very difficult to use results as the ones given in the theoretical outline above. Fortunately there are some alternatives. First of all there exists a commercial computer program which can do all the calculations. The name of this program is Expert Choice and it is available for all modern PCs.

Secondly there is a much easier and more straightforward method of obtaining the relative weights. This method is, of course, not as accurate as the one given in the theoretical outline but the results are usually sufficiently precise. The methods goes as follows:

1. Normalize all columns of the matrix so that they add up to one.
2. Compute the individual row averages. The resulting numbers are the relative weights.

For example let the prioritization matrix be:

$$A = \begin{bmatrix} 1 & 1/2 & 1/4 \\ 2 & 1 & 1/4 \\ 4 & 4 & 1 \end{bmatrix}$$

Now follow the procedure above and normalize all columns. In this case we get the following result:

$$A_{norm} = \begin{bmatrix} 1/7 & 1/11 & 1/6 \\ 2/7 & 2/11 & 1/6 \\ 4/7 & 8/11 & 4/6 \end{bmatrix}$$

From this we can calculate the row average and obtain an estimate of the relative weights of the three alternatives. The result is:

$$w = \begin{bmatrix} 0.13 \\ 0.21 \\ 0.66 \end{bmatrix}$$

which tells us that alternative A has been given a weight of 13%, alternative B a weight of 21% and alternative C a weight of 66%.

The degree of inconsistency is not as easy to calculate if you are not going to use the matrix calculations. The method is as follows:

1. multiply the columns of the original matrix by the weights of the alternatives;
2. compute the row sum of the new matrix;
3. divide the row sums by the weights of the alternatives;
4. compute the average of the new numbers. This average is an estimate of λ_{max}.

We will continue with the example from above. In step 1 we multiply the columns by the weights of the alternatives. This leads to the following matrix which we may call C:

$$C = \begin{bmatrix} 0.13 & 0.11 & 0.17 \\ 0.26 & 0.21 & 0.17 \\ 0.52 & 0.84 & 0.66 \end{bmatrix}$$

Now compute the sum of the rows and divide this sum by the weights of the alternatives. This gives.

$$\begin{bmatrix} 0.41/0.13 & 3.15 \\ 0.64/0.21 & = & 3.05 \\ 2.02/0.66 & 3.06 \end{bmatrix}$$

The average of the RHS is now equal to 3.09 from which follows that the *ICI* is:

$$ICI = \frac{3.09 - 3}{3 - 1} = 0.045 = 4.5\% \tag{8.10}$$

We believe that the use of prioritization matrices is going to grow dramatically in the years to come because of the growing complexity of

Table 8.4 Important measures

Intensity of importance	Definition	Explanation
1	Equal importance	Two activities contribute equally to the objective
3	Weak importance of one over the other	Experience and judgment slightly favour one activity over the other
5	Essential or strong importance	Experience and judgment strongly favour one activity over the other
7	Very strong or demonstrated importance	An activity is favoured very strongly over another; its dominance demonstrated in practice
9	Absolute importance	The evidence favouring one activity over another is of the highest possible order of affirmation
2, 4, 6, 8	Intermediate values between adjacent scale values	When compromise is needed

practical decision making. In order to ease the use of the matrices Saathy has suggested a scale to be used when filling in the matrices. This scale is given in Table 8.4 above.

Other scales have been suggested but we believe that the one suggested by Saathy is working reasonably well in practice. To give an example of the use of the scale, assume that alternative A is strongly favoured over alternative B, its dominance is however not demonstrated in practice. In this case the entry in the prioritization matrix at position 1,2 will be 5 and the entry at position 2,1 will be 1/5.

Apart from the use of prioritization matrices another important aspect of the analytical hierarchy process is that decisions are broken down into hierarchies which make it possible to make the decisions in a sequential way. An example of this is given in Figure 8.7 below in which the choice of future strategy was up for discussion. The board was discussing the following alternative in order to find an appropriate mix: price changes, advertising, product development, cost reductions, investments and job enrichment but they could not reach a conclusion just by considering the alternatives. Hence it was decided to break down the decision process into stages and try to evaluate the different stages individually.

The choice between the alternatives will now take place by going through all the levels of the hierarchy using prioritization matrices at each stage in order to evaluate the importance of the individual paths.

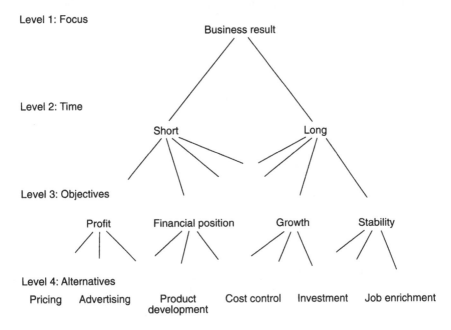

Fig. 8.7 Decision hierarchy for a textile company.

Eventually all paths have been ranked and you end up with a final ranking of the alternatives.

In the authors' experience it takes a little time to convince managers that this is a good way to make decisions. But as soon as they have experienced the value of having consistency measures at each stage, and when decision in this way become very well documented, the opposition disappears.

8.5 AN EXAMPLE

To finalize our demonstration of the use of these techniques we give you an example from a sports club. One of the committees of this club was given a sum of $100,000 to make new initiatives towards the members of the club. They started their work by breaking down the problem of choosing new activities using a tree diagram. This diagram is shown in Figure 8.8.

Based on this the committee started its prioritization by prioritizing between the elements of the first level of the tree: the professionals and the amateurs. This led to the result given in Figure 8.9.

The next step was to prioritize between the actions for the professionals on the one side and the actions for the amateurs on the other. These prioritizations are shown in Figures 8.10 and 8.11.

Now it is possible to complete the hierarchy. At each stage the relative importance is inserted and by multiplication we may now reach the final result. This is shown in Figure 8.12.

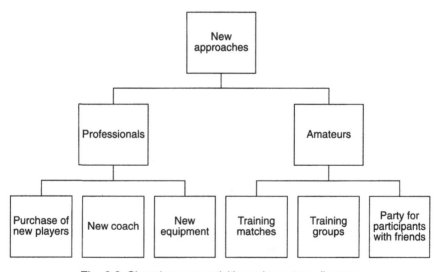

Fig. 8.8 Choosing new activities using a tree diagram.

	E	M	Weight
E	1	1/4	0.20
M	4	1	0.80

Fig. 8.9 Priority between professionals (E) and amateurs (M).

It can be seen from the figure that the budget has now been distributed between the alternatives. All members of the committee were satisfied with the solution because it was clearly based on consensus and it was later on easy to explain why the outcome was as shown.

Only one thing remained and this was to distribute the jobs between the members of the committee. To this end a special version of the matrix diagram was used. The diagram is shown in Figure 8.13.

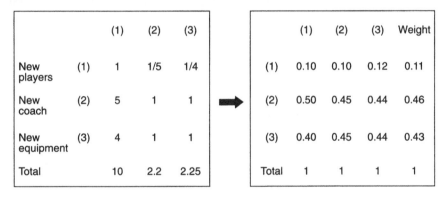

Fig. 8.10 Prioritization between actions for professionals.

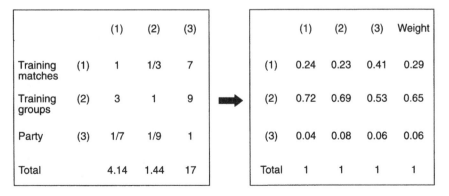

Fig. 8.11 Prioritization between actions for amateurs.

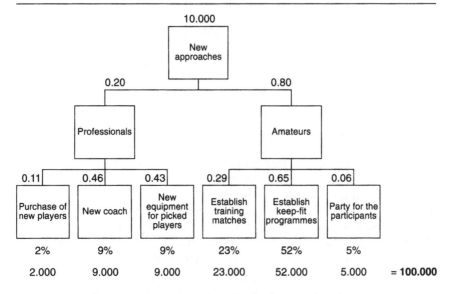

Fig. 8.12 Final hierarchy with distribution of budget.

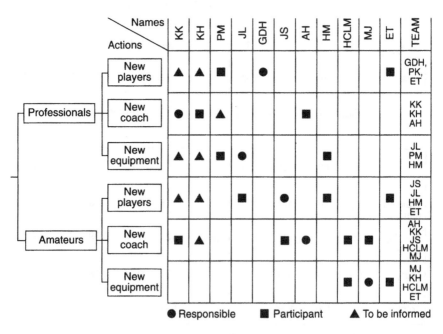

Fig. 8.13 Matrix diagram showing the distribution of jobs.

The conclusion made by the committee members on the use of these techniques in a situation like this was that the techniques are very efficient for reaching the goals fast. In other situations a problem like the one described would have been discussed for ages and when a conclusion had been reached nobody would really be able to explain how it was reached.

REFERENCES

Brassard, M. (1989) *The Memory Jogger Plus*, GOAL/QPC, Methuen, MA,USA.

Johnson, R.A. and Wichern, D.W. (1993) *Applied Multivariate Statistical Analysis*, Prentice-Hall, New York, USA.

Kanji, G.K. and Asher, M. (1996) *100 Methods for Total Quality Management*, SAGE, London.

Mizuno, S. (1988) *Management for Quality Improvement: The Seven New QC Tools*, Productivity Press, Mass., USA.

Saathy, T. (1980) *The Analytical Hierarchy Process*, McGraw-Hill, USA.

Senge, P.M. (1991) *The Fifth Discipline – The Art and Practice of the Learning Organization*, Doubleday Currency, New York, USA.

Measurement of quality: an introduction

9

Modern measurement of quality should of course be closely related to the definition of quality. As mentioned many times the ultimate judge of quality is the customer which means that a system of quality measurement should focus on the entire process which leads to customer satisfaction in the company, from the supplier to the end user.

TQM argues that a basic point behind the creation of customer satisfaction is leadership and it appears from previous chapters in this book that basic aspect of leadership is the ability to deal with the future. This has been demonstrated very nicely by, among others, Jan Leschly, president of Smith Kline, who in a recent speech in Denmark compared his actual way of leading with the ideal as he saw it. His points are demonstrated in Figure 9.1 below.

It appears that Jan Leschly argues that today he spends approximately 60% of his time on fire-fighting, 25% on control and 15% on the future. In his own view a much more appropriate way of leading would be, so to speak, to turn the figures upside down and spend 60% of your time on the future, 25% on control and only 15% on fire-fighting.

We believe that the situation described by Jan Leschly holds true for many leaders in the Western world. There is a clear tendency that leaders in general are much more focused on short-term profits that on the process that creates profit. This again may lead to fire-fighting and to the possible disturbing of processes that may be in statistical control.

The result of this may very well be an increase in the variability of the company's performance and hence an increase in quality costs. In this way 'the short-term leader' who demonstrates leadership by fighting fires all over the company may very well be achieving quite the opposite of what it wants to achieve.

To be more specific we are of the opinion that 'short-term leadership' may be synonymous with low quality leadership and we are quite sure that in the future it will be necessary to adopt a different leadership style in order to survive, a leadership style which in its nature is long term and which focuses on the processes that lead to the results rather than the results themselves. This does not of course mean that the results are uninteresting *per se* but rather that when the results are there you can do nothing about them. They are the results of actions taken a long time ago.

All this is of course much easier said than done. In the modern business environment leaders may not be able to do anything but act on a short-term basis because they do not have the necessary information to do otherwise. To act on a long-term basis requires that you have an information system which provides early warning and which makes it possible for you and gives you time to make the necessary adjustments to the processes before they turn into unwanted business results. In our view this is what modern measurement of quality is all about.

In order to create an interrelated system of quality measurements we have decided to define the measurement system according to Table 9.1 below, where measurements are classified according to two criteria: the stakeholder and whether we are talking about processes or results. (See also section 4.3.)

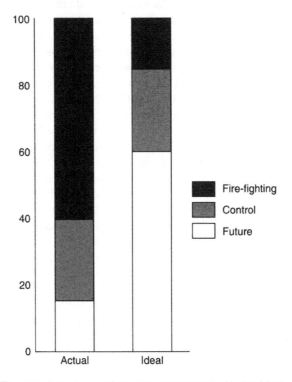

Fig. 9.1 Actual way of leading compared with the ideal.

Table 9.1 Measurement of quality – the extended concept

	The company	The customer	The society
The process	Employee satisfaction (ESI) Checkpoints concerning the internal service structure	Control and checkpoints concerning the internal definition of product and service quality	Control and checkpoints concerning, e.g. environment, life cycles etc.
The result	Business results Financial ratios	Customer satisfaction (CSI) Checkpoints describing the customer satisfaction	'Ethical accounts' Environmental accounts

As appears from Table 9.1 we distinguish between measurements related to the process and measurements related to the result. The reason for this is obvious in the light of what has been said above and in the light of the definition of TQM. Furthermore we distinguish between three 'interested parties': the company itself, the customer and the society. The first two should obviously be part of a measurement system according to the definition of TQM and the third has been included because there is no doubt that the focus on companies in relation to their effect on society will be increased in the future and we expect that very soon we are going to see a great deal of new legislation within this area.

Traditional measurements have focused on the lower left-hand corner of this table, i.e. the business result and we have built up extremely detailed reporting systems which can provide information about all possible types of breakdown of the business result. However, as mentioned above this type of information is pointing backwards and at this stage it is too late to do anything about the results. What we need is something which can tell us about what is going to happen with the business result in the future. This type of information we find in the rest of the table and we especially believe (and also have documentation for) that the first four squares of the table are related in a closed loop which may be called the improvement cycle. This loop is demonstrated in Figure 9.2.

This is particularly due to an increase in customer loyalty stemming from an increase in customer satisfaction. The relationship between customer satisfaction and customer loyalty has been documented empirically several times. One example is Rank Xerox, Denmark who, in their application for the Danish Quality Award, reported that when they analysed customer satisfaction on a five-point scale where 1 is very

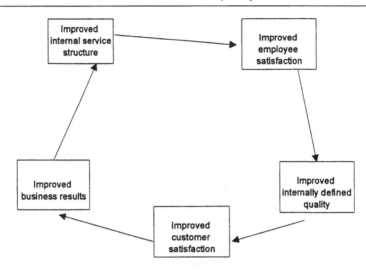

Fig. 9.2 The improvement loop.

dissatisfied and 5 is very satisfied they observed that on average 93% of those customers who were very satisfied (5) came back as customers, while only 60% of those who gave a 4 came back.

Another example is a large Danish real estate company who, in a customer satisfaction survey, asked approximately 2500 customers to evaluate the company on 20 different parameters. From this evaluation an average value for customer satisfaction (customer satisfaction index) was calculated. The entire evaluation took place on a five-point scale with 5 as the best score which means that the customer satisfaction index will have values in the interval from 1 to 5.

In addition to the questions on parameters, a series of questions concerning loyalty were asked and from this, a loyalty index was computed and related to the customer satisfaction index. This analysis revealed some very interesting results which are summarized in Figure 9.3 below in which the customer satisfaction index is related to the probability of using the real estate agent once again (probability of being loyal).

It appears that there is a very close relationship between customer satisfaction and customer loyalty. The relationship is beautifully described by a logistic model.

Furthermore it appears from the figure that in this case the loyalty is around 35% when the customer satisfaction index is 3, i.e. neither good nor bad. When the customer satisfaction increases to 4 a dramatic increase in loyalty is observed. In this case the loyalty is more than 90%. Thus the area between 3 and 4 is very important and it appears that even very small changes in customer satisfaction in this area may lead to large changes in the probability of loyalty.

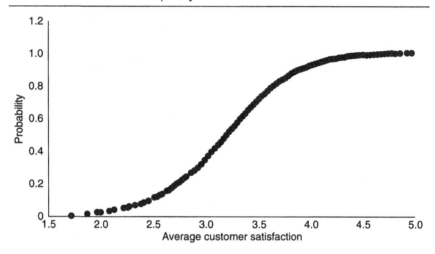

Fig. 9.3 Probability of loyalty as a function of customer satisfaction.

The observed relationship between business results and customer loyalty on one side and customer satisfaction on the other is very important information for modern management. This information provides early warning about future business results and thus provides management with an instrument to correct failures before they affect the business result.

The next logical step will be to take the analysis one step further back to find internal indicators of quality which are closely related to customer satisfaction. In this case the warning system will be even better. These indicators which in Table 9.1 have been named control points and checkpoints will of course be company specific even if some generic measure may be defined.

Moving even further back we come to the employee satisfaction measure and other measures of the processes in the company. We expect these to be closely related to the internally defined quality. This is actually one of the basic assumptions of TQM. The more satisfied and more motivated employees you have the higher the quality in the company.

An indicator of this has been established in the world's largest service company, the International Service System (ISS) where employee satisfaction and customer satisfaction have been measured on a regular basis for some years now (see Chapter 10). In order to verify the hypothesis of the improvement circle in Figure 9.2, employee satisfaction and customer satisfaction were measured for 19 different districts in the cleaning division of the company in 1993. The results were measured on a traditional five-point scale and the employee satisfaction index and the

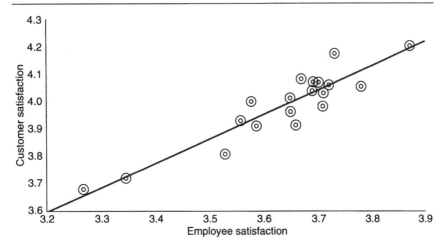

Fig. 9.4 Relationship between ESI and CSI.

customer satisfaction index were both computed as weighted average of the individual parameters. The results are shown in Figure 9.4.

The interesting figures shown in Figure 9.4 demonstrate a clear linear relationship between employee satisfaction and customer satisfaction. The higher the employee satisfaction the higher the customer satisfaction. The equation of the relationship is as follows:

$$CSI = 0.75 + 0.89 \, ESI \qquad (R^2 = 0.85) \qquad (9.1)$$

The coefficients of the equation are highly significant. Thus the standard deviation of the constant term is 0.33 and of the slope is 0.09. Furthermore we cannot reject a hypothesis that the slope is equal to 1.

It appears from this that a unit change in employee satisfaction more or less gives the same change in customer satisfaction. We cannot of course, just from these figures claim that this is a causal relationship but combined with other information we believe that this is strong evidence for the existence of an improvement circle like the one described in Figure 9.2. To us, therefore, creation of a measurement system along the lines given in Table 9.1 is necessary. Only in this way will management be able to lead the company upstream and thus prevent the disasters that inevitably follow the fire-fighting of short-term management.

In the following chapters we follow this up and will describe in detail the measurement of customer satisfaction, employee satisfaction and the control and checkpoints of the process in relation to the customer.

Measurement of customer satisfaction   10

10.1 INTRODUCTION

As mentioned in the previous chapters the concept of quality has changed dramatically during the last decade or so. Today increasing customer orientation has forced companies to use a definition of quality in terms of customer satisfaction.

This change, of course, means that the measurement of quality also has to be changed. It is no longer sufficient just to measure quality internally. Instead you also have to go to the market-place and ask the customers about their impression of the total set of goods and services they receive from the company. A number of companies, especially Japanese companies, have already realized this but many Western companies (especially European) are still lagging behind when it comes to quality measurements from the market-place. This has been demonstrated very clearly in our QED study. In Japan almost every member company of JUSE has a systematic way of measuring and reporting customer satisfaction. In Denmark this only holds true for two out of three comparable companies.

In this chapter we develop a theoretical framework for the measurement of customer satisfaction. Furthermore we suggest a practical implementation (see Kristensen *et al.*, 1992). A practical example is given in Chapter 20.

10.2 THEORETICAL CONSIDERATIONS

We assume that the company has a very simple delivery system in which the goods and services are delivered directly to the end user and where the company can obtain customer satisfaction information directly from the end user. Furthermore it is assumed that the goods and services are evaluated by the customer on n different parameters concerning importance of and satisfaction with each parameter. Let the rate of importance (weight) of the ith parameter be ω_i and let c_i be the individual satisfaction evaluations on an appropriate scale. We then define the customer satisfaction index (CSI) as follows:

$$CSI = \sum_{i=1}^{N} \omega_i c_i \tag{10.1}$$

We now assume that the revenue from customer satisfaction can be described as some function of the CSI, $\Phi(CSI)$. This function is of course assumed to be an increasing function of CSI – the larger the CSI the larger the revenue.

Furthermore, we assume that the cost of obtaining customer satisfaction is quadratic with k as a cost parameter. This is a standard assumption within economic theory and furthermore it is in accordance with, e.g. the philosophy of Taguchi. What the assumption means is that it becomes more and more expensive to increase customer satisfaction when customer satisfaction is already at a high level. To put it in another way, the marginal cost is not constant but instead is an increasing function of customer satisfaction.

From this it follows that the expected profit is given by

$$\Pi = \Phi\left(\sum_{i=1}^{N} \omega_i c_i\right) - \sum_{i=1}^{N} k_i c_i^2 \tag{10.2}$$

In order to balance the quality effort in the company the management problem is to maximize profit with respect to the mean value of the individual quality parameters. The first-order conditions of this maximization are equal to

$$\frac{\delta \Pi}{\delta c_i} = \Phi'(CSI)\omega_i - 2k_i c_i = 0 \qquad i = 1, \ldots, N \tag{10.3}$$

These conditions may be rewritten in several ways, such as

$$\frac{c_i}{\omega_i} = \frac{\Phi'(CSI)}{2k_i} \qquad i = 1, \ldots, N \tag{10.4}$$

The left-hand side of this equation may be interpreted as an index explaining how well the company fulfils the expectations of the customer. The right-hand side balances revenue and costs and tells us that the required degree of fulfilment will depend upon how much you get from customer satisfaction measured in relation to the costs.

Practical application of the results will depend upon the available information in the company. Weight and satisfaction can be estimated by sampling the market while it will usually be more difficult to get information about individual cost factors. Sometimes a rough estimate of cost ratios will exist but in many cases it will be necessary to assume identical costs.

These reflections lead to the suggestion that the company should balance its quality effort according to the rule:

$$\frac{c_i}{\omega_i} = \frac{c_j}{\omega_j} \quad \forall i, j \tag{10.5}$$

According to this simple rule which easily can be implemented in practice the degree of fulfilment should be equal for all quality parameters in the company.

An even simpler presentation of the result can be made if we assume that the right-hand side of equation (5) is equal to a constant. This will be the case, e.g. if k is equal to 0.5 and that the derivative of the revenue function with respect to CSI is equal to 1. In this case the following very simple rule will result.

This type of result will make it very easy to report the outcome of the customer satisfaction study in a graphical way as we shall see later.

All results have been obtained under the assumption that financial restrictions are without importance in the company. If costs are subject to a restriction this is easily incorporated in the results and it will not lead to dramatic changes.

10.3 A PRACTICAL PROCEDURE

A general practical procedure for the analysis of customer satisfaction will consist of the following steps:

1. determination of the customer and the process leading from the company to the customer;
2. pre-segmentation of the customers;
3. determination of relevant quality attributes (parameters);
4. choice of competitors;
5. design of questionnaire;
6. sampling;
7. post-segmentation of customers based on results;
8. determination of quality types;
9. construction of quality maps;
10. determination of cost points;
11. determination of sales points and customer loyalty;
12. SWOT analysis;
13. determination of corrective actions.

The structure of the procedure is given in the flow chart in Figure 10.1

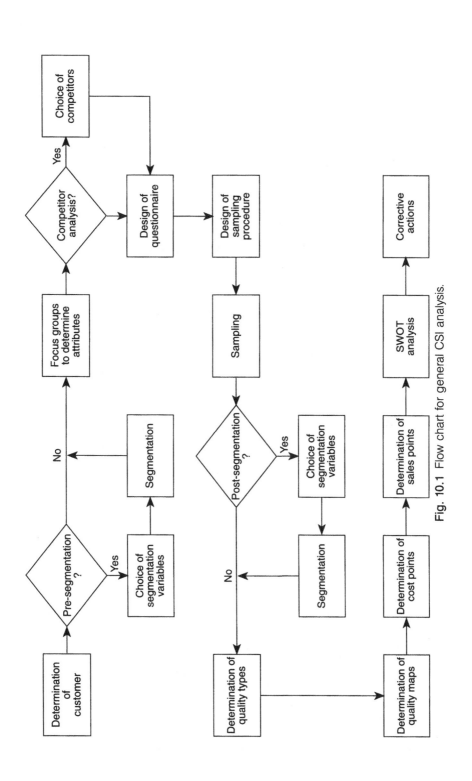

Fig. 10.1 Flow chart for general CSI analysis.

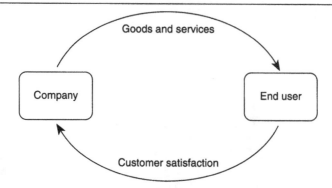

Fig. 10.2 Simple customer satisfaction.

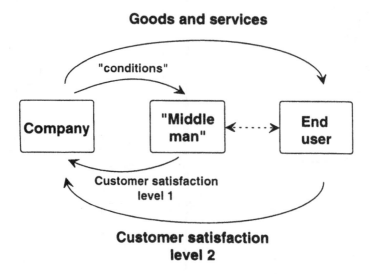

Fig. 10.3 Dual customer satisfaction.

10.3.1 STEPS 1 AND 2

The first crucial step is to determine the customer and the process leading from the company to the customer. In certain simple cases we have a situation like the one described in Figure 10.2 where the company delivers goods and services to the end user and gets information back concerning the satisfaction.

In most cases, however, the situation is more like the one described in Figure 10.3 where the delivery consists of a chain of so-called middlemen before the goods and services reach the final customer.

It is crucial of course that from the start it is well-known what the delivery system looks like. It may lead to very wrong conclusions if one forgets certain parts of the chain as the following example illustrates.

A major cleaning company in New York had contracts for the cleaning of large building complexes with a large number of tenants in each. The level of cleaning and the prices were discussed not with the individual tenants but rather with a building manager who decided everything in relation to the contract with the cleaning company. The cleaning company never really considered the individual tenants as their customers, instead they focused on the building manager. For a long time this went well. From time to time the cleaning company called up the building manager and asked him about his satisfaction and usually he was satisfied because in most cases the cleaning company lived up to the contract. After a time, however, the tenants became more and more dissatisfied with the services they received. In the first case they did not say anything to the building manager, instead they gathered and decided that they wanted another cleaning company to do the job. A spokesperson went to the building manager and told him that they were not satisfied with the cleaning company and he was left with no other choice but to fire the cleaning company. The company of course could not understand this because as far as it knew it had lived up to the contract and its customer was satisfied. It learned its lesson, however, and in the future it never just considered the middleman as its customer. Instead it went out all the way to the end users and asked them about satisfaction and it used this information not just to improve its own services but also to keep the building manager informed about the situation.

To sum up, it is extremely important that the customer is clearly defined from the start. The process must be clear and the possible points of measurement must be identified.

Apart from this it should also at this stage be decided if customers should be segmented. In most cases customers do not constitute a homogeneous group. Different segments will require different treatments. Hence it will usually be necessary to split up customers in groups based upon the information which is already used within marketing, e.g. size of customer, private or public customer, location etc. In this case we can direct corrective action as close as possible to the individual customer.

10.3.2 STEP 3

Determination of relevant attributes is the next important step. It is very important that this takes place in co-operation with the customer. In too many cases companies themselves define what is relevant to the customer. This is a very bad idea because experience shows that very often companies only have a vague impression of what is really relevant to the customer. It follows from this that customers should participate in defining the relevant attributes and the best way of doing this is usually by setting up focus groups. Groups with approximately eight members are usually efficient if they are led by trained psychologists or moderators. The groups come up with a list of relevant parameters and this list will be the starting point for the next step in which a questionnaire is designed.

10.3.3 STEPS 4, 5 AND 6

In this group of steps the sampling takes place but first of all it must be decided whether competitors should be included in the analysis. In many cases it will be a great advantage to have competitors in the analysis but this will of course make the entire customer satisfaction analysis somewhat larger. Furthermore it may complicate the analysis because in some cases it will be difficult to find respondents who know both the company in question and the competitors.

Depending upon the decision concerning competitors a questionnaire must be designed. The size of the questionnaire should be kept to a minimum in order not to annoy the customers. We usually recommend that the number of parameters should not exceed 30. The questionnaire must be professional in appearance and in the case of business-to-business research a contact person must be identified.

10.3.4 STEPS 7 AND 8

Before constructing quality maps it will usually be a good idea to go through the collected material in order to let the data speak. First of all it is very useful to find out whether there are any segments in the material other than the ones already defined. This can be done by using a variety of statistical tools. If significant groupings are found, these groupings will also be used when reporting the final results.

Furthermore the material should also be analysed in order to find out what kind of quality the different parameters represent. Is it expected quality or perhaps value-added? To this end different techniques have been developed by different market research companies. This kind of information will be very important when evaluating the possible outcome of actions taken later on.

10.3.5 STEPS 9, 10 AND 11

The following step will be to introduce the quality map. This map is based upon the theoretical result above in which the optimum was found

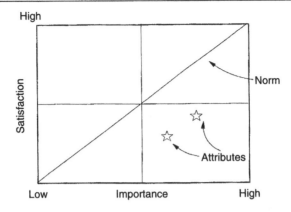

Fig. 10.4 A quality map.

when the importance is equal to the satisfaction for each parameter. An example of such a map is given in Figure 10.4.

The map is constructed by plotting the importance on the horizontal axis against the satisfaction on the vertical axis. To reach optimum profit, theory then shows us that the parameters should be placed on the principal diagonal of this map.

Very often, however, decision makers are not as strict as this. Instead the map is divided into squares by dividing each axis into two, using the average importance and the average satisfaction as dividing points. These four squares are then used for decisions concerning actions. The two squares with either high/high or low/low are of course the squares in which the parameters have a correct placing. The other two squares are more problematic. If the importance is high and the satisfaction is low the company is faced with a serious problem which may lead to loss of customers in the future. Similarly if the importance is low and the satisfaction is high the company has allocated its resources in the wrong way. Being good at something which the customers do not evaluate means a loss of money. Instead these resources could be used for improving the situation in the high/low square.

The reasoning above depends of course upon the assumptions made in section 10.2. A very important assumption is that the costs of improving the satisfaction of a parameter are equal for each parameter. If this is not the case we have to establish a cost index in the company and use this index as a correction factor for each parameter. Then the horizontal axis will no longer be the importance of the parameters but instead the importance per unit of the costs. This is demonstrated in Figure 10.5 below.

Another way of improving the analysis would be to introduce 'sales points' or 'loyalty points' in the analysis to see if there are any differences

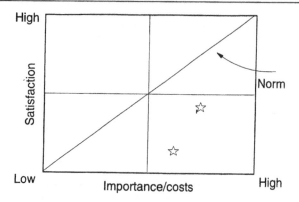

Fig. 10.5 Quality map with the introduction of costs.

between the importances established in the interview with the customer and the loyalty established from a different set of questions. This difference will usually reflect a difference between short-term and long-term importance of the parameters (see Kristensen and Mortensen, 1996).

In practice the loyalty points are constructed by using a series of questions concerning the loyalty of the customer towards the company. Will the customer buy again, recommend the company to others and similar questions. Using these questions it will then be possible, using statistical techniques, to determine the (short-time) loyalty effect of each parameter. The results may then be communicated as shown in Figures 10.6 and 10.7 below, depending upon whether competitors are included in the analysis or not.

These maps may be interpreted in the same way as the quality maps. The difference is that they tend to separate the short-term corrections from the more long-term corrections. There is no doubt that the theoretical results above should be followed but the loyalty maps will help you to find the best sequence of improvements by selecting the parameters

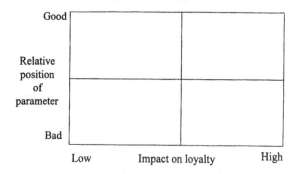

Fig. 10.6 Effect on loyalty and relative position.

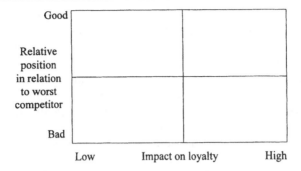

Fig. 10.7 Effect on loyalty and competitor analysis.

with the worst relative position (satisfaction/importance) and highest loyalty effect first.

10.3.6 STEP 12

The entire discussion until now has been on an operational basis. But the results of a customer satisfaction survey should also be used at the strategic level. The quality map is a perfect instrument for this. Usually strategic discussions will take place using a SWOT analysis, i.e. identifying strengths, weaknesses, opportunities and threats. Using the quality map the SWOT elements can be identified as shown in Figure 10.8 below.

Of course the threats will be found where the importance is high combined with a low satisfaction and strengths will be where both are high. Actions concerning these two are not very different at the strategic level from the operational level. It is somewhat different when we consider the other two elements of the figure. From an operational point

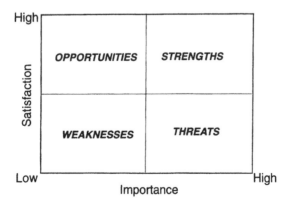

Fig. 10.8 SWOT analysis based on a customer satisfaction survey.

of view the actions will be to adjust the parameters in this part of the map in such a way that they will be concentrated in the low/low part. This will not necessarily be the case when we consider the map from a strategic point of view. From this point of view parameters in this part of the map should not exist or rather they should all be changed to become strengths. In this case the parameters with a high degree of satisfaction are our opportunities. With these parameters we are already performing well and consequently the job will be to convince our customers that this group of parameters is important to them. Concerning the low/low parameters these may strategically be seen as weaknesses. We are not doing very well. On the other hand the parameters are not very important but if the situation changes and customers change their evaluation then the parameters may become a threat. This could easily happen if our competitors find out that we do not perform very well in these cases. They may then try to convince the customers about the importance of the parameters and all of a sudden we are left with a threat.

REFERENCES

Hoinville, G. and Jowell, R. (1982) *Survey Research Practice*, Heinemann Educational Books, London.

Kristensen, K., Dahlgaard, J.J. and Kanji, G.K. (1992) On measurement of customer satisfaction, *Total Quality Management*, 3(2), 123–8.

Kristensen, K. and Martensen, A. (1996) Linking customer satisfaction to loyalty and performance, *Research Methodologies for the New Marketing*, ESOMAR Publication Series, vol. 204, 159–70.

Moser, C.A. and Kalton, G. (1981) *Survey Methods in Social Investigation*, Heinemann Educational Books, London.

Measurement of employee satisfaction   11

In section 4.3.2 we concluded that:

> One of the main control points of 'human quality' is employee satisfaction; which should be measured and balanced in the same way as customer satisfaction.

In this chapter we will show how employee satisfaction can be measured and how these measurements may be used as a tool for continuous improvements.

An employee satisfaction survey can be undertaken after carrying out the following eight-step guidelines:

1. Set up focus groups with employees to determine relevant topics.
2. Design the questionnaire, including questions about both evaluation and importance for each topic.
3. Compile presentation material for all departments.
4. Present the material in the departments.
5. Carry out the survey.
6. Report at both total and departmental levels.
7. Form improvement teams.
8. Hold an employee conference.

These points are discussed in greater depth in the following pages.

11.1 SET UP FOCUS GROUPS WITH EMPLOYEES TO DETERMINE RELEVANT TOPICS

It is crucial to the success of the survey that the employees feel that the survey is their own. They should therefore be included in designing the survey. It is naïve anyway to think that a survey meant to illustrate the areas/problems/improvement possibilities that are relevant to employees can be designed without their collaboration. The best way to involve the employees is to ask them which elements of their job are important to them and also which of these elements, in their view, should be improved.

One effective method for collecting such information is to set up employee focus groups with participants from different departments of the company. The aim is to collect the information from a small representative group of employees, usually two to three groups with six to eight participants each are enough to represent the employees.

When a group meets the agenda for the meeting is presented by the person who is in charge of setting up the system for measuring the satisfaction of the employees. After that we recommend that the employees receive a short introduction (30 minutes) to the rules of brainstorming with affinity analysis and then the group starts with its own brainstorm and affinity analysis. The issue to brainstorm might be formulated as follows:

What are the important elements of my job which should be improved before I can contribute more effectively to continuous improvements?

The result of each focus group will typically be 30–50 ideas which are grouped in 5–10 main groups (co-operation, communication etc.). An analysis of the two to three affinity diagrams will show overlapping ideas so there is a need to construct an overall affinity diagram which is the input to the next step: designing the questionnaire.

11.2 DESIGN THE QUESTIONNAIRE INCLUDING QUESTIONS ABOUT BOTH EVALUATION AND IMPORTANCE FOR EACH TOPIC

Experience shows that the questions in an employee survey may be grouped in the following main groups:

- Co-operation
  - between employees
  - between departments
  - helping others
- Communication and feedback
  - communication between employees
  - feedback from managers
  - feedback from customers
- Work content
  - independence
  - variety
  - challenges to skills

- Daily working conditions
  - targets for and definition of tasks
  - time frameworks
  - measurement of the end result
  - importance of the end result for the firm
  - education and training
- Wages and conditions of employment
  - wages
  - working hours
  - job security
  - pensions
- Information about goals and policies
  - information about the firm's *raison d'être*
  - information about the firm's goals (short- and long-term)
  - information about departmental goals
  - information about results
- Management
  - qualifications
  - commitment
  - openness
  - credibility
  - the ability to guide and support.

The actual questionnaire should not be too comprehensive. Experience has shown that there should not be more than 30–40 questions. One technique to use when reducing the number of questions is to run a pilot test with data from a small sample of employees. By using the statistical

Table 11.1 An example of a questionnaire to measure employee satisfaction

Job elements	Importance 1 2 3 4 5	Satisfaction 1 2 3 4 5
1. I can plan and decide by myself how my job is done	1 2 3 4 5	1 2 3 4 5
2. My job demands that I do several different activities so that I have to use all my creative abilities	1 2 3 4 5	1 2 3 4 5
3. I'm well trained before new work processes or new systems are introduced	1 2 3 4 5	1 2 3 4 5
4. The work flow between the different functions of the organization is simple	1 2 3 4 5	1 2 3 4 5
5. The co-operation and co-ordination between departments	1 2 3 4 5	1 2 3 4 5

technique 'factor analysis' the questions which correlate together can be identified and hence a selection from these questions can be done to be included in the final questionnaire. Another more simple technique is to select three to five ideas from the final affinity diagram and hence construct the questions from these ideas.

As with customer satisfaction surveys, employee surveys also ask about the evaluation and importance of each area, using, e.g. a five-point scale. In Table 11.1 the first page of the questionnaire used at Robert Bosch, Denmark, is shown. The questionnaire which has been used since 1994 contains 39 questions. As the table shows the employees are asked to evaluate both the importance and the satisfaction of each element specified in the questionnaire. Without such data it will be difficult in step 7 to decide which elements are most important to improve.

11.3 COMPILE PRESENTATION MATERIAL FOR ALL DEPARTMENTS AND PRESENT THE MATERIAL TO THE DEPARTMENTS

It is essential to avoid the creation of myths in connection with an employee survey. Openness is therefore a key word. It is the departmental manager's job (if necessary, assisted by a quality co-ordinator) to ensure that all employees understand the purpose of the survey and to inform them that they are guaranteed full anonymity.

The most important material to present to the employees is the questionnaire to be used. The manager should take time to present the questionnaire and discuss it with his employees. Besides the questionnaire, results from previous surveys may be valuable to present and discuss. Such examples may come from other companies, other departments or from the same department where the material is presented.

11.4 CARRY OUT THE SURVEY

The questionnaire should be filled out within the same time interval in all departments. To increase the response rate the questionnaire may be analysed by an external consultant who guarantees anonymity. The collection of the filled out questionnaires and check for 'everybody's participation' should be done by a person who has the trust of the employees. The department's quality co-ordinator may be the person who has the ownership of that activity.

To illustrate the importance of this step a company increased the response rate from approximately 60% to 90% by asking the departments' secretary to collect the filled in questionnaires. The year before the questionnaires had been collected by the company's central personal department.

11.5 REPORT AT BOTH TOTAL AND DEPARTMENTAL LEVEL

The result of the employee satisfaction survey should be reported in the same way as a customer satisfaction survey. Top management should receive the overall employee satisfaction index. This index shows the progress or the lack of progress in employee satisfaction. Together with the overall index top management should also ask for the employee satisfaction index from each department. Such results will help the top management group to identify the departments that need help.

At the departmental level each departmental manager needs the overall index from his own department plus group results and the details about the questions in each group. Such information will help the departmental manager and his employees to identify which elements of customer satisfaction should be improved first.

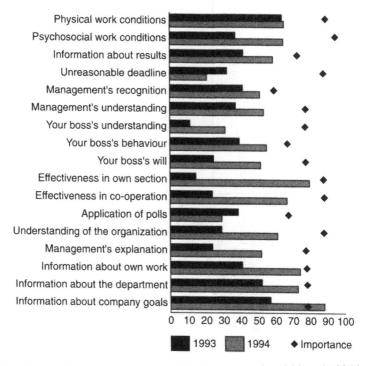

Fig. 11.1 The results of the employee satisfaction survey for 1993 and 1994 in L.M. Erickson, Denmark: satisfaction and importance (results shown are from one department only with 17 employees in 1993 and 15 in 1994).

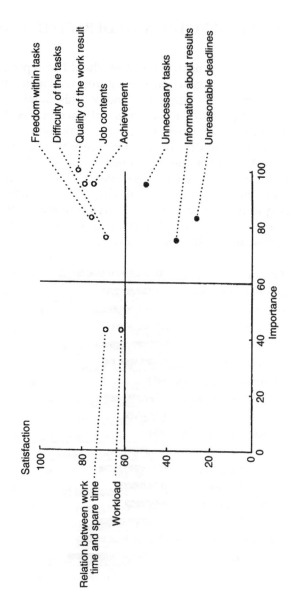

Fig. 11.2 Some results from the employee satisfaction survey.

11.6 FORM IMPROVEMENT TEAMS

As mentioned above, it is the employees' survey. They have helped to design it themselves and, through their answers, they have shown where possibilities for improvements exist. Therefore they should also be allowed a say in how to implement the improvements. Improvement teams should therefore be formed in those parts of the company where the survey has indicated opportunities for improvements. This means that improvement teams must be formed at both departmental level and cross-organizationally.

To show the effect of focusing on the results of an employee satisfaction survey we present in Figure 11.1 some of the results of the survey run at L.M. Erichson, Denmark, in 1993 and 1994. The results shown in Figure 11.2 are the data from one department in L.M. Erichson. The data show the average satisfaction in 1993 and 1994 in relation to 17 questions from the questionnaire. The questions were selected because a gap between satisfaction and importance (the stars) was identified. Hence improvement teams were formed in order to identify the causes behind the gaps and to implement improvements. After only one year there were considerable improvements in employee satisfaction.

11.7 HOLD AN EMPLOYEE CONFERENCE

The exchange of experiences is important as regards continuous improvements and general motivation in the firm. We therefore suggest that employees be given the opportunity at the conference to discuss the various areas they have dealt with and the suggestions they have made. The results of initiative (implemented suggestions) from earlier employee surveys can also be discussed at the conference.

Quality checkpoints and quality control points

12

In section 4.3.3 we defined and discussed the differences between quality control points and quality checkpoints. To recapitulate:

> When measuring the state of a process result, we say that we have established a 'quality control point'.

> When measuring the state of a process, we say that we have established a 'quality checkpoint'.

Massaki Imai argued in his book *Kaizen* (1986) that western managers were most interested in the results, i.e. different quality control points while Japanese managers also focused on the various process measures, i.e. various quality checkpoints which were expected to have an effect on the results.

With the introduction of TQM and the dissemination and application of the self-assessment material from the Malcolm Baldridge Quality Award and the European Quality Award it is our experience that much has changed in the West since Imai wrote his book. Western managers are now aware of the importance of establishing a measuring system which includes measurements from the process (management as well as production processes) which enable the results and also measurements of the results.

Of course there are problems in establishing a coherent measurement system which comprises the most important check and control points. The problem is not only to establish a model of the whole measurement system but also to have the employees involved in the identification and measurement of the critical control and checkpoints of the specific processes (administrative as well as production processes).

In establishing a model of the whole system, TQM models, e.g. the European Quality Award Model, may be of great help and if a company uses this model in a continuous self-assessment process where all departments are involved in the quality culture will gradually change to a culture where people become involved in the identification, measurement and improvement of their own critical check- and control points.

In the process of establishing an effective measuring system most companies need some inspiration from other companies. We will therefore conclude this chapter by showing some examples taken from different companies. Most of the examples are specific applications of the generic quality measure discussed in section 4.3.3:

$$\text{Total defects per unit} = \frac{\text{number of defects}}{\text{numbers of units produced or tested}}$$

It is our experience that most of the quality measures may be used together with control charts in order to be able to analyse and distinguish between specific causes and common causes of variation.

Examples of quality measures for the whole firm, i.e general quality measures (measures which can be used for both the firm as a whole and individual departments):

- Meeting delivery times as a % of filled orders.
- Number of complaints as a % of filled orders.
- Failure costs as a % of turnover or production value.
- Rate of personnel turnover.
- Number of absentee days as a % of total working days.
- Number of quality improvement suggestions per employee.
- Number of employees in quality improvement teams as a % of total employees.
- Number of hours allotted to education as a % of planned time.

Examples of quality measures in purchasing:

- Number of rejected deliveries as a % of total deliveries.
- Cost of wrong deliveries as a % of purchase value.
- Number of purchase orders with defects as a % of total orders.
- Production stops in time caused by wrong purchases in relation to total production time.
- Number of inventory days (rate of inventory turnover).

Examples of quality measures in production (in a broad sense, i.e. including the production of services):

- Used production time as a % of planned time.
- Failure costs as a % of production value.
- Number of repaired or scrapped products as a % of total produced products.
- Idle time as a % of total production time.
- Number of inventory days for semi-manufactured goods.
- Ancillary materials, e.g. lubricants, tools etc. as a % of production value.

- Number of invoiceable hours as a % of total time consumption.
- Number of injuries as a % of number of employees.

Examples of quality measures in administration and sales:
- Number of orders with defects as a % of total orders.
- Numbers of orders with errors as a % of total invoices.
- Number of credit notes as a % of total invoices.
- Service costs due to wrong use as a % of sales.
- Auxiliary materials/resources as a % of wage costs.
- Number of unsuccessful phone calls as a % of total calls.
- Number of debtor days.

Examples of quality measures in development and design:
- Number of design changes after approved design in relation to total designs.
- Number of development projects which result in approved projects in relation to total development projects.
- Failure costs due to the development departments as a % of production or sales value.
- Time consumed in development as a % of planned time consumption.

As the above examples show, there are plenty of opportunities for defining quality measures and establishing quality control/quality checkpoints throughout the firm. Such measures are important in connection with continuous improvements.

There are many more examples than the ones outlined above. So it is important that management and the employees in the various firms and processes take the time needed to determine whether the examples shown here can be used or whether there are alternative possibilities for both quality checkpoints and quality control points.

REFERENCES

Imai, M. (1986) *KAIZEN – The Key to Japan's Competitive Success*, The Kaizen Institute Ltd, London.
Motorola (1990) *Six Sigma Quality – TQC American Style*, Motorola, USA.

Quality measurement in product development

13

As apparent from the previous chapters, the quality concept is defined in several ways. The different quality organizations use different definitions and the definitions may also be changed over time. It is therefore understandable that among many practitioners there is considerable uncertainty in the definition that can enable the user of quality management to actually measure quality and especially quality in relation to product development.

Deming (1984) stated that 'quality can be defined only in terms of the agent'. In other words, it is the user of the product who is the final judge of the quality. This view dates as far back as Shewhart (1931 who stated that 'the difficulty in defining quality is to translate future needs of the user into measurable characteristics, so that the product can be designed and turned out to give satisfaction at a price that the user will pay'. Correspondingly, Oyrzanowski (1984) stated that 'the consumer is the final judge of the best quality of a given product. It can be defined through market research, marketing etc.'

With these views as our starting point, we will follow by giving a definition of the quality concept that can be directly related to the necessary statistical measurement. The measuring methods are outlined and a number of cases will be presented to demonstrate the use of the definitions in practice.

13.1 DEFINITION OF THE QUALITY CONCEPT FROM A MEASUREMENT POINT OF VIEW

In the practical measurement of quality there are two aspects to be clarified:

1. Are the properties manifest or latent? Manifest properties are directly measurable, such as the number of doors in a car, whereas latent

Table 13.1 Typologization of the quality concept

Type of consumer	Latent (not measurable)	Manifest (measurable)
Homogeneous	Semi-subjective quality: not directly measurable quality, but perception is the same for all consumers	Objective quality: directly measurable quality with the same perception for all consumers
Heterogeneous	Subjective quality: not directly measurable quality with different perception with consumers	Semi-objective quality: directly measurable quality but different perception with consumers

properties are not directly measurable, e.g. properties of a more artistic nature, such as the design of a tablecloth.

2. Are the users, i.e. the real quality judges, homogeneous or heterogeneous? Homogeneous users have a uniform attitude to or assessment of quality, whereas heterogeneous users have a differentiated perception of quality.

Combining these two facts gives an operational typologization of the quality concept which will make it possible to measure quality in practice. The four quality types appear from Table 13.1.

It appears from the table that the classical division of the quality concept into subjective and objective quality respectively is extended by two, so that now there are four division criteria: subjective, semi-subjective, objective and semi-objective quality. All four can in principle appear but homogeneity among consumers must generally be regarded as a rare phenomenon. We therefore regard the subjective and the semi-objective quality as the most interesting from a practical point of view and in the following we will therefore focus on these when measuring quality in relation to product development. The division between latent and manifest quality attributes is in accordance with the distinction between the first and second waves of TQM as expressed by Senge (1991). In the first wave the focus was on measurable aspects of quality, while the second wave introduced a new perspective of the customer. Senge sees the second wave as starting with the introduction of the seven new management tools (Chapter 8), and he wrote:

Along with these new tools for thinking and interacting, a new orientation toward the customer has gradually emerged. The new perspective moved from satisfying the customer's expressed requirements to meeting the latent needs of the customer.

Quality can, in principle, be measured in two different ways. Either by a 'direct' measurement of the consumer's preferences via statistical scaling methods (latent) and experimental designs (manifest) or by an indirect preference measurement from observing the reactions of the market, the so-called hedonic analysis. Subsequently, these methods of measuring will be described through a number of cases from practice and the emphasis will be on giving the reader an overall impression of the methods. A more specific discussion of the methods is beyond the scope of this book and is left to more specialized literature on the subject.

13.2 DIRECT MEASUREMENT OF QUALITY

By direct quality measurement consumers are interviewed about their attitude to and assessment of different products and their quality dimensions. The choice of method depends on whether the quality dimensions can be read directly from the product or whether it is necessary to measure the dimensions indirectly.

In the following, the technique of quality measurement will be described via two cases from Danish trade and industry. The first case describes the attempts made by a Danish producer of housing textiles (tablecloths, place-mats, curtains etc.) to uncover the quality dimensions in a market greatly characterized by subjective assessments (latent quality attributes). The other case describes the efforts of a Danish dairy to optimize the quality of drinking yoghurt based on manifest measurements of the properties of the yoghurt. In the first case, it is a question of latent quality attributes, whereas the quality attributes in the second case are regarded as manifest. In both cases the consumers are regarded as being heterogeneous, so what we see are examples of subjective quality and semi-objective quality respectively.

13.2.1 MEASUREMENT OF SUBJECTIVE QUALITY: CASE FROM A DANISH TEXTILE FACTORY

Some years ago one of the authors was contacted by a producer of housing textiles who wanted to have a detailed discussion of the quality concept in relation to the factory's product line. Until then, quality control had been limited to inspection of incoming raw materials and 100% inspection for misprints but they had become aware that in relation to the market they were hardly paying attention to the relevant quality dimensions.

To uncover the company's 'culture' in the area, the analysis started out with interviews with the mercantile as well as the technical managements of the company. The interviews were unstructured and unaided and the purpose of them was to uncover what aspects should be considered when assessing the quality of the products.

The mercantile manager, who had a theoretical business background and had always been employed in the textile industry, stated the following quality dimensions for his products:

1. smart design;
2. nice colours;
3. highly processed colours;
4. inviting presentation.

According to the mercantile manager, there must of course be a certain technical level but when this level has been reached, e.g. through a suitable inspection of incoming material, the technical aspects are not of importance to the customer's assessment of the quality. In the market under review, it is a question of feelings and according to the mercantile manager, it does not serve any purpose to use considerably more time on technical standards! Resources should be concentrated on uncovering what determines the quality of a design and on the development of alternative methods of presenting the products (packaging). Accordingly he was of the opinion that the technical aspects of a tablecloth could only be considered as expected qualities. In order to give the customer some value added it was necessary to concentrate on the aspects mentioned above.

The technical manager, who was engineer by education, had – not unexpectedly – a somewhat different attitude to the concept of tablecloth quality. He started the interview by the following definition of the quality concept:

Quality = The Degree of Defined Imperfection

The dimensions on which imperfection can be defined were stated as the following (unaided):

1. creasing resistance (non-iron);
2. shrinkage;
3. fastness of colours to wash;
4. fastness of colours to light;
5. rubbing resistance (wet and dry);
6. tearing strength;
7. pulling strength;
8. 'Griff'.

The first seven dimensions are defined as technical standards and the eighth is the only subjective element. 'Griff' is the overall evaluation of the cloth by an experienced producer when he touches the cloth.

After some aid, the technician extended his description with the following two points:

9. design and colour of the pattern;
10. design of the model.

The difference between the two managers' perceptions of the quality concept is thought-provoking and it is not surprising that the company felt very uncertain about the direction to choose for future product development. With the mercantile manager, all qualities were latent, while practically all qualities (to begin with) were manifest with the technical manager.

After a number of talks a consensus was reached on the future quality concept. It was decided to determine a technical level in accordance with the points listed above by using a benchmarking study of the competitors and then concentrating resources on an optimization of the quality of design.

The following procedure for a continuous optimization of the quality of design (including colour) was used from then on:

1. The design department produces n different design proposals on paper.
2. The proposals are screened internally and the proposals accepted are painted on textile.
3. The painted proposals are assessed by a consumer panel on an itemized five-point rating scale, using products from the existing product programme as well as competitors' products.
4. The results are analysed statistically by means of multidimensional scaling (internal procedure) and the underlying factors (latent quality dimensions) are identified if possible.
5. The results are communicated to the design department, which is asked to come up with new proposals in accordance with the results from point 4.
6. The new proposals are test-printed and manufactured.
7. The resulting product proposals are assessed again by a consumer panel and the best proposals are selected for production, supplemented, however, with marketing analyses of cannibalization, etc.

The statistical method mentioned, multidimensional scaling (MDS), covers a number of techniques the purpose of which is to place a number of products in a multidimensional space based on a number of respondent's attitudes to the products. It is assumed that neither respondent nor analyst in advance can identify the quality dimensions used by the respondents.

By means of the data from point 3. products as well as consumers are placed in the same diagram, the products as points and the consumers as vectors oriented in the preference direction. The diagram is examined by the analyst who, by means of his background knowledge, tries to name the axes corresponding to the latent quality dimensions.

Software for MDS is available in many variations. A relatively comprehensive collection of scaling techniques can be found in SPSS for

Windows (Professional Statistics) which in the module ALSCAL offers an extremely flexible approach to MDS. Furthermore the manual for the package gives a very good introduction to the concept of scaling.

Figure 13.1 shows the first result of an MDS run for the mentioned textile factory. The company analysed two existing designs (E1-E2), six new designs (N1-N6) and one competing design (C1).

The first run was used for determining the latent quality dimensions and revealing any gaps in the market which it might be interesting to fill. It became clear relatively quickly that the design quality is dominated by two dimensions. One distinguishes between whether the pattern is geometric or floral (romantic), the other whether the pattern is matched ('harmonious') or abstract '(disharmonious'). The first of the two dimensions mentioned divides the population into two segments of practically the same size, whereas for the other dimension there is no doubt that the quality harmony ought to characterize the design for tablecloths.

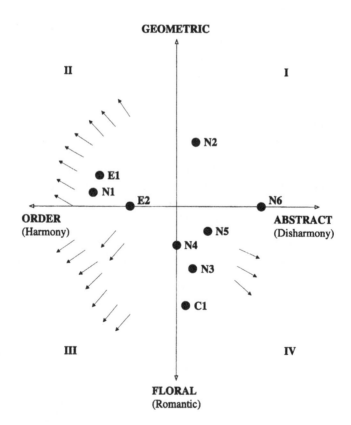

Fig. 13.1 Latent quality dimensions for tablecloths (before adjustment).

It further appears from the map that, apart from one, hardly any of the new proposals have a chance in the market. It is also clear that – as assessed by the products included – there is a substantial gap in the market for products with harmonious floral qualities.

This information went back to the design department, which was given the special task of finishing the floral area. It was decided to drop N6 and to stake on an adjustment of N5 from the fourth to the third quadrant. Besides, if possible, move N3 and N4 away from the competing product C1. The result can be seen from Figure 13.2.

It appears from the map that the company has succeeded in obtaining a better position in the third quadrant after the adjustment of N5. On the other hand, the adjustments of N3 and N4 were less successful in relation to the quality optimization.

The result for the company was that it chose to launch N1 and the adjusted version of N5. N2 was dropped completely, while the last two designs went back to the design department for further changes in order to be used at a later stage.

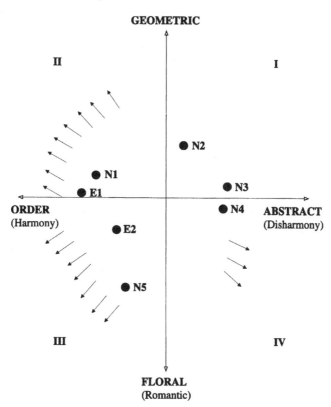

Fig. 13.2 Adjusted quality map for tablecloths.

It appears from the analysis that through the use of latent techniques like MDS it is possible to obtain considerable insight into the quality dimensions not directly measurable. The analysis phase itself is not very difficult and it will be easily mastered by persons who normally work with quality control. It is somewhat more difficult, however, to get analyst and designer to play together and it requires some experience to translate the results of the latent quality dimensions into practical design adjustments.

13.2.2 MEASUREMENT OF SEMI-OBJECTIVE QUALITY: CASE FROM A DAIRY

In certain production contexts one has the impression that one has a total overview of the quality dimensions on which consumers assess the product. This was the case when one of the authors was asked to assist a Danish dairy in optimizing the quality of drinking yoghurt.

For some time the dairy had been dissatisfied with the sale of drinking yoghurt which failed to hold its own in competition with other refreshing drinks. It was therefore natural to reason that the product quality did not live up to the demands of the market. Through market surveys the dairy knew approximately what quality dimensions the market generally valued in refreshing drinks but because of extremely strict legislative requirements the dimensions that could be played on were limited to the following:

1. The acidity (pH value) of the product.
2. The fat content (%) of the product.
3. The type of juice added.
4. The homogenization pressure (kg/cm^3) used.
5. The protein content (%) of the product.

On the basis it was decided to carry out an actual experiment with the above-mentioned factors as a starting point. In order not to incur too heavy test costs it was decided to carry out the experiment as a 2^5 factorial design which entailed that 32 different types of drinking yoghurt had to be produced. Like in the previous case, the results were assessed on an itemized five-point rating scale by a representative cross-section of the relevant market segment.

It soon proved impossible to carry out the experiment as a complete factorial design where all respondents assessed all types of yoghurt. No test person is able to distinguish between so many different stimuli. It was assessed that the maximum number of types that could be assessed per test person was four and it was therefore decided to carry out the experiment as a 'partially confounded 2^5 factorial design distributed on eight blocks with four replications'. In this way, certain effects are confounded but with an expedient test plan it is possible to design the test in such a way that all effects (main effects and interactions) can be measured. A classical reference at this point is the monumental work by Cochran and Cox (1957).

The data from such an experiment can be analysed in several different ways. External MDS is a possibility or, like here, a multifactor analysis of variance. The results showed that the type of fruit naturally plays a part but that this variable, so to speak, segments the market. Otherwise, the optimum quality appeared by using the following basic recipe irrespective of the type of fruit:

- pH value: high level;
- fat content: low level;
- homogenization: high level;
- protein content: high level.

Besides, the following interactions could be ascertained via the analysis of variance:

1. Products with lemon taste should without exception have a high pH value. The effect is not quite as marked for sweeter types of juice.
2. If yoghurt of a high fat content is produced, the homogenization pressure ought to be high.
3. If yoghurt of a high protein content is produced, the homogenization pressure ought to be high.
4. Products with a low fat content ought to have a low protein content.

It could be ascertained from the analysis that the existing drinking yoghurt was far from being of optimum quality. Primarily, the fat content was far too high and there was an undesirable interaction between the factors. A change of this situation would probably result in an improvement on the demand side and it would furthermore mean lower costs as a consequence of the reduction of the fat content if the excess butterfat could be put to use.

It appears also in this example that it was possible through direct preference measurements to obtain considerable insight into the actual quality of the product. In the latter case, the analysis followed the classical scientific road with actual experiments and a very straightforward analysis. In contrast to the optimization in the latent case, this procedure is very elementary and the whole process can be mastered without problems by persons with normal insight into quality control.

13.3 INDIRECT MEASUREMENT OF QUALITY

The direct quality and preference measurement as outlined above has been developed in a marketing context but the economic field has also been working with quality measurements for a number of years. In what follows we describe some of the micro-economic aspects of quality measurement and we outline how this may be used by quality managers in connection with product development. The exposition follows Kristensen (1984) closely.

It all started in 1939 when Court (1939) introduced the hedonic technique as a means of adjusting price indices for quality variations. Later, a number of empirical studies followed but the theory was not founded until Lancaster (1966) and Rosen (1974) made their contributions. In theory quality is measured indirectly through the reaction of the market as the starting point is to establish a connection between the qualities of a product and the market price of the product.

13.3.1 AN OUTLINE OF THE HEDONIC THEORY

In classical micro-economic consumer theory consumer choice is based upon maximization of a utility function specified in the quantities consumed subject to a financial constraint. This gives very good results but their realism has been questioned by market researchers and other practical people working with consumer demand and today the economic theory of consumer demand plays only a small role in management education. Thus, it is symptomatic that in a major textbook (Engel, Kollat and Blackwell, 1973) only two out of almost 700 pages are devoted to the economic theory of the consumer.

A major point of criticism is that the neoclassical theory of consumer demand does not take the intrinsic properties of goods (their characteristics) into consideration and is hence not able to deal with problems like the introduction of new commodities and quality variations unless, as Lancaster (1966) put it, you make 'an incredible stretching of the consumers' powers of imagination'.

A way out of some of the problems is to adopt the hedonic hypothesis that goods do not *per se* give utility to the consumer but instead are valued for their utility-bearing attributes (Lancaster, 1966). Such an extension will make it possible to study heterogeneous goods within the framework of the classical theory of the consumer and will produce a direct link between the market price of a complex good and its attributes (quality).

This was shown by Rosen (1974) who provided a framework for the study of differentiated products. His point of departure is a class of commodities that are described by n attributes, z_i, $i = 1, ..., n$. The attributes are assumed to be objectively measured and the choice between combinations of them is assumed to be continuous for all practical purposes, i.e. a sufficiently large number of differentiated products are available in the market.

Each differentiated product has a market price which implicitly reveals the relationship between price and attributes and it is a main object of the hedonic theory to explain how this relationship is determined. To simplify things, it is assumed that consumers are rational in the sense that if two brands contain the same set of attributes, they only consider the cheaper one and the identity of the seller is of no importance.

To explain the determination of market equilibrium, Rosen (1974) assumed that the utility function of the household can be defined as

$$U = U(x, z_1, ..., z_n, \alpha), \tag{13.1}$$

where x is a vector of all other goods than the class of commodities considered and z_i, $i = 1, ..., n$, are the attributes for this class. The vector α represents taste-determining characteristics and hence differs from person to person. Constrained utility maximization then leads to the bid function indicating the maximum amount a household would be willing to pay for different combinations of attributes at a given level of utility:

$$\theta = \theta(z_1, ..., z_n, y, \alpha) \tag{13.2}$$

where y is the household income.

Symmetrically, Rosen (1974) shows that by means of ordinary profit maximization it is possible to define the producer's offer function indicating the minimum price he is willing to accept for different combinations of attributes at a given level of profit:

$$\phi = \phi(z, ..., z, \cdot M, \beta), \tag{13.3}$$

where M and β describe the level of output and the characteristics of the producer regarding production.

Market equilibrium is then obtained by the tangency of the offer and bid functions resulting in a common envelope denoted $p(z)$. This envelope or function is the implicit price function or the hedonic price function as it is often called (Griliches, 1971) and it shows the market relationship between the price and quality attributes of the class of differentiated commodities considered (Figure 13.3).

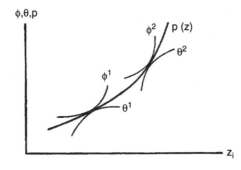

Fig. 13.3 Offer and bid functions and the hedonic function.

The hedonic function represents the available information in the market on which the agents base their decisions. This, of course, means that knowledge of the function is of great importance to the suppliers in the market if an optimal product development is going to take place. But apart from this, how should $p(z)$ be interpreted?

As shown above, $p(z)$ represents a joint envelope of families of offer and bid functions. Hence, it may be said to represent the market's consensus about marginal rates of substitution among the quality attributes (Noland, 1979).

Associated with the hedonic function is the concept of implicit price which is defined as the partial derivative of $p(z)$ with respect to z_i, $i = 1, ..., n$. The implicit prices show what value the market implicitly attaches to marginal amounts of the individual quality characteristics of a product (*ceteris paribus*); a very useful piece of information when interpreting the overall correlation between price and quality of a product.

The assumptions behind the hedonic model may still seem somewhat heroic to practical people and it must be admitted that the model does not explain everything about price formation and the consumer choice process. Still, there is no doubt in the mind of the authors that the hedonic hypothesis is a significant improvement on the classical theory and one that will be of value to, e.g. quality management researchers trying to obtain insight into the relationship between price and quality.

What then can be obtained by including this type of analysis in the quality manager's tool box?

One of the answers to this question can be found in the way that standard analysis of the relationship between price and quality is presently conducted. Either the list price is correlated with a quality composite constructed by someone other than the researcher (e.g. Consumers' Union in the USA), or it is correlated with each quality dimension and then the overall correlation between price and quality is found as an average. In all cases linear measures of association are used. As examples of all the cases linear measures of association are used. As examples of the first type of study Riesz (1978) and Sutton and Riesz (1979) can be mentioned.

A second reason for introducing hedonic theory lies in the fact that no uniform definition of quality has been adopted by market researchers. As mentioned earlier, some researchers use quality composites, more or less arbitrarily defined, while others use the individual quality dimensions in an averaging process. These methods will, however, lead to different results, and hence studies using different methods are not compatible. This is explained in detail in Kristensen (1984).

In the authors' opinion, we need an overall quality index or quality composite when studying the relationship between price and quality. But such an index with a solid theoretical background is formed by the hedonic function and hence we have found yet another reason for dealing with hedonic theory in quality research. In this connection, it should be stressed that the hedonic function is not a measure of quality to any given consumer (unless all consumers have the same utility function). The hedonic function measures the opportunity set facing both consumers and producers and hence expresses some kind of market consensus concerning the relationship between price and quality.

Some researchers might object that it is obvious that price is strongly related to, e.g. the size of a differentiated product, and this is not what they are interested in. Their definition of quality does not include such obvious quality characteristics and hence these characteristics should not be included when measuring the relationship. The answer to this is that, when analysing the relationship between price and attributes, all relevant attributes must be included, otherwise the results for the group of attributes in which the researcher is interested will be biased. The relationship between the researcher's concept of quality and price appears from the value and variability of the implicit price obtained for the attribute or group of attributes the researcher is considering.

The above-mentioned reasons for introducing hedonic theory in quality research all focus on an improved measurement of the relationship between price and quality but a set of more practical reasons with implications for the agents (i.e. buyers and sellers) in the market are just as important. In practice, the evaluation of complex goods like houses, cars, antiques etc. in both primary and secondary markets is a very big problem. For the seller it is a question of price determination and, of course, product development and for the buyer it is a question of determination of the efficient offers in the market. Consider, e.g. a real estate agent who gets the job of selling a certain house. What should he demand for the house? If his offer is not efficient he cannot sell the house and if he gets too little for the house he will lose customers in the future. A buyer of a new house on his part will obtain offers from a number of different real estate agents and pick out the best offers. But how should he do this in a rational manner?

The answer to these questions for both buyers (which of course could very well be companies) and sellers is to obtain knowledge about the existing relationship in the market between price and attributes for the good in question. With the help of this information the seller will be in a good position when pricing a new product or when determining the viability of prices for existing products. When pricing a new product, one possibility is to identify the characteristics of the product, substitute these into the hedonic function and then price the product at the level of $p(z)$. Likewise, the viability of current prices can be judged by a comparison with $p(z)$. To the buyer, the information will show whether an offer is under or overpriced by looking at the residuals when substituting the characteristics into the hedonic function. In this way, the buyer will be able to pick out the set of efficient offers for further analysis before making a final decision. This again brings the hedonic function into focus with emphasis this time on the process of estimation and interpretation. In fact, the background to the empirical part of this chapter was an inquiry from a group of real estate agents who wanted a tool for a more systematic pricing of their houses.

The hedonic technique will also be of value to those business people who are doing different kinds of price research, e.g. calculating and estimating price indexes in order to forecast future prices. This is due to the fact that by help of the hedonic technique it is possible, by using time dummies or some other specification of time in the hedonic function, to separate the quality part of a price movement from the actual inflation and thus make it possible for the market analyst to adjust existing price indexes for quality variations and to make a prediction of future prices that also takes changes in quality into consideration.

13.3.2 A STUDY OF THE DANISH HOUSING MARKET: THE MATERIALS AND VARIABLES UNDER CONSIDERATION

The collection of data for this example took place around 1980 and consisted (in principle) of the total number of house transactions completed through a specific estate agent in the city of Aarhus, Denmark. In total, 528 transactions were examined in detail, resulting in a database containing information about the financial terms of the transaction, the attributes of the house and the time of sale. These data were supplemented with secondary data collected from official sources in order to make an economic evaluation of the terms of the transaction possible.

The method of sampling chosen has a consequence that the material cannot be said to give a representative picture of the total number of house transactions in the city of Aarhus in the time period under consideration. Thus, it would be unreasonable to postulate that the special characteristics of the estate agent who has supplied the material should be without importance to the composition of the group of customers. This means that unbiased estimation of different population characteristics such as proportions and averages cannot take place. On the other hand, there is no reason to believe that the price-forming mechanisms should depend on the agent, which means that the study of the implicit price function is hardly affected by the non-representativeness of the sample. This conclusion is supported by some results obtained from a smaller control sample taken from a different agent. As expected, this sample diverged from the original as regards composition but it was not possible to detect significant deviations as regards the relative prices of the attributes of the house.

Normally (Noland, 1979) housing attributes, i.e. the explaining variables of the hedonic price function, are divided into the following groups with typical representatives given in parenthesis:

1. Attributes relating to the house
   1.1 space (number of rooms, room size, lot size)
   1.2 quality (age and type of the building).
2. Attributes relating to the location
   2.1 accessibility (access to employment)
   2.2 neighbourhood quality (geographical area).

The number and type of attributes included vary depending on the type of housing under consideration. In most cases, variables are either nominally or intervally scaled but sometimes also ordinal variables are included. Even latent variables obtained from principal components or factor analysis are used from time to time, especially when expressing special quality attributes.

Table 13.2 contains a list of the variables chosen for this study. It appears that the variables are divided into three groups of which two relate to the attributes of the house and one relates to the price.

Table 13.2 The variables under consideration

Name	Description
Price variables	
MPRICE	Mortgaged price
CPRICE	Cash price according to (4)
PMT	Yearly payment of instalments and interest
r	Average nominal interest rate
i	Average effective interest rate (end of month of sale)
DPMT	Down payment
Location	
PLACE 1	Eight city districts, medium quality
PLACE 2	Two city districts, high quality
PLACE 3	Surrounding area
Attributes	
LOT	Lot size in m^2
SPACE	Living space (m^2) exclusive of basement
BASE	Size of basement (m^2)
GARAGE	Number of garages
AGE	Age of building when sold
BATH	Number of extra bathrooms
FIRE	Number of fireplaces
TYPE	Dummy indicating a terrace house (0) or not (1)

(a) Price variables

The concept of price in connection with a Danish house transaction is not unique. Usually one speaks of a mortgaged price composed of down payment and a number of mortgages at interest rates below or above the market interest rate. From an economic point of view, this means that price should be considered a vector consisting of:

MPRICE: mortgaged price
DPMT: down payment
r: nominal interest rate
i: market interest rate
n: duration

so that from a formal point of view, when studying the relation between price and attributes, one should be talking about multidimensional dependent variable. However, when estimating marginal prices, traditional theory requires a unique relationship between the elements of the vector so that price appears as a scalar.

To show how the problem is solved in this case and to demonstrate some of the peculiarities of the Danish mortgaging market we have included Table 13.3 showing an example of the financial structure of a Danish deal.

The official price appearing in all documents is DKK 496 000, but this is not equal to the price that the house would cost if it were paid for in cash because the market rate of interest is different from the nominal rate. The reason for this difference is found in the institutional practice in Denmark. When a house is sold, the major part of the deal is usually financed through the mortgage credit institute in the way that the institute issues bonds at a maximum interest rate of 12% p.a. and then hands over the bonds to the debtor who must sell the bonds on the exchange. The quotation of the bonds is usually below their nominal value and since the loans are annuities, it can be calculated from the following equation:

$$L(1 - (1 + r)^{-n})/r = QL(1 - (1 + i)^{-n})/i \qquad (13.4)$$

Table 13.3 Price structure of a Danish house deal

Financial institution	Size of loan (DKK)	Nominal rate of interest p.a. (%)	Yearly payment (DKK)
Mortgage credit institute	110 000	10	17 820
Private	286 000	15	47 932
Total	396 000	–	65 752
Down payment	100 000	–	–
Mortgaged price	496 000	–	–

where L is the loan, Q is the quotation, r is the nominal rate of interest, i is the market rate of interest and n is the duration. It will be seen that for large n the quotation is simply equal to $Q = r/i$.

From this it follows that the cash price of a house can be calculated by multiplying the different loans by the relevant values of Q and then adding the down payment. Assume that the house described in Table 13.3 was sold in December 1981. At this time, the official market rate of interest published by the Stock Exchange was 19.96% p.a. for loan #1 and 20.38% for loan #2; the difference due to differences in duration (10 and 16 years respectively). By help of the formula above, Q can be calculated at 0.6819 and 0.7810 respectively for the two loans, from which it follows that the cash price is:

$$CPRICE = 110\ 000 \times 0.6819 + 286\ 000 \times 0.7810 + 100\ 000$$

$$= 398\ 375 \tag{13.5}$$

In the study this was not done for each loan. Instead, the average value of r was calculated as

$$\bar{r} = (0.10 \times 110\ 000 + 0.15 \times 286\ 000)/396\ 000 = 0.1361 \tag{13.6}$$

and similarly, the average market rate of interest was used. In this case $i = 20.17\%$. By means of $\bar{r}$, $\bar{n}$ was calculated from the formula

$$L = PMT(1 - (1 + \bar{r})^{\bar{n}})/\bar{r} \tag{13.7}$$

and then the average value of Q could be calculated. After this, the cash price was found as

$$CPRICE = \bar{Q}(P - U) + U. \tag{13.8}$$

In our case $\bar{n} = 13.43$ and $\bar{Q} = 0.7533$. Then

$$CPRICE = 0.7533(496\ 000 - 100\ 000) + 100\ 000 = 398\ 307. \tag{13.9}$$

The difference between the two methods is in general very small. The advantage of the method used is that we only have to deal with one value of r, i and n.

(b) Location variables

Originally 12 different location categories corresponding to the postal districts of the area were used. In order to obtain information about the two location attributes mentioned earlier, accessibility and neighbourhood quality, these were divided into three groups of which two consisted of city districts (PLACE 1 and PLACE 2) and one of the surrounding districts (PLACE 3). This division should reflect accessibility as well as quality, since the groups, PLACE 1 and PLACE 2, were formed in accordance with neighbourhood quality. Thus the difference between the price of PLACE 1 and PLACE 3 should be an estimate of the implicit price of good accessibility, while the difference between PLACE 1 and PLACE 2 should be an estimate of the implicit price of a good neighbourhood quality. This, of course, assumes that there is no inter-action between these two location attributes.

(c) Housing variables

This group of variables is almost self-explanatory. It should, however, be mentioned that AGE is measured in whole years and that in those cases where the house has been renewed AGE is measured as a weighted average with weights based on the value of the house before and after the renewal. Those houses that were described as 'older' were given an age of 30 years according to the agent.

Originally, the material also contained information about the type of roof but a number of tests showed no significance for this attribute and hence it was excluded.

(d) Results of the regression analysis

As mentioned earlier, the object of the following is to determine the functional relationship between the price and the quality attributes of a house in order to determine the implicit price of the individual attributes and in order to be able to predict the value of a house on the basis of its attributes. Formally

$$CPRICE = f(LOT, SPACE, BASE, GARAGE, AGE,$$
$$BATH, FIRE, TYPE, PLACE, TIME) \qquad (13.10)$$

where a variable describing the time scale (TIME) has been included.

Specification of the relation and the functional form plays a vital role for the results (Palmquist, 1980). Regarding the specification, the discussion in the relevant literature is centred around the problem of aggregation in connection with the variables representing time of sale and location (Griliches, 1971; Straszheim, 1974; Palmquist, 1980). It is recognized that aggregation over time may lead to wrong conclusions but since some aggregation is necessary in all cases, it is normally accepted to aggregate over time if the time period is not too long. On the other hand, there is much more doubt whether it is reasonable to aggregate different geographical areas. In this chapter the consequences of this are taken, which means that aggregation over time is used in all analyses, while the reasonableness of geographical aggregation is tested. It should be stressed that aggregation over time does not mean that time is excluded from the equation. What it does mean is that relationship is assumed to be stationary over the period of aggregation and that different time periods can be distinguished by shifting intercepts alone.

(e) Choice of the functional form

As mentioned previously, theoretical economics does not give very much advice regarding the functional form. There is, however, some indication from the market-place. Thus, the authors have learned from several sources (estate agents) that according to their experience, within certain limits, 'price goes up twice as fast as the hardware one puts into the house'. How exactly a prosaic statement like this should be interpreted is not clear but it is certainly tempting to let it mean that the elasticity of the price with respect to quality in a broad sense should be equal to 2.

In order to test this hypothesis the so-called Box-Cox theory is used on the following class of transformations:

$$(CPRICE)^\lambda = \beta_0 + \sum_{i=1}^{14} \beta_i x_i \qquad \text{for } \lambda \neq 0 \tag{13.11}$$

$$\ln(CPRICE) = \beta_0 + \sum_{i=1}^{14} \beta_i x_i \qquad \text{for } \lambda \neq 0 \tag{13.12}$$

where x_i ($i = 1, ..., 14$) indicates all attributes of the house. The object is then to estimate the parameters λ and β_i ($i = 0, ..., 14$) and to test the hypothesis that $\lambda = \frac{1}{2}$.

Results of the Box-Cox analysis for the geographically aggregated material show that the optimal λ value is 0.59 covering a set of acceptable hypotheses on the 95% level equal to (0.46; 0.73). Hence the material strongly supports the practical experience from the market-place mentioned earlier. It should be mentioned that the results obtained by Goodman (1978) are very similar to the results obtained here. Thus, Goodman's result for an overall λ value is 0.6 and he also effectively rejects the linear and semilog forms.

The results of the Box-Cox analysis in combination with the prior knowledge obtained from the market-place has given the author great confidence in the sqrt-model and hence we shall proceed with a presentation of the estimation results for this model.

(f) Results of the sqrt-model

The results of the sqrt-model are displayed in Table 13.4. In the table regression coefficients for the aggregated material and for each of the three geographical areas are shown together with the average implicit prices and their standard deviations.

The mean values of the attributes were used as the basis for this computation.

Looking at the average implicit prices one finds that the prices of LOT, SPASE, BASE, GARAGE, AGE and BATH are in perfect accordance with what could be expected from knowing the Danish market. Thus, the estimated prices of the size variables are somewhat lower than the costs of an extra m^2, indicating, as expected, that it is cheaper to buy a new house than to build an extension to an existing house (*ceteris paribus*). The implicit prices of an extra garage and an extra bathroom are very close to

Table 13.4 Results of the sqrt-model

Variable	Aggregated material	Place 1	Place 2	Place 3	Average implicit price (kroner)
Lot	0.020[b]	0.027	− 0.002	0.017	24.4 (8.6)
Space	0.841[a]	0.583[a]	1.331[a]	1.218[a]	1024.7 (83.0)
Base	0.456[a]	0.456[a]	0.566[a]	0.398[a]	555.4 (71.7)
Garage	17.775[a]	19.022[b]	29.351[a]	14.654[b]	21 943.0 (4903.4)
Age	− 1.621[a]	− 1.708[a]	− 1.943[a]	− 1.295[b]	− 1971.1 (230.9)
Bath	9.326[c]	9542	1.373	9.064	11 420.5 (5742.2)
Fire	32.026[a]	43.858[a]	2.742	27.719[a]	39 991.0 (6868.5)
Type	0.080	− 9.659	22.045[c]	8.002	62.5 (7195.2)
Place 1	30.299[a]	–	–	–	36 031.9 (6347.8)
Place 2	49.399[a]	–	–	–	59 693.9 (7879.5)
1975	75.872[a]	94.673[a]	54.982[a]	60.599[a]	84 448.1 (8820.3)
1976	90.177[a]	109.365[a]	70.343[a]	70.262[a]	101 669.1 (8875.7)
1977	103.246[a]	122.397[a]	90.996[a]	84.229[a]	117 756.2 (9324.3)
1978	146.411[a]	164.224[a]	140.393[a]	121.366[a]	173 322.5 (10 187.8)
Constant	342.100[a]	392.096[a]	337.658[a]	304.824[a]	–
$\bar{R}^2$	0.771	0.726	0.849	0.812	
F	110.8[a]	51.9[a]	47.0[a]	46.7[a]	
N	458	231	99	128	

[a] Significant at level 0.001.
[b] Significant at level 0.01.
[c] Significant at level 0.05.

the actual costs of these attributes when building a new house according to a construction company that was interviewed about these matters. On the other hand, the implicit price of approximately DKK 40 000 for FIRE comes as a surprise. This price is much higher than the costs of a new fireplace and probably indicates that the variable FIRE works as a general quality indicator.

The area prices (PLACE 1 and PLACE 2) take a house placed in the surrounding area as a starting point. If this house is moved to a medium-quality city area, the price goes up to approximately DKK 36 000 corresponding to an estimate of the capitalized value of good accessibility. If the house is moved to a high-quality city area, the price goes up approximately DKK 60 000. From this it follows that the implicit price of a good area quality is approximately DKK 24 000.

The implicit prices stated in connection with the years 1975 to 1978 indicate the hedonic price changes in relation to the year 1974. As an example, the figures show that a house costing DKK 450 000 in 1978 corresponding to a relative increase of 63% or 13% p.a. This is in very good accordance with the official statistics, which for the period in question showed an increase of 68% for MPRICE. As mentioned earlier, time dummies can be used to adjust nominal prices for quality changes, since the coefficient of a dummy is equal to the change in the dependent variable, other things being equal. Thus, the price change from 1974 to 1978 at constant quality was 63%. In the same period the material showed a nominal increase in CPRICE equal to 68%, indicating an increase in quality from 100 to $168/163 = 103.1$ during the period. An extensive account of the use of the hedonic method for constructing quality-adjusted price indexes can be found in Griliches (1971).

Turning to the individual areas, it will be seen that statistical tests reject regional homogeneity as regards the quality variables. The most distinctive difference between the three areas is found for the variable FIRE; a difference which strongly supports the interpretation of this variable as some kind of quality indicator. Other differences are relatively small apart from the price increases which, as was expected when knowing the market, have been strongest for PLACE 1. Otherwise, the structure of the relative prices is the same for the three areas, and the differences are not so marked that further analysis based upon the aggregated material will be invalidated.

In conclusion of the preceding study of the relationship between price and quality of Danish single-family houses we find the following:

1. A special treatment of price was necessary in order to establish compatibility between prices of the individual houses. This is in general necessary when financing is a part of the deal and when the market rate of interest differs from the nominal rate.

2. A rather strong but non-linear overall relationship between price and quality was discovered. Regarding the individual quality elements, it turned out that of those originally considered only two (the type of the roof and TYPE) were not related to price. On average, the relative prices of the rest were in good accordance with what was expected.

3. Since neither consumers nor sellers are identical, the established relationship between price and quality cannot in this case be assigned to one of these groups, but is rather an expression of the market's consensus about the relationship between price and quality and it represents the information available to the agents in the market on which they should base their decisions.

It appears from the analysis that by introducing the hedonic technique it is possible to obtain much more information about the nature of the relationship between price and quality than would be the case if a traditional correlation study were used. In addition to a measure of the association between price and quality, the hedonic technique provides information about the actual economics of the price/quality relationship, information which will be of great practical value to both quality management researchers and practitioners when designing new profitable products.

REFERENCES

Cochran, W.G. and Cox, G.M. (1957) *Experimental Design*, J. Wiley, USA.

Court, A.T. (1939) Hedonic price indexes with automative examples. In: *The Dynamics of Automobile Demand*, New York.

Deming, W.E. (1984) *Quality, Productivity and Competitive Position*, MIT, USA.

Engel, J.F., Kollat, D.T. and Blackwell, R.D. (1973) *Consumer Behaviour*, New York.

Goodman, A.C. (1978) Hedonic prices, price indices and housing markets. *Journal of Urban Economics*, 5, 471–84.

Griliches, Z. (ed.) (1971) *Price Indexes and Quality Change*, Cambridge, MA, USA.

Kristensen, K. (1984) Hedonic theory, marketing research and the analysis of consumer goods. *International Journal of Research in Marketing*, 1, 17–36.

Lancaster, K.J. (1966) A new approach to consumer theory. *Journal of Political Economy*, 74, 132–57.

Noland, C.W. (1979) Assessing hedonic indexes for housing. *Journal of Financial and Quantitative Analysis*, 14, 783–800.

Oyrzanowski, B. (1984) *Towards Precision and Clarity of the Concept of Quality.* EOQ Quality, pp. 6–8.

Palmquist, R.B. (1980) Alternative techniques for developing real estate price indexes. *The Review of Economics and Statistics*, 62, 442–8.

Riesz, P.C. (1978) Price versus quality in the marketplace: 1961–1975. *Journal of Retailing*, 54, 15–28.

Rosen, S. (1974) Hedonic prices and implicit markets: product differentiation and pure competition. *Journal of Political Economy*, 82, 34–55.

Senge, P.M. (1991) *The Fifth Discipline – The Art and Practice of the Learning Organization*, Doubleday Currency, New York, USA.

Shewhart, W.A. (1931) *Economic Control of Quality and Manufactured Products*, D. van Nostrand & Co. Inc., New York, USA.

Strazheim, M. (1974) Hedonic estimation of housing market prices: a further comment. *The Review of Economic and Statistics*, 56, 404–06.

Sutton R.J. and Riesz, P.C. (1979) The effect of product visibility upon the relationship between price and quality. *Journal of Consumer Policy*, 3, 145–50.

Quality costing $\quad$ 14

14.1 THE CONCEPT OF TQM AND QUALITY COSTS

In Chapter 4 we defined TQM as being the culmination of a hierarchy of the following quality definitions:

Quality is to continuously satisfy customers' expectations;
Total Quality is to achieve quality at low cost;
Total Quality Management is to achieve Total Quality through everybody's participation.

The concept quality costs, i.e. the sum of failure costs, inspection/appraisal costs and prevention costs is very important to understand when you try to implement Total Quality Management and in this respect try to establish and fulfil strategic goals. But it is not so easy to get a profound understanding of the concept. The problem is that because the majority of these costs are invisible there is a risk that the following deadly disease may break out: 'Management by use only of visible figures, with little or no consideration of figures that are unknown or unknowable'. As Deming told us (1986): 'The figures which management needs most are actually unknown and/or unknowable. In spite of this, successful managements have to take account of these invisible figures.'

In relation to TQM we know that the level of quality will be improved by investing in the so-called quality management costs. These consist of:

1. Preventive quality costs. These are costs of activities whose aim is to prevent quality defects and problems cropping up. The aim of preventive activities is to find and control the causes of quality defects and problems.

2. Inspection/appraisal costs. The object of these costs is to find defects which have already occurred, or make sure that a given level of quality is being met.

'Investment' in so-called quality management costs will improve quality and result in the reduction of so-called failure costs.

Failure costs are normally divided into the following two groups:

1. Internal failure costs. These are costs which accrue when defects and problems are discovered inside the company. These costs are typically costs of repairing defects.
2. External failure costs. These are costs which accrue when the defect is first discovered and experienced outside the firm. The customer discovers the defect and this leads to costs of claims and as a rule, also a loss of goodwill corresponding to the lost future profits of lost customers.

We know now that a large part of failure costs, both internal and external, are invisible, i.e. they are either impossible to record, or not worth recording. We know too that, for the same reasons, a large part of preventive costs are also invisible. This leaves inspection costs which are actually the most insignificant part of total quality costs, inasmuch as these costs gradually become superfluous as the firm begins to improve quality by investing in preventive costs.

Investing in preventive costs has the following effects:

1. Defects and failure costs go down.
2. Customer satisfaction goes up.
3. The need for inspection and inspection costs goes down.
4. Productivity goes up.
5. Competitiveness and market share increases.
6. Profits go up.

This is why we can say that

Quality is free

or more precisely

The cost of poor quality is extremely high.

It cannot be emphasized too strongly that, in connection with TQM, the concept of failure should be understood in the broadest possible sense. In principle, it is a failure if the firm is unable to maintain a given level of quality, i.e. maintain a given level for total customer satisfaction. Some examples of this are given below.

Example 1: A firm's products and services do not live up to the quality necessary to maintain or improve customer satisfaction. The result is:

1. Market share goes down.

2. Profits decline, because the invisible failure costs rise. These do not show up in the firm's balance sheet, though their effect can possibly be read on the 'bottom line', i.e. by looking at the change in profits – provided that management does not 'cheat' both auditor and readers of the financial statement by 'creative bookkeeping'.

Example 2: The production department is not always able to live up to product specifications. The result is:

1. More scrap and more rework.
2. Chaos in production. Productivity declines.
3. More inspection.
4. More complaints.
5. More loss of goodwill.
6. Profits go down. Some failure costs are visible and do show up in the balance sheet. Some are invisible and therefore do not show up directly in the accounts. The 'bottom line' of the financial statement shows the effect of both visible and invisible failure costs.

Example 3: The firm's marketing promises the customer more than the product can deliver. The result is:

1. The customer's expectations are not fulfilled.
2. More complaints.
3. More loss of goodwill.
4. Profits go down. Some failure costs are visible (costs of claims) and show up on the firm's balance sheet. Others are invisible (loss of goodwill) and can perhaps be read indirectly by looking at the trend in the company's profits.

It will be clear from the examples we have discussed that the traditional classification of quality costs into:

1. preventive costs,
2. inspection/appraisal costs,
3. internal failure costs and
4. external failure costs

does not directly include these crucial 'invisible figures'. This oversight could be one of the reasons why, according to Deming (1986), this deadly disease afflicts most Western companies. In proposing a new classification of quality costs, we hope to make good this deficiency.

By comparing these examples it is also clear that much has happened since 1951 when Dr J.M. Juran published his first *Quality Control Handbook* in which Chapter 1 ('The Economics of Quality') contained the famous analogy of 'gold in the mine' and also the first definition of quality costs:

The costs which would disappear if no defects were produced.

This definition uses a very narrow failure concept as a failure happens when a defect is produced. The failure concept used in these days was a product oriented failure concept. For many years the product oriented failure concept was dominant and the total quality costs were often calculated as the costs of running the quality department (including inspection) plus the cost of failures measured as the sum of the following costs:

1. cost of complaints (discounts, allowances etc.);
2. cost of reworks;
3. scrap/cost of rejections.

It is interesting to compare Juran's definition of quality costs from 1951 with his definition from his *Executive Handbook* which was published 38 years later (1989, p. 50):

> Cost of poor Quality (COPQ) is the sum of all costs that would disappear if there were no quality problems.

This definition uses the broad failure concept which we advocate in this book and it is also very near to 'the TQM definition of Total Quality Costs' presented by Campanella (1990, p. 8):

> The sum of the above costs [prevention costs, appraisal costs and failure costs]. It represents the difference between the actual cost of a product or service, and what the reduced cost would be if there was no possibility of substandard service, failure of products, or defects in their manufacture.

This definition is a kind of benchmarking definition because you compare your cost of product or service with a perfect company – a company where there is no possibility of failures. We have never met such a company in this world but the vision of TQM is gradually to approach the characteristics of such a company. In practice we need other kinds of benchmarks as the perfect company. We will propose a method to estimate a lower limit of the total quality costs in section 14.2 which use a best in class but imperfect company as a benchmark.

The gold in the mine analogy signals first of all that the costs of poor quality are not to be ignored. These costs are substantial. Secondly the analogy signals that you cannot find these 'valuables' if you do not work as hard as a gold digger. The 'gold digging process' in relation to quality costs will be dealt with in section 14.4.

Because of the problem with the invisible costs, we have found it necessary to introduce a new classification of the firm's total quality costs – one which takes account of 'the invisible figures'. This new classification is shown in Table 14.1.

As Table 14.1 shows, total quality costs can be classified in a table, with internal and external quality costs on the one side and visible and

Table 14.1 A new classification of the firm's quality costs

	Internal costs	External costs	Total
Visible costs	1a. Scrap/repair costs 1b. Preventive costs	2. Guarantee costs/costs of complaints	1 + 2
Invisible costs	3a. Loss of efficiency owing to poor quality/bad management 3b. Preventive/appraisal costs	4. Loss of goodwill owing to poor quality/bad management	3 + 4
Total	1 + 3	2 + 4	1 + 2 + 3 + 4

invisible quality costs on the other. In the table, we have classified total quality costs into six main groups (1a, 1b, 2, 3a, 3b and 4). Apart from the visible costs (1a + 1b + 2), the size of the individual cost totals is usually unknown.

It is often claimed in quality literature that total quality costs are very considerable, typically between 10–40% of turnover. This is why these costs are also known as 'the hidden factory', or 'the gold mine'. We believe that these costs can be much higher, especially if the invisible costs of 'loss of goodwill' are taken into account.

14.2 A NEW METHOD TO ESTIMATE THE TOTAL QUALITY COSTS

Since quality costs are considerable in most firms, it is hardly surprising that management is interested in them. The question is, how can they be estimated?

The traditional method is to record costs as they arise (e.g. wage costs, material etc.) or are thought to arise (e.g. depreciations). However, this method is only applicable in calculating visible costs. We will therefore propose a new method for the indirect measurement of total quality costs – a method which we believe may be invaluable in connection with the strategic quality management process.

The method builds on the basic principle of benchmarking (Chapter 15) where differences in quality and productivity may be revealed by comparing firms competing in the same market. The method was first proposed by the authors of this book in 1991 and has later been proposed by Karlöff (1994) when identifying a benchmarking partner.

The method is as follows.

Let P_{jt} stand for the ordinary financial result of company j at time t, and let P_{jt}/N_j stand for the ordinary financial result per employee. N_j

denotes the number of employees, converted to full-time employees, in company j. Assume also that there are m comparable firms competing in the same industry/market.

Now let the m competing firms be ranked as follows:

$$P_{1t}/N_1 < P_{2t}/N_2 < \ldots < P_{mt}/N_m \qquad (14.1)$$

Based on this ranking, the lower limit of company j's total quality costs at time t can now be calculated:

$$C_{jt} = (P_{mt}/N_m - P_{jt}/N_j) \times N_j = (N_j/N_m) \times P_{mt} - P_{jt} \qquad (14.2)$$

The limit in (14.2) is a lower limit in the short term.

It can be seen from (14.2) that this lower limit is calculated as the difference between the ordinary financial result per employee of the most profitable firm (per employee) and company j, multiplied by the number of employees in company j.

We call this limit a lower limit because the method builds on a comparison with the best company, i.e. the company which has achieved the highest profits per employee. This company is used as a benchmark for the other firms being compared, a consequence of this approach being that its lower limit of quality costs is zero. It does not have zero quality costs, of course, which is why, with the help of equation (14.2), we call it a lower limit.

In conclusion, we present an example of the use of the method in the Danish printing industry.

The example is based on an analysis of the financial statements of printing firms with at least 20 employees. Initially, there were 80 such firms who were thought to be comparable with company j, a printing firm with 64 employees.

The most profitable firm had a profit of 199 966 kroner per employee, while the most unprofitable firm had a loss of 254 142 kroner per employee. 30%, i.e. 24 of the 80 firms had losses. The lower limit for total quality costs thus varies considerably between the 80 firms.

This variation is shown in Figure 14.1. It can be seen that the correlation between the lower limit of the total quality costs and company size, measured in number of employees, can be shown by a straight line with a positive slope. It can also be seen that there is a surprisingly small variation around this line. The coefficient of determination, which is a measure of how well this straight line shows the relationship, is as high as 0.97.

The model in Figure 14.1 thus tells us that the biggest firms in the printing industry also have the highest quality costs. Not surprising, perhaps. What is surprising, though, is that there is almost a perfect linear relationship between company size and the indirectly measured quality costs. However, this is a consequence of the correlation between the ordinary profit and company size. One would normally expect a positive correlation, in other words, that the biggest firms also have the highest profits. However, this is not the case in the Danish printing industry. The figures here show that the ordinary business result (profit) tends to fall as firms get bigger. This relationship is shown in Figure 14.2.

It can be seen from Figure 14.2 that, unlike Figure 14.1, there is a big variation around the straight line which shows the relationship between quality costs and company size. The conclusion is that, although we cannot definitely prove that there is a correlation, if there is one, then this straight line is our best estimate of it. A more detailed analysis, based on this straight line, shows that for each new employee in a firm in the printing industry, the ordinary financial result falls by about 19 000 kroner.

A very obvious explanation for this is that growing firms use ineffective management methods. We are convinced that TQM can change this. Firms must make an immediate start on the quality journey. Only in this way can total quality costs be reduced which in turn is the best means of improving profits.

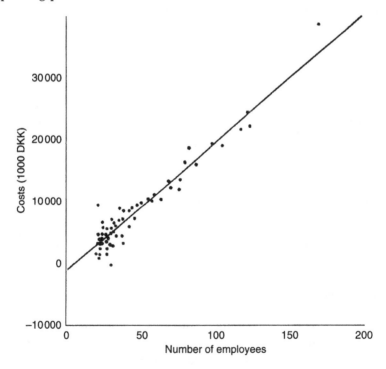

Fig. 14.1 The relation between the lower limit for quality costs and number of employees among 80 firms in the printing industry ($r^2 = 0.97$).

Following this analysis of industry-wide quality costs, we will now show how an analysis in a specific company, company j, has been carried out.

Initially, company j's 'limit' was calculated as:

$$C_{jt} = (199\ 966 - 35\ 384) \cdot 64 = 10\ 533\ 248 \text{ kroner,}$$

corresponding to about 13% of turnover.

After a more detailed analysis of those firms which had bigger profits per employee than company j, the management objected that some of these firms were incommensurable with company j. This resulted in the following revised 'limit':

$$C_{jt} = (109\ 185 - 35\ 384) \cdot 64 = 4\ 726\ 976 \text{ kroner,}$$

corresponding to roughly 6% of turnover. This 6% must now be related to Table 14.1, which showed how total quality costs could be classified into visible and invisible quality costs. If the 6% is a reasonable lower limit, then a lower limit for invisible costs can now be calculated as the difference between the 6% and the visible costs, measured as a

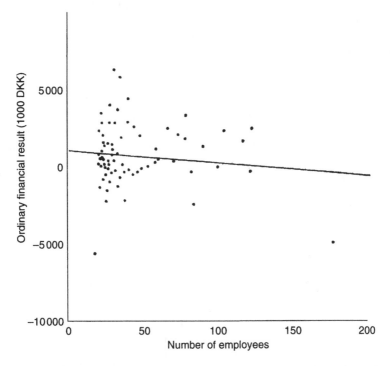

Fig. 14.2 The relation between the ordinary profit and number of employees among 80 firms in the Danish printing industry.

percentage of turnover. If the percentage for the visible costs is large compared to the 6%, then the screening method used should be critically reviewed.

To end this chapter, we present a problem which three groups at a management seminar on TQM were given to analyse.

The problem, presented by an external consultant, is as follows.

- Quality costs can be divided up into:
  - red kroner: internal and external failure costs
  - blue kroner: preventive and monitoring costs
  - green kroner: losses connected with loss of image, reduced sales, etc.
- Every firm has all three types of costs to a greater or lesser extent.
- At a brainstorming session, the group is asked to draw up lists of cost items within each of the three types of costs.
- Each group is then asked to estimate the size of the three types of costs – red, blue and green kroner – plus the total quality costs.
- The results are then discussed at the full meeting.

The three groups each presented their results at the full meeting and their evaluation of the size of the various types of quality costs are shown in Table 14.2 below.

The three groups were unaware of the above results, where equation (14.2) was used in the calculation of a lower limit for quality costs and their discussions and evaluations took place independently of each other.

In view of these initial results, the firm found the method for calculating the lower limit of total quality costs useful in connection with the strategic planning process. The method was used the following four years when comparing the financial results with the most important competitors' results. Figure 14.3 shows how the company used the method for one of the years (1992). It is obvious that we have the same strong linear relationship for the whole industry.

Table 14.2 The three groups' evaluation of the firm's quality costs (million kroner)

Group	Red kroner	Blue kroner	Green kroner	Total
A	3.5	3.0	0.5	7.0
B	5.2	0.65	0.65	6.5
C	3.25	1.95	1.3	6.5

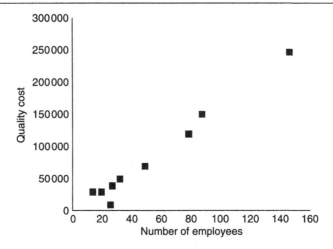

Fig. 14.3 The relation between the lower limit for total quality costs and number of employees among 10 firms in the printing industry.

14.3 ADVANTAGES AND DISADVANTAGES OF THE NEW METHOD TO ESTIMATE TOTAL QUALITY COSTS

The advantage of the method, apart from being simple to use, is that a firm is forced to compare itself with its competitors.

The firm can see directly whether it is in the premier division, the first, second or third division, or whether it is struggling at the bottom of the fourth division. Such comparisons are 'worth their weight in gold' to top management and boards of directors in setting overall quality goals for strategic quality management, not to mention their use in quality audits, which are top management's most important means of checking the firm's total quality activities. In this connection, there is actually little difference between a football club and a business.

Football clubs set goals for the next season, e.g. to move up to the premier division next year and be among the three best premier division clubs within three years. In the same way, businesses have to set overall quality goals which all employees in the firm can accept and strive for. We believe that this new method of calculating quality costs has a number of advantages which make it very useful for this purpose.

The hierarchy of goals which are subsequently set for all the firm's departments should be based on the same quality cost philosophy which has been the leitmotif of this book. The type of questions outlined in section 14.4 are a good point of departure for setting quality cost goals in the various departments or functions in the firm.

An important criterion for the choice of our new method is that it must be simple to use and understand. The drawback of our new method on the other hand is that the method is not foolproof. There may be other causes (non-controllable factors) behind a low ranking than poor quality management (controllable factors).

Let us finish with an example which may clarify the problem. At a presentation we were opposed by a student who argued that he could not accept the method because a company may be able to improve the ranking and hence decrease the lower limit of its total quality costs by changing the input to the processes from a labour intensive input to a machine intensive input.

The student's example showed a company that had a total profit of 10 million kroner. After having changed the input the company still had a total profit of 10 million kroner but the number of employees had been reduced by 50%. By using the new method to estimate the total quality costs the result may show that the company has increased the ranking and decreased the lower limit of the total quality costs significantly. The student's comment was that such a change in the process input did not improve the quality of the company so the method could not be accepted.

Let us think about this argument. What might be the reasons why the company decided to change from a labour intensive input to machine intensive input? We can see no other reasons than quality reasons or cost reasons, i.e. reasons which all may be related to the definitions of total quality:

> Quality is to continuously satisfy customers' expectations
> Total Quality is to achieve quality at low cost.

When the company decided to change the input from labour intensive to machine intensive input the expectation was that the investment was profitable, i.e. the total profit would be improved compared to a non-investment situation.

The example above does not show such an effect on the surface. But behind the figures the profit may have been positive compared to a non-investment situation. The profit in fact may have been reduced to five million kroner if the company did not invest in machine intensive input.

If the company were the only company in the market which were able to identify the opportunity for investment in machine intensive input then of course the effect is that the company has increased Total Quality dramatically in the short run. The competitors will sooner or later 'wake up' and use the same investment opportunity. In the meantime our 'pioneer company' might have improved its ranking and decreased its quality costs.

So the answer to the student and other opponents of the new method to estimate the total quality costs is that the method is a 'benchmarking method' which cannot be used independently of a company's competitors because the method is built not only on the definition of quality but also on the definition of total quality.

An alternative to the proposed method will be to use 'value added per employee' instead of 'ordinary profit per employee' in (14.1) and (14.2) where 'value added' is defined as shown below:

Value added = Ordinary Profit + Wages + Depreciation

Using value added instead of profit in (14.1) and (14.2) will not be analysed in this book. For further understanding of our new method, see section 15.2.

14.4 QUALITY COST MEASUREMENT AND CONTINUOUS IMPROVEMENTS

> If we can define it – we can measure it;
> If we can measure it – we can analyze it;
> If we can analyze it – we can control it;
> If we can control it – we can improve it.
> R.M. McNealy (1994)

This quotation tells us in condensed form why it is necessary to measure quality costs and also that before you start to measure them it is necessary to define exactly what you want to measure.

The question now is how can measurement of quality costs be made a more integral part of continuous improvements? Is it possible to make the invisible quality costs visible and hence to set quality goals for these costs? We will attempt to answer these crucial questions below.

In connection with the annual or biannual quality audit, the following sequence of questions would be appropriate in each department of the company:

1. Which quality problems/defects have you observed during the past year?
2. Which additional quality problems/defects are likely when it is remembered that the goal of quality management is to maintain or improve customers' satisfaction of needs?
3. Which preventive activities have been introduced to prevent the problem, or defect, from occurring?
4. Which inspective activities have been introduced to discover problems which have occurred?

These preliminary questions are necessary in order to 'get at the root' of the problems which have to be controlled if the firm's goal is Total Quality and TQM. They are also important in determining the hierarchy of quality goals which must be systematically set throughout the whole firm in connection with strategic quality management. These questions guarantee that new and possibly even more ambitious quality goals are not set without first considering the methods which can be used to fulfil them. Questions 3 and 4 force people to think about quality control activities, i.e. methods which prevent problems arising in the first place, or which discover defects or problems which have already occurred.

The following extract is an example of the quality problems which were identified in a printing firm by several work groups discussing the first two of the above questions:

1. The quality of the various orders fluctuates too much.
2. Customer film not good enough.
3. Insufficient information on order bags.
4. Too many defective printing plates sent to press room.
5. Poor communication.
6. Inferior raw materials and customer materials.
7. Poor control of various departments' work.
8. Poor control of received articles/materials.
9. Instructions/order bags not read properly.
10. Inadequate check of own work.

These examples are from one of the foremost firms in the Danish printing industry as regards quality and profit, so they are probably typical of the industry as a whole.

In planning quality improvement projects, it is essential that a starting point is taken in these examples. This means carrying out an analysis of causes and, in this connection, an analysis of existing methods for preventing or discovering quality problems would be invaluable. Thus questions 3 and 4 above.

Apart from these four questions, it would also be natural to ask about the consequences of individual quality problems. In other words, a form of quality cost evaluation ought to be carried out. The following three questions force people to 'think' about quality costs:

1. What are the consequences and thus the estimated failure costs per problem/defect?
2. How often does the problem/defect occur?
3. What are the failure costs per year?

These are not easy questions to answer. Both questions 1 and 2 are problematical. Answering question 1 demands, e.g. a consideration of the invisible consequences, i.e. taking account of invisible quality costs, which is not that simple. Notwithstanding, according to Deming (1986), these 'invisible figures' are the most important of all. If they are ignored just because it is hard to estimate their size, then management will soon 'have neither company nor figures'. These questions force both management and employees to systematically take account to invisible figures in their efforts to fulfil the firm's quality goals. In this connection, the important thing is not so much whether we can accurately predict the consequences of a quality problem but that these consequences are evaluated and the chief problems identified. The estimation of quality costs is used to rank identified problems in order of importance. This ranking eases group discussion, in that it makes it much easier to agree which problems to tackle first. Ranking is a good starting point for the setting of quality goals.

The above method enables the firm to identify the most important opportunities for improvement (OFIs) and thus also enables it to estimate the most important contributions to total quality costs. The method also helps the firm to decide which quality cost contributions ought to be regularly measured and recorded. The basic philosophy of the method is that quality costs only have value if they are recorded or estimated in connection with continuous improvements. The method has therefore been developed so that it is natural to use it in connection with quality improvements.

One source of inspiration in connection with the application of the above method, i.e. when a company decides to identify and measure quality costs, is the work carried out by the American Society for Quality Control and British Standard. BS 6143 and the ASQC publication *Principles of Quality Costs* (Campanella, 1990) contain detailed descriptions of quality cost elements and suggestions for charts of accounts. Such standard charts of accounts should only be used as a source of inspiration in determining which quality cost elements are central in a given company.

The important thing is that as more and more employees become actively involved in continuous improvements, the main quality elements are gradually identified throughout the firm, thus the decision about which quality cost element to measure and record can be made in connection with this. The firm's own chart of accounts for quality costs thus becomes a tool in its efforts to improve quality. In Chapter 19 a case example will show how a Danish company started up with only four accounts and how after eight years they increased the number of accounts to nine.

REFERENCES

Campanella, J. (1990) *Principles of Quality Costs*, ASQC, Milwaukee, Wisconsin, USA.

Dahlgaard, J., Kristensen, K. and Kanji, G.K. (1992) Quality costs and total quality management. *Total Quality Management*, 3(3), 211–22.

Dahlgaard, J., Kristensen, K and Kanji, G.K. (1994, 1995) *The Quality Journey*, Carfax, London, UK and Productivity Press, Madras, India.

Deming, W.E. (1986) *Out of the Crisis*, MIT, Cambridge, Mass., USA.

Juran, J.M. (1951) *Quality Control Handbook*, 1st edn, McGraw-Hill, New York, USA.

Juran, J.M. (1989) *Juran on Leadership for Quality – An Executive Handbook*, The Free Press, New York, USA.

Karlöff, B. and Östblom, S. (1994) *Benchmarking – A Signpost to Excellence in Quality and Productivity*, John Wiley & Sons, New York, USA.

McNealy, R.M. in *Readings in Total Quality Management* (ed. H. Costin), The Dryden Press, Harcourt Brace College Publishers, New York, USA.

Womack, J.P., Jones, D.T. and Roos, D. (1990) *The Machine that Changed the World*, MIT, USA.

Benchmarking   15

In the 1960s Rank Xerox appeared to be 'the sweetheart of Wallstreet'. The company had developed a product – the photocopying machine – which was a real milch cow. Each time the counter clicked, it meant money to Xerox. The company entered the Fortune 500 in 1962 as number 423 and worked its way up to Number 70 in 1970.

The result of this rising was, however, that the company fell asleep. Much money was lost on adventures outside the 'core business' and the control of vital functions such as product development and production were lost. Furthermore, the company forgot to keep an eye on the real competitors. Of course, it had an eye on the progress of IBM and Kodak but the danger from the Far East was overlooked.

The situation became more and more critical and as Mr Peter McColough, the former managing director of Xerox, put it:

> The Kodak machine combined with IBM's superior marketing skills could have killed us.

The situation reached its preliminary climax when Canon declared open war with Xerox in an advertisement of 12 January 1981:

> Waging total war against Xerox.

Obviously, Canon was sure that, at this time, Xerox was an easy target for a direct attack. However, Xerox had faced the danger and would not accept the attack. Mr David Kearns, the managing director, said 'We are determined to change significantly the way we have been doing business.' The challenge was accepted and as Canon had declared war, Xerox could also respond in the same way. The company sought advice and guidance in the classical art of war and found in Sun Tzu, a Chinese philosopher who lived around 500 BC, the strategy which should be used in the fight against the competitors:

> If you know your enemy and know yourself, you need not fear the result of a hundred battles.

By this, the groundwork for Xerox's future strategy was laid. They would fight the competitors by systematically gathering information on the market, the competitors and themselves for the strategical fixing of means and methods necessary to win the declared war. We know today that this procedure was the main reason why Rank Xerox could ride against the tide and regain the lost market shares.

They called this procedure **benchmarking** and this is the subject of this chapter.

15.1 WHAT IS BENCHMARKING?

15.1.1 DEFINITION

As stated above, benchmarking is based on Sun Tzu's rule of the art of good war: 'To know yourself and your enemy'. This was combined with an ancient Japanese word DANTOTSU, meaning striving towards becoming the best of the best. These two things united form the core of benchmarking as it also appears from the following definition given by Mr David Kearns, the former managing director of Rank Xerox, in the childhood of benchmarking:

> Benchmarking is the continuous process of measuring products, services, and practices against the toughest competitors or those companies recognized as industry leaders.

The definition opens up the possibility that you should not only look at your toughest competitors but also to other companies from which you may learn something. However, as this is not evident from the definition, it has been necessary to make a more explicit definition of benchmarking.

The new definition was published by the American Productivity and Quality Center in 1992 and is the following:

> Benchmarking is a systematic and continuous measurement process; a process of continuously measuring and comparing an organization's business processes against business process leaders anywhere in the world to gain information which will help the organization take action to improve its performance.

It is important to underline that benchmarking is not the same as copying. As W.E. Deming (1993) put it in a speech at Hewlett Packard: 'It is a hazard to copy. It is necessary to understand the theory of what one wishes to do.'

Benchmarking may form the basis of a renewed development in a company as this tool helps to identify the processes in which the best possibilities of improvements lie. The solutions used in other companies, however, can only very seldom be transferred directly to the company in question. Adjustments in some form will be made but the understanding of the 'theory' behind the solutions should always form the basis of current improvements.

Benchmarking has had many definitions since Xerox started. One of the more suggestive has been made by Mr Fred Bowers of Digital Equipment Corporation in a conference paper at American Productivity and Quality Center in 1992. Bowers see benchmarking as a company's attempt to model the human process of learning.

Human beings are exceptionally capable of identifying and using 'best practice' everywhere they meet it. From the world of sport we have many fine examples. The Fosbury Flop (high jump) which became known all over the world in connection with the Olympic Games in 1968, is one of the best. Today high jumpers all over the world use their own version of this jump. They have understood the theory behind the jump and where the centre of gravity lies.

15.1.2 TYPES OF BENCHMARKING

Dependent on the object of analysis, benchmarking is normally divided into the following three types:

1. internal benchmarking
2. competitor benchmarking
3. functional/generic benchmarking.

The objects of analysis of internal benchmarking are departments, divisions, or sister companies of the same concern in order to identify the best performance of a given activity within the company.

In many companies the same activity is displayed in many different places, e.g. order booking, stocking, distribution and product development. In this case, it would be natural to start seeking the 'best practice' internally in the company. The advantages thereof are firstly to ease the admittance to information and data. Secondly, this form of benchmarking opens up the possibility of a deep understanding of how benchmarking can be implemented. The procedure can – so to speak – be practised internally. Furthermore, experience shows that internal benchmarking improves the internal level of performance and the internal customer satisfaction through reduction of the variations of quality and productivity and it improves at the same time the ability to communicate and co-operate in the company. If you examine the disadvantages of internal benchmarking, it must be that only very rarely are 'world class performances' found internally in the company. The consequences thereof are that internal benchmarking cannot stand alone but is the first step on the road towards the final goal of benchmarking: to be the 'best in class'.

By competitor benchmarking the company compares itself directly to present and potential competitors within the same range of products (e.g. competitors at foreign markets) in order to gather information on the competitors' products, processes and results to be able to compare this information with the company's own results and to learn from the differences.

Gathering information about the behaviour of competitors is naturally always of supreme interest for a company. When Rank Xerox started its benchmarking analysis in the early 1980s its production costs per unit were higher than Canon's sales price. Obviously there was something which Canon could do which Xerox could not. To gather information about this was crucial to Xerox. Consequently, Xerox made an investigation of the conditions of production in a wider sense, not only with Canon, but also with Minolta, Toshiba and Ricoh. In doing this, Xerox was helped to a great extent by its Japanese joint venture named Fuji Xerox Co. Ltd. They discovered that the Japanese producers of photocopying machines had sought their ideas from *inter alia* Toyota and Honda, one of which was the 'just in time principle' and they were very fast at adapting their ideas to their own production.

The advantages of competitive benchmarking, beside the fact that the company puts itself in a certain position in comparison with its competitors, is that at a very early stage, the company's attention is drawn to the expectations which the customers may rightly have from it. Furthermore, the results have a high degree of comparability as the products and thus the basic production structures are identical. The disadvantage of this form of benchmarking is that the gathering of data is difficult. In many cases, you have to consult indirect sources as direct information from the competitors is unattainable.

In the third type of benchmarking, called functional/generic benchmarking, the potential comparative partner is any company which has obtained a reputation of being excellent within the area which is benchmarked. In this case, it means that the company does not necessarily have to limit itself to its own trade but keep its eyes open to 'best practice' everywhere. If, for instance, you want to study the dispatch of orders, it may be natural to compare with a mail order company or other companies which handle a great number of orders every day. If instead you want to study information systems, it could be a computer company with which you should compare yourself.

The advantage of this form of benchmarking is that the probability of finding world class practice grows as the number of potential benchmarking partners is expanded. On the other hand, it is obvious that the possibility of transferring the found practice directly to one's own company is smaller than by the other types of benchmarking. Another advantage is that the collection of data in this case is considerably easier

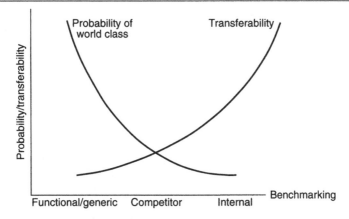

Fig. 15.1 Characteristics of the three types of benchmarking.

than by competitive benchmarking as it is much easier to get a co-operation going with companies from other lines of business than your own line.

As a final conclusion concerning the three types of benchmarking, we refer to Figure 15.1.

The figure distinguishes on the horizontal axis between three types of benchmarking. On the vertical axis is measured the probability of finding world class practice AND the extent of the possibility of direct transfer (that is without adjustment) to one's own company of the practice found.

As previously mentioned, it can be seen that usually the procedures found internally can to a large extent be transferred directly. On the other hand, the probability of finding world-class practice internally is usually small. It is the exact opposite by functional benchmarking. Here the probability of finding world class practice is large. On the other hand, it is usually necessary to adjust 'best practice' to the conditions of one's own company. Competitive benchmarking lies in the middle of these two extremes.

15.2 WHAT CAN BE BENCHMARKED?

In the previous section we defined the three types of benchmarking while in this section we shall describe what can be benchmarked. Table 15.1 shows what can be benchmarked and which types of benchmarking can be applied.

The purpose of this table is to show that at a superior level, three main areas exist which can be benchmarked and that in principle all of these

Table 15.1 Types of benchmarking and what can be
benchmarked

Type/what	Quality	Productivity	Time
Internal benchmarking Competitive benchmarking Functional benchmarking	√ (√) √	√ (√) √	√ (√) √

three main areas can be combined by one or more of the three types of
benchmarking. This is not the same as saying that the procedure is
identical for the various combinations in the table as the difficulties of
applying each single combination can vary considerably from one combination to the other, for which reason the detailed benchmarking procedure will also vary considerably. The parentheses in the table imply that
difficulty in applying especially competitive benchmarking can be
expected.

It is shown from Table 15.1 that at a superior level there are three
answers to the question 'what can be benchmarked?' These three
answers are (Karlöf, Bengt and Östblom, 1994, p. 35):

1. quality
2. productivity
3. time.

However, it can be argued that only two main areas can be benchmarked
– quality and productivity – as time will always be a part of either
quality or productivity. When we have chosen time, despite this fact, as a
special area which can be benchmarked, the reasons are the following:

1. The time concept is simple and easy to understand and is thus easily
   accepted by all employees.
2. The time concept is by definition related to processes and will thus
   automatically force the participants to focus on processes and process
   relations. Consequently, it will, by definition, invite a better
   co-operation between processes and departments.
3. Reduction of times (e.g. times of delivery) means increased productivity and increased quality perception by customers.

Examples of times used for benchmarking are listed below:

1. Turn-around times, e.g. time from order taking to delivery.
2. Time of development for new products.
3. Installation time.
4. Time for debugging.
5. Time for handling of claims.

6. Time for handling of inquiries.
7. Time for dealing with employees' suggestions for improvements.
8. Punctuality of deliveries in percentage terms.

Many companies have obtained major results by focusing on times. One of these is Electrolux Cleaning Services in Västervik, Sweden, which has reduced the time of delivery of vacuum cleaning motors by more than 90%. Another company, ABB, has launched a new quality improvement programme named 'Customer Focus'. The aim of this programme is, *inter alia*, to halve all turn-around times.

Regarding benchmarking of productivity we would like to mention that comparisons by means of productivity measures are a common and often effective means of identifying potential benchmarking partners. A common productivity measure in this connection is:

Ordinary net profit per employee =

$$\frac{(\text{turnover} - (\text{purchase} + \text{expenses} + \text{depreciations} + \text{interests}))}{\text{average number of full-time employees}}$$

The application of this productivity measure in connection with benchmarking is often applied by analyzing the results of the following three steps:

1. The ordinary net profit per employee is calculated as described above. The potential benchmarking partners can be identified by means of this measure.
2. A breakdown of the ordinary net profit per employee into its components is made, i.e. the following key figures are calculated:
   a. turnover per employee
   b. purchase per employee
   c. costs per employee
   d. interest per employee
   e. depreciations per employee.
   By comparing the above key figures with the key figures for the potential benchmarking partners, it will be possible to minimize the number of potential partners. At the same time, this comparison creates the possibility of identifying the processes which will be valuable to benchmark.
3. A further breakdown of the key figures of step 2 is made, if possible. The aim is to minimize the number of benchmarking partners further and to increase the possibility of identifying the relevant processes for benchmarking.

The application of the productivity measure 'ordinary net profit per employee' will be dealt with later in connection with benchmarking of the total quality costs of a company.

Benchmarking of quality will either be a natural extension of time or productivity being applied first in connection with benchmarking or it can be the area which for some reason has been focused on as the first.

Benchmarking of quality can be divided into the same main areas which are normally used in connection with the division of the concept of quality:

1. External quality:
   a. customer satisfaction
   b. the technical quality of the product.
2. Internal quality:
   a. employee satisfaction
   b. process quality.

In relation to external quality it can be interesting to look into the following questions:

1. How can need and expectations be identified ('Expected Quality')?
2. How can 'value added' qualities be identified ('Charming Quality')?
3. How are dissatisfied customers identified?
4. How are dissatisfied customers dealt with?
5. How is customer satisfaction measured?
6. Which qualities are included in the customer satisfaction measuring?
7. How are customer satisfaction measurings applied?
8. How are comparisons to competitors carried through ('Relative Quality')?

The earliest form of benchmarking we know is that under point 8. The most common way to do it is simply to become customer of the competitor, buy the competitors' products and compare them with your own products.

In relation to employee satisfaction it can be interesting to look into the following questions:

1. How is employee satisfaction measured?
2. How are measurings applied?
3. How are employees educated and trained?
4. How do you ensure that employees are involved in quality improvements?
5. How is employee involvement measured?

Benchmarking of process quality can be divided up into a row of key processes which in relation to a production company may consist of the following key processes:

1. Research and development.
2. Production and distribution.
3. Administration supporting processes.

In relation to research and development it is important to look into the following questions:

1. How is research and development carried through?
2. How is design review carried through?
3. How are customer demands translated into construction demands?
4. Does the company have a system for shortening the time for development?
5. How is the quality of the development work measured?

In relation to production and distribution the following questions may be important:

1. How are the processes designed?
2. How can times of delivery be minimized?
3. How can process quality be measured?
4. How are the measurings applied?
5. How are continuous improvements ensured?
6. How are defects and problems dealt with?
7. How is quality audit carried through?
8. How are quality plans made?

Finally, in relation to administrative supporting processes the following could be important:

1. How can supporting processes be identified?
2. How can the quality of supporting processes be measured?
3. How are measurings applied?
4. How can continuous improvements of the supporting processes be ensured?
5. How are defects and problems dealt with?
6. How can quality audits be carried through?
7. How are quality plans of supporting processes made?

The questions mentioned above must not be considered as exhaustive. Beyond the examples mentioned, there will be a number of things which can be benchmarked, all dependent on the exact company and the market in question. However, we are of the opinion that the questions above form a good basis for the beginning of a benchmarking procedure.

15.3 HOW IS BENCHMARKING CARRIED THROUGH?

There are many ways in which benchmarking can be applied. Rank Xerox, for one, has its own procedure divided into 10 steps. This procedure is based on the pioneer work laid down by Camp (1989) in the early 1980s. In our opinion, it can be advantageous to look at benchmarking in

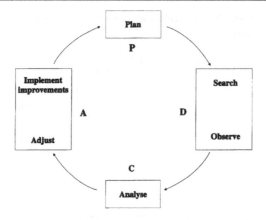

Fig. 15.2 The PDCA circle of benchmarking.

the same light as other continuous improvements. In Figure 15.2 we have consequently made a model for the implementation of benchmarking based on the ideas behind the so-called Deming cycle or the PDCA cycle.

It appears from Figure 15.2 that, firstly, benchmarking is considered an eternal process (a closed loop) meaning that as soon as the benchmarking procedure is implemented and the improvements started, a new plan and search for improvements starts. Secondly, the benchmarking is implemented in four natural stages:

1. PLAN: planning
2. DO: search and observe
3. CHECK: analyse the results
4. ACT: adapt results and carry through improvements.

The planning stage (Plan) comprises the initial activities in connection with benchmarking. The stage will typically consist of the following four points:

1. Determination of what shall be benchmarked.
2. The determination of criteria for the selection of benchmarking partners.
3. The determination of methods for data collection.
4. The determination of use of resources.

As regards point 1 it will, in principle, be a question of choosing between the items mentioned in section 15.2. The choice will of course reflect the perception of a certain weakness in a given area, e.g. distribution.

As regards the choice of a partner, the criteria must be determined on the basis of the superior consideration that the results found will be

Table 15.2 Methods for data collection in benchmarking

	Data collection	
	Direct	Indirect
Internal	1. Direct observation of the processes chosen 2. Studies of internal material	(Indirect data collection is normally not used in connection with internal benchmarking)
External	1. Site visit 2. Questionnaire	1. Trade analyses 2. Studies of literature 3. Conferences 4. Consultants 5. Experience groups

transferable to one's own company and at the same time, the practice found should reflect 'world class' (Figure 15.1).

As regards the data collection, it must be determined from where the data should be collected and how it should be collected. In principle, the benchmarking can be internal or external and the data collection can be direct or indirect. If these are combined, the methods for data collection can be found as shown in Table 15.2.

By and large, Table 15.2 explains itself and consequently, we will not explain the single elements in detail.

In the next phase, the Do phase, you search and observe as per the criteria laid down under the Plan phase. The phase comprises the following steps:

1. The concrete choice of a benchmarking partner.
2. Data collection.

In connection with this phase it may be necessary to return to the Plan phase, as the planned data collection may be impossible with the partner chosen. The two phases will consequently interplay before you can progress to the third phase of the model.

This phase, the Check phase or the analysis phase, comprises the following steps:

1. Data correction.
2. Identification and quantification of differences of performances (gaps).
3. Identification of causes for differences of performances.

Under the first item, the data are corrected with regard to systematical errors which make the data not immediately comparable. They may be corrected with regard to differences in market conditions, level of costs, etc. Under the second and third items, the differences of performances in quality and productivity are identified and you must try to explain the reason for these differences. Some of these will often be technological causes, some systems causes, or be of a human nature.

The final phase is the Act phase. During this phase, the results are adjusted to your own situation and improvements are implemented. The phase comprises the following steps:

1. Communication of the results found.
2. Ensuring acceptance with the involved parties.
3. Adjustment of the obtained results to one's own situation and the arrangement of functional aims.
4. Making of a plan of action.
5. Implementation of the plan of action.

The last step of the phase, implementation, is not always easy to carry through. Changes are always met with resistance and item 2 is therefore crucial. Furthermore, it is important that the implementation is carried through with its own PDCA cycle in such a way that the steps of the process can be surveyed all the time.

A successful passage through the PCDA cycle of benchmarking depends to a large extent on the commitments of the management. Naturally, benchmarking leads to changes and it is the responsibility of management to lead these changes. There is a saying in Japan that 'Management's job is to manage change. If management fails, we must change management.'

REFERENCES

Camp, R.C. (1989) *Benchmarking – The Search for Industry Best Practices that Lead to Superior Performance*, ASQC Industry Press, Milwaukee, Wisconsin; Quality Resources, New York, USA.

Deming, W.E. (1993) *The New Economics*, MIT Centre for Engineering Study, USA.

Karlöff, B. and Östblom, S. (1994) *Benchmarking – A Signpost to Excellence in Quality and Productivity*, John Wiley & Sons, New York, USA.

PART THREE
Process Management and Improvement

Leadership, policy deployment and quality motivation

16

16.1 INTRODUCTION

Today everybody agrees that leadership is a necessary condition for TQM and any book about TQM will say this. But what is leadership in relation to quality management? The answers to this question are not so easily agreed upon and vary considerably from author to author and from manager to manager.

The purpose of this chapter is to present a leadership model which we find useful in connection with the policy deployment process of TQM. The model is highly people-oriented since we have found this aspect of leadership especially weak in current Western management.

16.2 THE PDCA LEADERSHIP MODEL – A MODEL FOR POLICY DEPLOYMENT

In Chapter 4 the TQM pyramid was presented and discussed. It was shown that the foundation of the pyramid was management's commitment or leadership. In the light of the discussion in Chapter 4 we conclude that the aim of TQM leadership is to build the TQM pyramid.

Our experiences, however, tell us that such an aim is not a sufficient condition for TQM leadership – it is only a necessary condition. Management needs a model which is process oriented, i.e. a model which follows management's yearly and follow-up cycle (the 'Hoshin Kanri' or policy deployment cycle). We call this model the PDCA Leadership Model. The model is shown in Figure 16.1.

The cycle of the PDCA Leadership Model begins with the Check phase, because the development of the plan for quality improvements requires an understanding of the present situation (where are we now?).

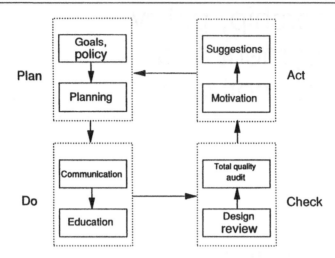

Fig. 16.1 The PDCA leadership model.

The TQM leadership model is to consist of two key elements based on Deming's well-known points 1 and 5: continuous improvement of products and services and continuous improvement of processes. Hence, the model will consist of the following two elements: design review and total quality audit.

The process of design review consists of checking the product and service development at various important stages – a preliminary stage, one or more intermediate stages and a final stage.

Total quality audit consists of checking the concordance between quality plans and quality results in order to identify future opportunities for improvements. In short, total quality audit is checking the quality of the processes of the company including the product development process.

When checking the concordance between plans and results the primary objective is to understand:

1. Why results did not live up to the expectations (plans)?
2. Why results were better than expected?

In other words the causes behind the measurements should be understood. In this context a thorough analysis and evaluation of measurements are a must. That means building up a coherent measurement system is a prerequisite for an effective quality audit (Chapter 12).

When checking the product development process it is important to integrate results from design review. These results should be evaluated in exactly the same way as results from other business processes in order to identify future opportunities for improvements.

Before the revolution of TQM top management participation in design review and quality audit was not common. These activities were usually considered to be the responsibility of the quality department. Today it is widely realized that these two activities cannot be delegated. Both are key elements of leadership and policy deployment.

The next phase of the leadership model is the Act phase, which consists of two elements – motivation and suggestions.

If top management participates wholeheartedly in the check phase an important signal has been sent out to the whole organization that quality and quality improvements are top priority. The effect will be people who are motivated for quality improvements. For each key process suggestions for quality improvements will be generated as input to the next phase of the PDCA Leadership Model. Section 16.2 will focus on these elements of the PDCA Leadership Model.

The Plan phase consists of two main elements – deciding on the quality goals and policies and design of the quality plans.

When deciding on the goals and policies management should have the four sides of the TQM pyramid as a reference. The goals and policies act as a picture (a vision) showing where the company wants to be (the goal of the journey). It is vital that this picture is updated from time to time as a result of the previous two phases (check and act). Chapters 19 and 20 give two examples on how world class companies have formulated their goals and policies.

Planning is the process of designing the detailed plans for quality improvements, i.e. the road map to follow on the quality journey. This planning process should be done on the same premise as the 'Hoshin Kanri' policy deployment process, i.e. people who are responsible for executing the plan should also participate in the planning process itself. This foundation will, through group dialogue, secure a stronger plan and will ensure that the company's quality culture will be changed into the direction needed. It will also secure that planning is not finished until the necessary implementation resources have been discussed or negotiated between top management, middle management and the implementation teams (QC circles, quality improvement teams etc.).

The design of the detailed plan for quality improvements starts with a top management decision on which areas should have the highest priority for improvements in the next year (waste reduction, cost reduction, customer satisfaction, education and training etc.). The results of the total quality audit combined with the results of a self-assessment and/or benchmarking are the natural input to this decision process.

The chosen priorities for improvement are 'thrown' to the divisional and departmental managers who 'catch the ball' and start a process where the overall goals of the quality improvements are analysed and evaluated. The aim of the process is to give feedback to top management and to design the detailed plans which are the means to reach the overall goals decided by top management.

Both at top management level and also at divisional or departmental level it may be a help to classify the plan for quality improvements into the following eight categories:

1. improvements in customer satisfaction;
2. improvements in employee satisfaction;
3. improvements in products and services;
4. improvements in processes (systems and technology);
5. improvements in people (education/training);
6. improvements in customer relationships;
7. improvements in supplier relationships;
8. improvements in the measurement system.

These overlapping categories are an efficient check-list during the 'catch ball' process of policy deployment (Hoshin Kanri). They may inspire management at different levels to identify meaningful opportunities for improvements and then decide on meaningful targets to achieve.

The last phase of the PDCA Leadership Model is the Do phase. Here we also have two elements. The final quality plan has to be communicated to everyone concerned and the necessary education has to be achieved.

Besides the need to educate the employees (including management) in the use of quality tools there is also a need to educate and train all the employees in human motivation – theory and practice.

If the previous three phases have been executed 'in the right way', i.e. by employee involvement, the Do phase will be executed under control of 'the local people'. They will function as an orchestra directed by their team leaders who are directed by their departmental leaders who are directed by divisional leaders or divisional quality steering groups which are directed by the company's overall steering group for quality improvements. The notes to play are in the quality plan. The only remark to 'the orchestra' is that the divisional steering group is the company's cross-functional committee in respect to the quality improvement process.

A model of this orchestra is shown in Figure 16.2. The model has been developed at Robert Bosch, Denmark and used in their Policy Deployment Process. CIP means Continuous Improvement Process, which has the highest priority in Robert Bosch worldwide.

16.3 LEADERSHIP AND QUALITY MOTIVATION

People are the key to quality. If their actions and reactions become quality related, then expensive failures and the accumulation of hidden costs may be reduced to an acceptable minimum or even prevented altogether.

Total Quality is a holistic concept which requires quality motivation of all people in an organization towards a common goal. Whatever the structure and management process of the organization the necessary links must be built up between people. We must learn to accept that employees are not only our greatest and most expensive asset but that they alone are the creators of quality, i.e. 'People make Quality' (Kanji and Asher, 1993).

The belief is that when people are well motivated then they can overcome any difficulties they experience in solving their problems. Further, whatever work we are associated with, we must motivate ourselves in order to achieve our work objective.

Quality motivation is all about people because it is people who make quality. We have a common saying that 'an organization is as good as its people'. It is well-known that the majority of quality-related problems within our organizations are not within the control of the individual employee. As many as 80% of these problems are caused by the way the people are organized and managed.

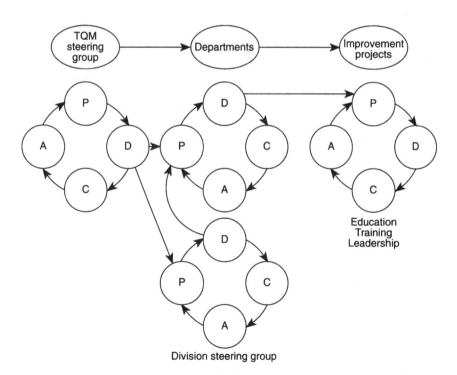

Fig. 16.2 The CIP orchestra.

Some examples of this bad management can be seen as follows:

- When people are not given the right training to do the job and have to learn the job of others.
- When the job itself is not properly defined and those doing it have to 'make it up' as they go along.
- When paperwork is out of date or otherwise inaccurate.
- When systems do not reflect the work that actually takes place or are not designed to help to do the job.

The role of managers within the organization is to ensure that everything necessary is in place to allow people to make quality.

Organizations are run by various systems and procedures in order to manage their activities smoothly and in an orderly fashion. However, in recent years the business world has changed rapidly and business processes have accordingly changed with it. The major activities of managers these days are therefore to manage these organizational changes. Most of them are due to the modern quality revolution which, in turn, has created the customers' higher quality expectation of products and services.

For the adaptation of these changes many organizations have followed a streamline route, i.e. a method to eliminate unnecessary work processes, duplication of workloads and extra cross-functional co-operation. Although streamline routes are desirable for many organizations, nevertheless, our human system organized in this way could easily create some negative and undesirable activities, e.g. loss of enthusiasm, lack of creativity and motivation. It is therefore the leadership of the organization that must play an active role in preserving the positive aspects of the human system and stimulate the individual in its real desire to work.

Leadership is the beginning of the quality improvement process which starts with vision, mission, values, policy and strategy, systems etc. and further continues with other principles and concepts of Total Quality Management. According to the European Model for Total Quality Management, leadership is the driving force behind policy and strategy, people management, resources and processes, leading ultimately to excellence in business results.

The European Model for Total Quality Management also suggests that customer satisfaction, people satisfaction and impact on society can be achieved through leadership. The model has used various criteria to demonstrate leadership including (EFQM, 1996):

- visible involvement in leading Total Quality;
- a consistent Total Quality culture;
- timely recognition and appreciation of the efforts and successes of individuals and teams;

- support of Total Quality by provision of appropriate resources and assistance;
- involvement with customers and suppliers;
- active promotion of Total Quality outside the organizations.

16.3.1 ASPECTS OF LEADERSHIP AND THE PDCA LEADERSHIP MODEL

Clear leadership and vision are considered to be the most important critical success factors of TQM. If TQM is adopted as a positive business strategy a substantial upfront investment of management time must be made before a return is seen. The model we presented in Figure 16.1 is an attempt to point out and to systematize some of the key tasks for leaders committed to the TQM process.

The PDCA cycle is an obvious choice as a frame of reference. The Plan phase and the existence of well developed communication reflect the degree of deployment in the firm while education and training reflect the degree of empowerment. When TQM has been incorporated into the firm's strategic and operational plans, communicated to all employees and delegation of responsibility has been undertaken as a consequence of education and training, then a need to measure the correspondence between plans and results is the next managerial step on the quality journey.

The Plan, Do and Check phases in our model reflect top-down leadership but to modify existing quality plans or establish new quality objectives, participation of the workforce is crucial. The Act phase reflects the bottom-up principle. It is a very important managerial task to create a motivational environment to ensure that the employees perform according to quality goals and make suggestions about quality improvements. As stressed by many authors motivation is increased and commitment is shown if management takes immediate action on good ideas from the workforce. Chapter 19 shows how a world-class company (Milliken Denmark) has had success in building up an effective suggestion system.

(a) Education and training

As regards education and training, with the purpose of giving people empowerment to do their own jobs, we have observed considerable differences in our QED study (Figure 16.3). Japan, Estonia and India report that between 65 and 80 hours per year are used for educational and training activities per employee. All other countries use 30–40 hours per year per employee.

The Indian and Estonian results reflect an obvious necessary investment in people to increase know-how. This is a signal of increasing

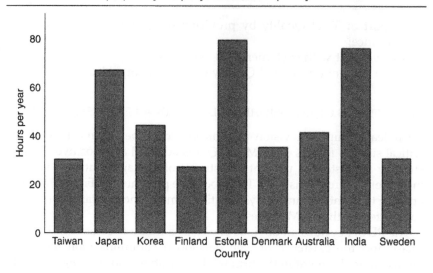

Fig. 16.3 Number of hours per year used for education and training per employee.

competition from the developing countries. Japan may be regarded as the country furthest ahead on the quality journey (Dahlgaard, Kristensen and Kanji, 1994). When the most obvious changes in the organization have been made it becomes more and more obvious to management that new opportunities for improvement depend upon empowerment. Satisfaction of the workforce and hence motivation and ability to act as a constructive part in the process of continuous improvement depend upon education and training. This is known and acted upon in Japan as seen in Figure 16.3. In Western countries less resources are invested in education and training and this could cause a bottleneck on the quality journey.

(b) Quality motivation and suggestions for improvements

In the TQM leadership model the aim of the Act phase is to create an environment which motivates people for quality and which encourages them to participate in making suggestions about quality improvement.

Motivation for quality may be done in many different ways (Kristensen, Dahlgaard and Kanji, 1993). It appears from Figure 16.4 that the respondents have especially focused on five different areas. The main observation is that the highest level of activity directed towards the five quality motivation areas is found in the East Asian countries of Taiwan, Korea and Japan. The main instrument for quality motivation in these

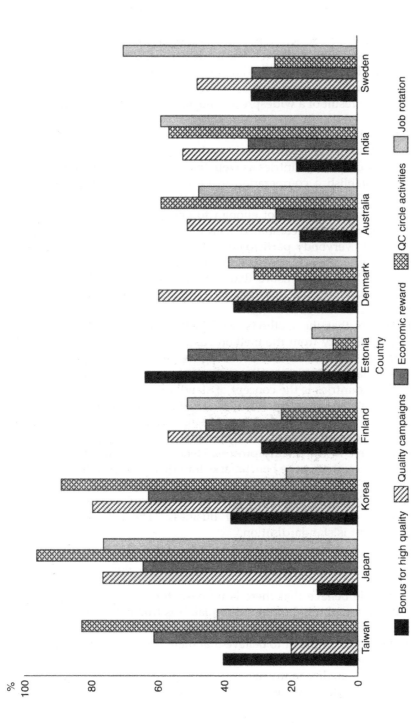

Fig. 16.4 Quality motivation and suggestions for improvement. (Source: QED study, 1992.)

■ Bonus for high quality ▨ Quality campaigns ▨ Economic reward ▨ QC circle activities ☐ Job rotation

countries is QC circle activities and this instrument is also widely used in India and Australia. It is well-known that the QC circle idea originates from Japan but it is not so well-known how the spread of the 'gospel' has taken place. The high use of QC circles in these countries is, in our opinion, the result of a widespread co-operation between countries in the Pacific area which started in 1978 with the first International Conference on QC circles. We know that the idea of teams and QC circles is very useful within quality management and we hope that the idea is going to spread to European countries as well. In order for this to happen we may need to establish a co-operation in Europe along the lines mentioned above.

Quality motivation is not enough to ensure a TQM culture. Quality motivation should be combined with a number of methods in order to ensure that everybody participates actively in improving the quality of products, services and processes. In our study we asked the participating companies how they ensure that the employees are active in making suggestions. From this question we obtained the results presented in Figure 16.5.

It appears that the methods used in the three East Asian countries differ significantly from the methods used in the other countries. Again we see that the level of activities is highest in the East Asian countries – especially Japan. The main discriminator between East Asian countries and other countries is the concept of standardization. In this connection, standardization means establishing a system for handling suggestions and setting goals for the number of suggestions. We believe that this reflects the degree of leadership commitment concerning integration of the workforce in the quality process. Hence we consider the figures for East Asian countries to be benchmarks for other countries. As Imai (1986) points out: 'There can be no improvement where there are no standards'. Similarly, Professor Yoshio Kondo (1992) pointed out at a series of lectures at the Aarhus School of Business: 'The entrance to quality improvement is standardisation.'

16.3.2 BASIS FOR MOTIVATION (MOTIVATION THEORIES)

Some people believe that there is no basis for motivation because it is only the frame of mind of an individual. It is true that you have to deal with people's minds and treat them fairly in order to motivate them, nevertheless it is difficult to believe that there is no basis for the development of motivation theory.

These days quality motivation is seen as a vital factor towards achieving work objectives using human resources and considering human needs. The basis for motivation theory therefore can be developed by considering some common elements of human needs.

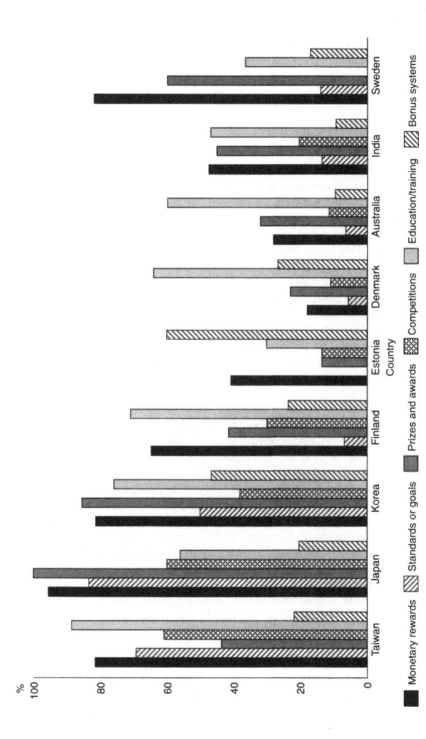

Fig. 16.5 Methods for quality suggestions in different countries. (Source: QED study, 1992.)

Maslow (1943) has described the hierarchy of human needs as follows:

- physiological needs
- safety needs
- social needs
- ego or esteem needs
- self-fulfilment needs.

According to Maslow an individual starts with physiological needs and when he fulfils that need, he then moves on to the next hierarchy, i.e. safety needs and so on.

Frederick Herzberg (1969), another Western expert, suggested that the motivation is governed by two types of factor, namely satisfiers and dissatisfiers. For some people, dissatisfaction at work is caused either due to low pay, noisy working environments or unsuitable office accommodation or similar other reasons. To eliminate dissatisfaction from such people it is necessary to satisfy them by providing higher pay and suitable office accommodation etc.

It is debatable whether by simply removing the sources of dissatisfaction from people one can motivate them to work with full commitment. On the other hand, one can easily use a satisfier effectively for the preparation of work standards, setting work goals and appraising the results etc.

According to Herzberg, fulfilling low level needs suggested by Maslow is equivalent to fulfilling the needs of a dissatisfier and similarly fulfilling high level needs requires a genuine satisfier. It is therefore understandable that to motivate people we need to have both dissatisfiers and satisfiers. That is to say, to motivate people we must not only remove sources of dissatisfaction but also take positive steps to provide sources of satisfaction.

In 1973, a task force headed by O'Toole in the USA published its findings about work in America. In this report he proposed that work should be defined as 'an activity that produces something of value for other people'.

At the same time Dr Nishibori of Japan suggested (Kondo, 1991) that the human work should include the following elements:

- creativity (the joy of thinking);
- physical activity (the joy of physical work);
- sociality (the joy of sharing pleasure and pain with colleagues).

In a real sense, there is no difference between O'Toole's and Nishibori's ideas regarding the elements of human work. As a matter of fact both of these ideas can be present under one heading as shown in Figure 16.6.

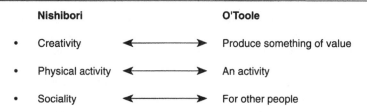

Fig. 16.6 Elements of human work.

Usually, we understand that work involves activity and the humanity in work means the creativity, i.e. natural fulfilment of the activities. Therefore the development of motivation requires both the creativity and sociality which incorporates some elements of humanity.

We will now look at this joint approach by Nishibori and O'Toole to understand the present development of quality motivation within the Eastern countries.

16.3.3 THE STRUCTURE OF A JAPANESE QUALITY MOTIVATION TRAINING PACKAGE

Kondo (1991) has pointed out that the managers and supervisors must motivate the co-workers continuously as a part of their normal duties. According to him, people must develop motivation through on-the-job training and the structure of the motivation theory can be seen as a large roof resting on three pillars mounted on a solid base as shown in Figure 16.7.

Here the base represents self-development (i.e. to motivate other people we must motivate ourselves). The first pillar is getting the job

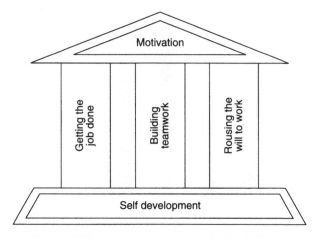

Fig. 16.7 Structure for human motivation training.

done (i.e. learning how to complete a difficult task). The second pillar is building teamwork (i.e. working together to achieve a common goal). The third pillar is rousing the will to work (i.e. creating the desire to work).

According to Kondo, motivation is affected by different factors and requires various responses depending on person, time and place. However, these factors have certain commonalities and the structure described above incorporates many of these characteristics.

16.3.4 QUALITY MOTIVATION IN JAPAN, TAIWAN AND KOREA

Quality motivation is the major task for modern business management. Without quality motivation it is impossible to implement Total Quality Management. In our questionnaire in the OED project (Dahlgaard, Kristensen and Kanji, 1992) we asked companies to inform us about their methods of motivation. The following main groups for their answers were chosen:

- bonus for high quality (create the desire to work);
- quality campaigns (create the desire to work);
- economic rewards (create the desire to work);
- QCC activities (building teamwork);
- job rotation (getting the job done).

The results obtained from the QED project regarding the main methods of motivation from Japan, Taiwan and Korea are given in Figure 16.8. The purpose of this result is to understand the motivation methods used by the various organizations in order to develop their Total Quality Management culture.

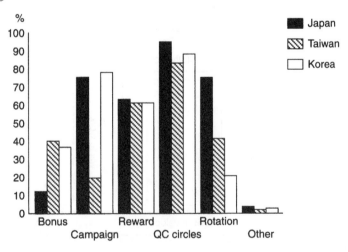

Fig. 16.8 Quality motivation in Japan, South Korea and Taiwan.

From Figure 16.8 it is clear to us that 90% of the companies suggested that the QC circles (i.e. building teamwork) are an important factor for the quality motivation. We therefore strongly believe that in all three countries QC circle activities are regarded as the major quality motivator. In Japan and Korea quality campaigns (create desire to work) are regarded as the second most important motivator and in Japan job rotation (getting the job done) also plays a very significant role.

Figure 16.8 also points out three major areas of difference between the countries:

1. bonus systems
2. quality campaigns
3. job rotation.

In our opinion job rotation is a necessary condition for implementing TQM and we believe that Japan is on the right track in this respect. This can be seen in Figure 16.9 where the percentages of active QC circles are given for both with and without job rotation.

The high correlation (Figure 16.9) between the job rotation and the percentage of active QC circles indicates that it will be necessary for both Taiwan and Korea to increase the use of job rotation in the future in order to achieve further quality development. The modest use of job rotation in

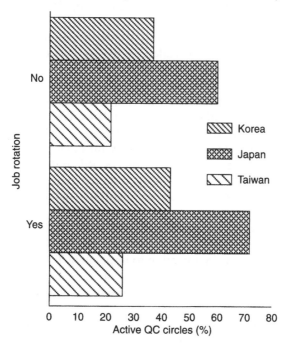

Fig. 16.9 The importance of job rotation with respect to QC circle efficiency.

Korea can probably be explained by the management structure mentioned in (Dahlgaard, Kristensen and Kanji, 1993).

With respect to quality campaigns (Figure 16.8), it is not clear from the information available to us why this approach is so little used in Taiwan. Only 20% of the companies in Taiwan have used it which is dramatically lower than Japan and Korea, where the figures are very high, i.e. 76% and 79% respectively.

Regarding bonus systems the figures are relatively small for all countries but still significantly lower for Japan. We know that in both Korea and Japan, bonus systems are frequently used but obviously they are not considered to be quality motivators to any great extent, which is fully in accordance with the basic motivation theory.

16.4 CONCLUSION

In section 16.1 of the chapter we asked the question 'what is leadership in relation to quality?' and we concluded that the answers to this question are not so easily agreed upon and vary considerably from author to author and from manager to manager.

Even if a common definition of leadership is not easily agreed upon there is one lesson which is very clear (Juran, 1989): 'The most decisive factor in the competition for quality leadership is the rate of quality improvement.'

In this chapter we have presented a new (dynamic) model of leadership (Figure 16.1) which we called 'a PDCA Leadership Model'. The elements of the model are linked together by using the most widespread model for quality improvements: the PDCA cycle also called the Deming cycle. The Model has been used to compare survey data from manufacturing companies in nine different countries. We recommend that the results of this comparative study could be used for benchmarking purposes where the data from the countries with the highest rate of quality improvements may be used as benchmarks. When doing this our PDCA Model for leadership may be an easy and effective model for managers to follow when they really try to institute leadership according to Deming's point 2.

Further, it has been shown that quality motivation is very important for modern business management. Without proper quality motivation it will be difficult for any organization to implement Total Quality Management. For development of the motivation it is essential to fulfil the leadership role and to have real commitment by the top management of the organization.

The evidence in this study indicates that in order to motivate people within an organization the leadership must consider job rotation as one of the most important management strategies. In conclusion we feel that this study has demonstrated that QC circles, i.e. teamwork, are regarded as the most successful approach for the systematic development of human motivation in Japan, Korea and Taiwan.

REFERENCES

Akao, Y. (1991) *Hoshin Kanri – Policy Deployment for Successful TQM*, Productivity Press, Inc., Cambridge, MA, USA.

Dahlgaard, J.J. Kristensen, K. Juhl, H.J. and Kanji, G.K. (1994) TQM leadership in different countries – a comparative study. *European Quality*, 1(2).

Dahlgaard, J.J., Kristensen, K. and Kanji, G.K. (1992) Quality and economic development project. *Total Quality Management*, 3(1), 115–18.

Dahlgaard, J.J., Kristensen, K. and Kanji, G.K. (1995) *The Quality Journey – A Journey Without An End*, Productivity Press (India) pvt. Ltd, Madras, India.

EFQM (1996) *Self-Assessed Guidelines for Companies*, Brussels, Belgium.

Herzberg, F. (1969) *The Motivation to Work*, John Wiley and Sons, New York, USA.

Imai, M. (1986) *KAIZEN – The Key to Japan's Competitive Success*, The Kaizen Institute Ltd, London.

Juran, J.M. (1989) *Juran on Leadership for Quality – An Executive Handbook*, The Free Press, New York, USA.

Kanji, G.K. (1990) Total Quality Management: the second industrial revolution. *Total Quality Management*, 1(1), 3–12.

Kanji, G.K. and Asher, M. (1993) *Total Quality Management: A Systematic Approach*, Carfax Publishing Co., Oxford.

Kano, N. (1984) Attractive quality and must be quality. *Quality*, 14(2).

Kondo, Y. (1991) *Human Motivation: A Key Factor for Management*, 3A Corporation, Tokyo, Japan.

Kristensen K., Dahlgaard J.J. and Kanji, G.K. (1993), Quality motivation in East Asian countries, *Total Quality Management*, 4(1), 79–89.

Maslow, A.H. (1943) A theory of human motivation. *Psychological Review*, No. 50, 370.

O'Toole, J. *et al.* (1973) *Work in America*, MIT Press, Cambridge MA, USA.

Implementation process[1]

17

17.1 INTRODUCTION

This chapter discusses how to implement Total Quality Management in the competitive business world where the customer no longer accepts the traditional approach to quality. In general it has been accepted that the basic problems which prevent both manufacturing and service industries from being quality organizations are seen to be the same.

In this modern world the implementation of the TQM process is one of the most complex activities that a company can undertake, because it requires cultural change for everybody. It is well-known that it is difficult to change people rather than things, nevertheless it is necessary for the top managers to take an active leadership role involving everybody in the organization in order to fulfil the quality goal. Kanji and Asher (1993) developed a four-stage implementation process for their TQM model. In the critical analysis stage they indicated that output will be the continuous improvement cycle, i.e. PDCA cycle.

17.2 FOUR STAGES OF IMPLEMENTATION

We believe that, among other things, two of the most common driving forces behind implementation of TQM within an organization are competition and the need to keep the customer happy. Kanji and Asher (1993) used the four-stage process of implementing TQM in an organization. The stages are:

1. identification and preparation;
2. management understanding and commitment;

[1] The authors would like to thank Mr Daniel Psaila for his contribution to this chapter.

3. scheme for improvement;
4. critical analysis.

At the critical analysis stage the output is Deming's cycle, i.e. Plan-Do-Check-Act. However, the above four stages of implementation can be modelled according to Deming's PDCA cycle as follows (Figure 17.1).

17.3 PLAN

Identifying and collecting information about the organisation in the prime areas where improvement will have most impact on the organisation's performance. Preparing the detailed basic work for the improvement of all organisation's activities (Policy Deployment)

Kanji and Asher, 1993

In order to discuss the above implementation process we will consider a service industry which specializes in the installation of heating and ventilation work. At the plan stage, after a period of induction and the appointment of external quality consultants, the SDL company embarked on a quality improvement programme. The company needed to embark on the quality improvement process because it had to change from managing growth to survival in the face of deep recession.

More precisely, by the end of 1989, the company's growth had escalated; more contracts were being won, more labour was being hired,

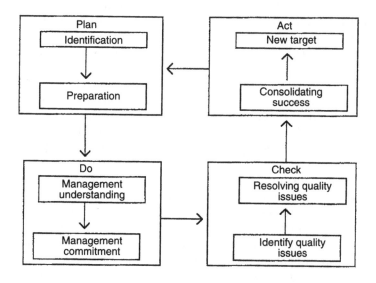

Fig. 17.1 PDCA model for implementation.

annual turnover (£2.5 million per annum) had reached an all-time high and the company appeared to be experiencing its best ever phase.

However, this boom period certainly had its downside. The increasing number of contracts required more financing which, in turn, increased the company' overdraft facility (drain on profits). The calibre and control of labour (particularly site labour) came to be more and more variable (customer dissatisfaction). The increase in workload brought with it a concomitant increase in errors, defective work and non-quality costs. Whereas the increased annual turnover should have meant an increase in profits, the non-quality costs of inefficient operations were eating into the profit margins instead.

The practical method of identifying the basic problems affecting the company's activities was applied. An initial survey of all head office (Mitcham) personnel revealed the three main areas for improvement as being:

1. accountability
2. communication
3. quality awareness.

Initial attempts at concentrating on the approach of effective problem solving at the early stage of the quality improvement programme revealed a serious organizational weakness. Department heads were embroiled in a fire-fighting culture, often responding to problems with costly knee-jerk reactions and seeking to blame others. Attempts at identifying the cause of problems were usually met with obstruction and at times open hostility. A problem that appeared in one department was invariably traceable back through the internal supply chain to one or more departments. The issue was further clouded by the absence of objective documentary records of errors, error investigation and corrective action.

It was clear that many of the problems experienced in the company were traceable through the management structure or rather lack of a clearly defined management structure. The company's rapid growth resulted in an *ad hoc* internal expansion characterized by blurred lines of accountability and protectionist internal barriers to effective communication.

Progress in tackling these issues was made by the managing director agreeing to formalize the organizational structure. An organization chart was constructed which reflected the current operations/departments: accounts and administration, estimating and surveying, contracts, drawing office, Mitcham works, Haverhill works and site operations plus suppliers (manufacturers). One of the most powerful concepts for the company-wide principle is the realization that a complex set of customer–supplier relationships exists. Each department of the company needed to concentrate on the effectiveness of the internal customer–supplier relationship, i.e. working together, before any significant progress would be made at improving interdepartmental efficiency.

To address this issue, a steering group comprising all heads of department was established to drive the quality improvement programme. The group initially focused on clarifying areas of responsibility, avoiding unnecessary overlaps and improving interdepartmental communication.

The group also approved the implementation of a company-wide training programme aimed at raising quality awareness and improving quality control throughout all operations. It was agreed that incidents of non-conformance with operational procedures would be recorded (on NCRs) for analysis and review.

The cost implications of non-quality were debated and it was agreed that the estimating department would cost all NCRs. It was pointed out that reducing the level of non-quality costs, by tackling the causes of problems not merely dealing with the symptoms, would lead to improved competitiveness and increased profitability.

However, initial analysis of non-quality costs is usually understated and the real costs can be staggering (estimates vary but can be as high as between 40 and 70% of sales turnover).

Establishing the steering group enabled the prime areas where improvement would have most impact on the company's performance to be identified and the data collection method (NCRs) agreed.

A programme of reviewing and improving process capability was approved primarily targeted at the contracts, drawing office, Mitcham works, Haverhill works and site operations departments. In this way, the detailed basic work for improving the company's activities was prepared.

17.4 DO

Making sure that the management understands the objective and methodology of TQM and are prepared to adopt them all the time.

Kanji and Asher, 1993

It is necessary that management understanding of TQM principles, error prevention, costs of poor quality etc. is addressed through the quality improvement teams.

Changing management style was essential to creating a continuous improvement culture. As this is not easily achieved it was important that an effective programme of training be implemented, starting with the steering group itself whose leadership would be essential to the success of the quality improvement programme.

As part of this process, management needed to move from its reactive style to a proactive one and prevent rather than solve problems.

Also, as internal competition is wasteful, it was necessary to break down existing internal barriers and to encourage a teamwork culture across the departments. It was emphasized in the quality group meetings that the company's management strategy needed to reinforce the teamwork approach as part of a TQM implementation.

According to the pyramid principle (Chapter 4), there are four principles that govern the basic philosophy of TQM:

1. customer focus;
2. continuous improvement;
3. focus on facts;
4. everybody's participation.

To counter the scepticism detected in some quarters, the potential results of a successful TQM process was continually stressed in steering group meetings:

1. reduction in wastage;
2. process control improves;
3. company morale gets better.

It was emphasized that improvement in quality would lead to increased (right first time) productivity which, in turn, would result in greater (external) customer satisfaction.

The challenge of TQM implementation is very much dependent on the commitment and will of the company's senior management to carry it through. The company had embarked on its road to quality voluntarily whilst in a healthy state.

However, the subsequent failure of its senior management, particularly the managing director, to adopt the objective and methodology of the quality improvement programme at all times eventually weakened the company's ability to deal effectively with the pressure of competition and downturn in financial performance when the effects of recession worsened.

17.5 CHECK

By a process of involvement of management and supervision in a proper scheme of training and communication, identifying quality issues and effecting a resolution of them by management led improvement activities.

Kanji and Asher, 1993.

The education of departmental heads continued through the steering group meetings, which occurred monthly for the first six months and quarterly thereafter. The purpose of each department in relation to the others was defined in departmental quality policy statements, translating the corporate policy in departmental terms which were communicated to all personnel.

All personnel were encouraged to report/record problems as they arose and this data was collected, investigated and analysed. This data and process capability studies enabled improvements to be made where these were most required. Although this approach was applied to situations where errors and their consequences, were readily visible and costly (traditional approach), this at least provided a starting point for changing to an error prevention culture. This, however, required a real change of individual and management approach which was only going to occur over time; even then certain individuals proved very resistant to change.

As (Kanji and Asher, 1993) point out 'In many ways the problem solving approach is the easiest and the cultural change is by far the most difficult aspect of the TQM process.'

The focus on problem solving was supported by a company-wide training programme aimed at creating quality awareness, followed by practical assistance to improve the control of key operational processes. This area of activity, at least, was adequately resourced and all personnel (approximately 120 permanent and casual staff) were included in the process.

Not surprisingly, the majority of problems showed up either in the two manufacturing plants or, worse, on customer sites. These were invariably traced back to drawing office and contract departments. During the period 1990/91, problems/errors were recorded on NCRs, investigated and improvements actioned. This provided comparative data for the period 1991/92, to assess which areas were actually improving.

17.5.1 CONTRACTS-DRAWING OFFICE

Although the drawing office was actually the responsibility of the contracts department, the draughtsmen had been poorly managed, often with costly results. The two contract managers were directed to work more closely with the draughtsmen and a series of inspection checks was built into the contracts – the drawing office supply chain. The draughtsmen were directed to cross-check each other's work wherever feasible and to provide regular progress reports on their project drawings.

This process was supported by the instigation of formal contract reviews, where the contract managers were directed to record and diligently pursue/resolve any ambiguities or discrepancies between the company's tender and the customer's specification. This area was found to be a significant cause of problems which resulted in company/ customer disputes and fed incorrect (from the customer's viewpoint) drawings, manufacture and site installation specifications into the system.

Additionally, monthly project review meetings were instigated which enabled actual potential problems to be identified and acted upon. Previously these were overlooked or not acted upon in a timely fashion.

One of the initial problems which had to be confronted here was the siting contract manager who had tried to excuse the growing number of problems by claiming to have too much work to contend with. A second contract manager was therefore appointed who had been the siting manager's assistant, although in practice he had been impeded in his attempts to share the workload. This structural move helped to remove this line of obstruction to the quality improvement initiative.

17.5.2 SITE OPERATIONS

In the worst instances, problems/defective work showed up at the installation stage at customer sites. One of the initial problems to be tackled here was to distinguish between errors due to site operatives and errors which site operations had little control over. Again, the NCR recording system was instrumental in determining the origins of the causes of errors.

As the majority of reported problems originated outside the site operation's sphere of control, these were tackled with the departments concerned.

However, the increase in the company's workload had led to site labour being taken on who were not always up to standard; in some cases the labour recruited comprised of chancers (inexperienced) or liberty takers (unreliable). This compounded the existing situation where long-standing site labour were assigned to projects more on the basis of their friendship with the managing director rather than their ability to manage projects and other site labour.

This situation was improved when an experienced site manager was appointed. He readily took the quality message on board and proceeded to reorganize the hitherto chaotic state of affairs. This included allocating site labour to projects on the basis of capability, shedding undesirable labour, giving a clear message to labour agencies that provision of substandard labour would not be tolerated and restructuring the pay/remuneration system to reflect actual performance and ability.

Together we persuaded the managing director to register fitters' mates on the industry's log book training scheme as a means of improving all round technical performance, as well as investing in the individuals themselves. This scheme proved very successful at motivating the individuals concerned, who were assured that they would receive proper training and not, as had been the case, be used as skivvies. As a result, both performance and morale significantly improved among trainees and experienced fitters, who were encouraged to impart their skills and assess their mates' competence in the field.

By the above means, it was not long before site operations had progressed to a preventive method of working which was reflected by a significant decrease in site originated errors.

17.5.3 MITCHAM WORKS

The manufacturing plant at Mitcham was predominantly staffed by very experienced sheet metal workers (SMWs) who had spent many years in the trade. It did not take long, therefore, to establish that this plant was not a major contributor to the causes of defective work; in the majority of cases defective work was traceable to inaccurate drawings or drawings produced to incorrect contract specifications.

However, the plant had a history of uneasy labour relations. The staff was a mixture of directly employed and self-employed SMWs who appeared (to the directly employed staff) to enjoy more favourable rates of pay, freedom and treatment, which at times led to friction and resentment. This situation was compounded by recurring conflicts between the self-employed SMWs and the managing director over the setting of rates of pay.

A recent dispute over this issue had resulted in an uneasy truce; the managing director considered he had been held to ransom by the self-employed SMWs and resolved to turn the tables when the company enjoyed the more favourable bargaining position! This conflict characterized the nature of dialogue between the parties in various shop-floor meetings I observed and did little to foster a co-operative teamwork spirit.

Another source of manufacture error was the estimating department's production scheduling, where the manufacturing locations for various drawings were decided by the managing director and general manager.

The main sources of problems here were identified as:

1. drawings which were split between the Mitcham and Haverhill works, where the standard of SMWs was inferior;
2. drawings which were offered to the self-employed SMWs on a price work basis;
3. drawings which were subcontracted to external manufacturing suppliers.

Taking these issues in reverse order, it was all too easy to blame defective manufacture on outside suppliers. However, in many cases it transpired that these problems with (external) suppliers originated within the company, typically through incorrect or ambiguous manufacturing specifications. Where drawings were split between the company's own works and external suppliers and where externally manufactured drawings were shipped directly to customer sites, it became that final inspection was either absent or ineffective.

This situation was improved by introducing inspection and test records for all manufacture drawings, indicating in-process and final inspection. It was agreed that all external manufacture would be returned to the Mitcham works for final inspection prior to delivery to customer sites. Where this policy was followed, the situation significantly improved by allowing errors to be detected and rectified prior to shipment (rectification was far more costly post-shipment).

There was a need to improve working relationships with external suppliers – along the lines of partnership and co-operation – and I was able to liaise closely with the company's preferred supplier (TNM). A quality control package was developed which dovetailed with the company's quality assurance system requirements; this was installed in the supplier organization, whose SMWs were inducted into the system's requirements and audited on a regular basis. Working closely with the supplier enabled manufacturing methods to be harmonized, which provided uniformity of finished product (the significance of which was readily apparent when two separately manufactured duct-work runs were joined together on-site).

In time, TNM came to regard the QC package as invaluable; it enabled them to claim for variation work, deal with queries/information requests efficiently and improve the quality of finished product.

Secondly, drawings which were offered to the self-employed SMWs on a price work basis often gave rise to problems. Investigating this issue revealed that while the standard of manufacture was high, certain items were either double manufactured or not made at all; this was due to the work method employed by the SMWs where duct-work runs were allocated to small teams to manufacture, with nobody taking overall responsibility for co-ordination.

Again, the inspection and test records helped to improve this situation as it was accepted by the SMWs that the job included inspection and co-ordination.

This episode revealed a potential for improving productivity in the works – an issue that increasingly occupied the managing director's thoughts! I noticed that when the SMWs were responsible for how the work was carried out, i.e. price work, their allocation of tasks among themselves led to the work being completed in about half the time normally achieved. I knew this to be the case as I had earlier persuaded the managing director and the SMWs to use the clocking-in cards to time how long jobs took to complete (this was an attempt to inject some objectivity into the management/shop floor dispute over job completion time estimates).

As a result, it was recommended to the managing director that the workshop be reorganized to accommodate manufacture by small teams, as opposed to individual work benches. I was appalled when the workshop was reorganized – the individual work bench approach was reinforced by the new layout and the job-timing was applied to each SMW to find out who the culprits were. My conclusions, after questioning the managing director on this development, were that (a) my attempts at improvement were being corrupted and (b) that each means of improvement I came up with was likely to be used by the managing director against the SMWs as part of his hidden agenda of getting his own back.

17.5.4 HAVERHILL WORKS

Thirdly, the problems caused by drawings which were issued to the Haverhill works for manufacture appeared to be a major cause for concern. Unlike Mitcham, the workforce at Haverhill was largely unskilled – young operatives taken on from school/college and trained on-the-job by the works manager and his two supervisors. The situation was compounded by excessive workloads, inadequate manufacture progress recording systems and inaccurate manufacture specifications.

The quality manager visited this plant once a month and he started working with the manager to improve the situation. An independent manufacture progress recording system was set up which gave the plant greater control over its own operations (whenever items were overlooked by head office or went missing it was always the Haverhill works who were blamed). An administrator was appointed to run this system which soon proved its value to the works manager. Additional SMWs were taken on to cope with the increased workloads.

The initiative which brought about the greatest improvement in performance, however, was the introduction of a key stage inspection system, which incorporated the kanban principle (JIT). The key manufacturing stages were identified by means of a process walk through and these were included as compulsory inspection points on the inspection and test record. These stages were assessed against the types of errors recorded by the plant on NCRs to ensure that the common problems would be tackled. Once the inspection stages had been defined training sessions were held to induct the SMWs into the system's requirements.

The main message that was emphasized was that the SMWs were not to proceed to the next stage of work until the present stage had been inspected and signed off on the inspection and test record – even if at times they had to wait until a supervisor was free. Achieving this required something of a change in culture, as getting the job done as quickly as possible had been the *modus operandi*.

Eventually, this new method of working became established as the norm. Where the procedure was not followed, this invariably showed up further down the manufacture line as defective work. These instances further reinforced the value of operating to the new system (and embarrassed the SMW concerned).

Also, more authority for managing the manufacture operations were delegated to the two supervisors, freeing up the works manager's time to focus more on checking manufacture instructions and drawings received from head office. Between the improvement efforts at the contracts-drawing office department end and more thorough drawing checks at the Haverhill works end, fewer errors were fed into the Haverhill manufacturing chain.

Cumulatively, the effect of these measures was to alleviate the workload pressures as a significant amount of manufacturing time had actually been spent on renewing defective manufacture, which in turn reduced the time available for new manufacture. In many ways, the improvement achieved by this plant was the most remarkable and showed what could be achieved when the objective and methodology of TQM was understood and consistently adopted by a management prepared to train and involve the workforce in identifying and resolving quality issues.

17.6 ACT

Starting a new initiative with new targets and taking the complete improvement process to everybody indicating supplier and customer links in the quality chain. Obtaining information about progress and consolidating success.

Kanji and Asher, 1993

By the end of the 1990/91 period, the quality improvement programme had enabled information about each department's success to be collected and quantified. This in turn enabled new targets for improvement to be set and communicated to all customer–supplier links in the company's internal quality chain.

The information was reviewed and discussed by the steering group and future improvement action statements were agreed and distributed to all departments. These statements set the tone for a new initiative which monitored progress and consolidated the success achieved.

This initiative saw an overall improvement in the performance of all departments, when assessed at the end of 1991/92. Main improvement results included:

1. overall reduction in NCRs from 99 to 64;
2. 43% reduction in non-conformities by Mitcham works;
3. 83% reduction in non-conformities by Haverhill works including a near total elimination of the most significant causes of error (applying the Pareto principle);
4. 35% reduction in non-conformities by site operations.

Attempts at quantifying the costs of non-quality were only partially successful. While all NCRs received (during the period 1991/92) were costed by the estimating department, these were the only known costs and related to those failure activities which happened to be reported. Efforts to obtain wider cost data, including prevention and appraisal cost figures, were invariably frustrated by the managing director who indicated that this area was very much out of bounds.

Even taking the effects of improvements achieved into account, the reported failure costs (between 10–15% of annual sales turnover) for the year period 1991/92 were difficult to assess as attempts to get the estimating department to clear the backlog of NCRs awaiting costing (relating to the 1990/91 period) proved fruitless. Either way, there was a serious under reporting of problems and one suspects, of assigning costs (especially as the most expensive errors seemed to implicate the managing director).

However, the comparative Haverhill data showed that the improvement initiatives implemented led to a reduction in scrap/defective work valued at approximately £50 000. It is no coincidence that the greatest cultural change occurred at this plant. This was due in no small measure to the fact that the plant was located some 60 miles away fiom the head office and was therefore less likely to be affected by head office interferences in effecting change and implementing quality improvement.

Elsewhere, the degree of cultural change which was achieved varied, dependent on each department head's commitment to the initiative. While overall this improved as visible results were obtained, there remained much work to be done in this area at the time that I parted company with the firm. The individual most resistant to the desired cultural change happened to be the managing director, who took an ambivalent attitude to quality and tried to cherry-pick the parts of TQM that suited his viewpoint and ignore the parts that did not.

When the effects of recession impacted upon the company, there was an increasing drift back to the bad old ways and much of the quality gains were squandered.

This became evident in the fluctuating customer satisfaction levels. Whereas customer complaints had decreased over the two-year period, they suddenly began to rise again.

REFERENCES

David, A.J. (1990) The customer/supplier relationship – the Nissan way. *Total Quality Management*, **1**(1), 59–68.

Kanji, G.K. and Asher, M. (1993) *Total Quality Management: A Systematic Approach*, Carfax Publishing Co., Oxford; paperback (1996) Productivity Press (India) Ltd., Madras, India.

Quality culture and learning[1]

18

18.1 INTRODUCTION

'Total Quality Management is the culture of an organization committed to customer satisfaction through continuous improvement. This culture varies both from one country to another and between different industries but has certain essential principles which can be implemented to secure greater market share, increased profits and reduced costs (Kanji, 1990).'

Creating a quality culture within an organization is increasingly recognized as one of the primary conditions for the successful implementation of Total Quality Management. It requires uncovering current underlying culture and examining the appropriateness of the objectives in order to adopt Total Quality Management. To close the gap between the old and the required new culture one must also explore the new quality improvement process for achieving customer satisfaction.

Taking its starting point in recent literature on quality, quality management and corporate culture, the purpose of this chapter is to introduce a new concept within management theory, namely the concept of quality culture. This concept is then discussed within the framework of Total Quality Management, providing some suggestions about practical procedures for developing quality culture.

In general, culture represents the way in which members of a business group control their behaviour in order to communicate with each other and with other groups in that society. It reveals their pattern of behaviour, customs and practices and the beliefs that are shared. Most of the countries in the world therefore have their own cultures based on several such factors.

Like countries, business organizations also have their own cultures. It is the totality of the norms, beliefs and values that controls the behaviour

[1] Part of this chapter is based on Hildebrandt, Kristensen, Kanji and Dahlgaard (1991).

of individuals and groups within any given organization. However, many organizations are not even aware of their own culture or its distinct characteristics. They become aware of it when they have to communicate with managers from other organizations with different cultures. Sometimes individuals realize their own culture when mergers and acquisitions take place and a great deal of cultural adjustment is thrust on them.

We also know that traditional and long established organizations have their own cultures which have evolved over the long period of their existence. These cultures are influenced by the culture of the country and the nature of its business of the organization, e.g. British chemical companies combine British culture with some characteristics of chemical companies throughout the world. British banks and financial institutions combine their customs with many of the global norms which are shared by their counterparts all over the world. It is therefore necessary for the newly developed industrial nations to combine their particular ways of doing business with the global practices of the businesses they are involved in.

There is always a question of how fast an organization should attempt to modify its culture. The wise thing is to change as fast as is practicable but certainly not as slow as the organization may find comfortable and cosy. That can run the risk of the boiled frog phenomenon. If you put a frog in water and warm up the water gradually, the frog will be so comfortable as the water warms up that it will not realize when the water becomes too hot and it is boiled to death. That is what a cosy culture can do to an organization.

The importance of organizational culture, generally accepted by many people, can be summed up by Peters and Waterman (1982) in their book *In Search of Excellence*, where they said 'without exception, the dominance and coherence of culture within these organizations proved to be the essential quality of success'.

Many managers these days pay proper attention to their organizational culture because they view culture as an asset (Egan, 1994). In some studies it has been suggested that organizations with adaptive cultures, geared to satisfy the changing demands of customers, employees and shareholders can outperform organizations without such culture. Companies with sound culture can increase their sales three times more than the organization without a sound culture. Therefore a successful company needs more than just sound business strategy, it needs a culture to support the strategy.

It is our understanding that sometimes organizations reflect the personality and character of the founder member's norms and beliefs. This can be seen easily by considering Henry Ford who is known for his immeasurable impact on the shape of his organization's culture; other examples include Walt Disney at Disney Productions, David Packard at Hewlett-Packard etc. However, according to Schein (1985), when the founder moves on, the culture they have embedded does not lose its momentum. The process and people in the company have become the carriers of the culture and the culture continues in the organization.

18.2 THE CONCEPT OF CULTURE

The concept of corporate culture has been used in recent years to develop and understand the concept of culture in connection with the study of organizations. In this section the concept of quality culture is introduced and developed for the better understanding of the way quality manifests itself in companies.

There are many definitions of culture. However, the concept of culture which is now considered for the theory of organizations has its origin within anthropology and is given by Tyler (1871–1958) as follows:

Culture or civilisation, taken in its wide ethnographic sense, is that complex whole which includes knowledge, belief, art, morals, law, custom, and any other capabilities and habits acquired by man as a member of society.

In recent years a number of behavioural scientists have used the above definition in the area of corporate culture. In 1956 Juran also proposed the application of the anthropological concept of culture in order to create a meaningful change within the organization.

18.3 ORGANIZATIONAL THEORY AND CORPORATE CULTURE

In discussing quality culture, first of all we will introduce the concepts of formal and informal organization and later the corporate culture which is one of the most important aspects of Total Quality Management.

The theory of organizations is often described through different types of organizational models. These models may be mutually different but have certain characteristics which are based on a stable structure. The traditional model of an organization is therefore most often a model emphasizing characteristics of hierarchy, division of labour and communication.

It is a well-known fact that the organizational structure is traditionally described in an organization chart and this is important in the understanding of an organization, but has a limited perspective.

Therefore, it is traditional to supplement the description of the formal organization with a description of the informal organization. By informal organization we mean non-planned management, often unknown but stable patterns of behaviour which fulfil the major parts of the daily routines. The informal organization is described in different ways, e.g. the human group, where the informal aspect is described as norms and roles in the sociocultural system and the concept work group, describing a shadow organization established by the workers in defence of management's infringements.

In recent years, another important source of understanding of an organization has been demonstrated through different forms of environmental relationships. It provides a model, which includes the importance of the environment to organizational structure and behaviour emphasizing some important variables in the environmental relations, e.g. market, technology, politics, financing and manpower.

Understanding both the formal, the informal and the environmental-related framework of description is important in order to understand Total Quality Management and quality culture.

18.4 CORPORATE CULTURE

The concept of culture has been the subject of considerable interest in the recent literature on organizational theory but has not to any significant degree been discussed in literature on quality. The introduction of the concept of culture may be seen as the culmination of a long trend of development in organizational theory. At first, this development meant that the conception of the organization as merely a tool was abandoned in favour of the independent social formation or social units with inner dynamics of their own. Further, the fundamental social unit in the organization and the idea of the organization as a cultural community was introduced and has gained ground.

There are many definitions of the concept of corporate culture. A few examples will be given in the following:

- 'Corporate culture can be defined as a set of commonly held attitudes, values, and beliefs that guide the behaviour of an organisation's members' (Martin, 1985).
- 'Culture can be defined as the shared philosophies, ideologies, values, assumptions, beliefs, experiences, attitudes and norms that knit a community together' (Kilman, Saxton and Serpa, 1985).
- 'Culture will be used here to mean the belief's top managers in a company share about how they should conduct their business' (Lorsch, 1985).
- 'Culture is the set values, behaviours and norms which make an organisation ticks' (Atkinson, 1990).
- 'How things are done around here' (Ouchi and Johnson, 1978).
- 'The ways of thinking, speaking and inter-acting that characterise a certain group' (Braten, 1983).

- 'Culture reflects assumptions about clients, employees, mission, products, activities and assumptions that have worked well in the past and which get translated into norms of behaviour, expectations about what is legitimate, desirable ways of thinking and acting. These are the focus of its capacity for evolution and change' (Laurent, 1990).
- 'A pattern of basic assumptions invented, discovered or developed by a given group as it learns to cope with its problems of external adaptation and internal integration that has worked well enough to be considered valid, and to be taught to new members as the correct way to perceive, think and feel in relation to these problems' (Schein, 1985).
- 'Culture is the shared beliefs, values and norms of a company in so far as these drive shared patterns behaviour' (Egan, 1994).

Formulated broadly, it applies that corporate culture deals with values and norms in organizations. The company's culture is expressed in visible terms in many different ways: through physical conditions like buildings, the company's stationary, the quality, including design, of the products, the colour of the company cars, etc. It is also expressed through the way people in the organization co-operate and solve problems. Generally speaking, the concept of visible management is closely associated with the use of the concept of culture in management theory.

Deal and Kennedy (1982), in discussing the corporate culture, have listed the following conceptual elements:

- corporate climate
- values
- heroes
- rites and ceremonies
- the cultural network

and further suggested: 'A strong culture is a system of informal rules which explain in detail how people should behave most of the time' and 'A strong culture enables people to get a better idea of what they do so that they are more motivated to work harder.'

Schein (1985) argues that the concept of culture ought to be reserved for the deeper-lying level of basic assumptions and convictions that are common to members of an organization (Figure 18.1). These assumptions and convictions are acquired responses to a group's problems of surviving in their external environment and its problems of internal integration. According to Schein, a distinction should be made between assumptions, systems and values which are the form of manifestation of culture in day-to-day life but not the epitome of culture.

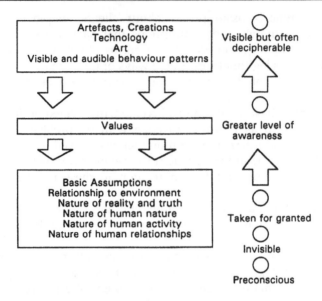

Fig. 18.1 Schein's three levels of culture.

As indicated above, culture is an acquired product of group experience and therefore can only appear where there is a definable group with a significant history. It should be noted that this is a considerable modification in relation to the management-oriented concept of culture. It is a conception of culture which is rooted more in theories of group development and group dynamics than in anthropologic theories of how cultures develop. This entails the assumption that it is possible in this context to take advantage of learning theories and to develop a dynamic conception of corporate culture. It also entails the assumptions that it is possible to integrate knowledge from other fields of theory with a view to gaining both a broader and deeper understanding of the extremely complex phenomena involved.

It should be noted that the corporate culture mentioned above does not comprise obvious patterns of behaviour. Schein argues in this context that obvious behaviour is always determined both by cultural conditions and by the haphazard situations arising in the external environment. Regularities in behaviour may thus reflect the environment as much as culture and therefore should not be used as the primary basis of defining culture. This does not mean that behaviour is of no importance in this context, it simply suggests that we have a deeper understanding. It will be difficult to decide whether it is a symptom reflecting culture or not.

The concept of culture as a tool of control and change has been at the centre of interest in recent years. However, the culture which reflects the management-inspired way of thinking, i.e. looking optimistically at the possibility of change, has created some controversy with a more anthropology-inspired way of thinking, i.e. relatively resistant to conscious change.

Therefore, in discussing the concept of quality culture it is necessary to look at these two extreme points of view, where the management-oriented viewpoint in its most extreme form regards culture as something coming from above in the organizational hierarchy i.e. something created through management decisions and management actions and therefore which can also be changed through management decisions, whereas the anthropology-oriented approach regards culture as something spontaneous, growing up from below as the result of many people's individual actions and experience and which therefore cannot be easily changed through any centralized process.

Like in so many other fields these viewpoints are not as reconcilable as it might appear on the face of it. This question will be taken up later but at this point it may be suggested that a so-called management-oriented viewpoint does not necessarily entail the type of top-down view mentioned above but might have connection with the above-mentioned anthropology-orientation.

An example of cultural change is the Xerox case. The Xerox company was forced to a radical change of corporate culture due to a collapse of its market shares in the world. To overcome this problem the company did not minimize the extent of the cultural change necessary. Some of the changes it adopted for this purpose are given in Table 18.1 as a result of which they have recaptured their world market shares.

In sections 18.5 and 18.6 we will discuss how a change like this may be achieved.

18.5 CLASSIFYING A CULTURE

Harrison (1972) and Handy (1976) prove that we can classify the culture of an organization into four broad ranges. The formation of culture depends on a number of factors including company history, ownership, organization structure, technology, critical business incidents and environments etc. The four cultures they discuss are power, role, task and atomistic. The purpose of an analysis would be to assess the degree to which the predominant culture reflects the needs and constraints of the company. They use diagrammatic examples to illustrate their ideas of cultural types with high versus low formalization and high versus low centralization (Figure 18.2).

The role cultures are typically bureaucratic organizations managed by time and motion studies and precise mechanical specifications with authority based on job descriptions. An example of a role culture would be government departments.

Table 18.1 Xerox cultural change

From	To
Incomplete or ambiguous understanding of customer requirements	Use of systematic approach to understand and satisfy both internal and external requirements
An orientation to short-term objectives and actions with limited long-term perspective	The deliberate balance of long-term goals with successive short-term objectives
Acceptance of a certain margin of error and subsequent corrective action as the norm	Striving for continuous improvement in error-free output in meeting customer requirements and doing things right first time
Unstructured individualistic problem-solving decision-making	Predominantly participative and disciplined problem-solving and decision-making using a common approach
A management style with uncertain objectives that instils fear or failure	An open style with clear and consistent objectives which encourages problem-solving and group-derived solution

The power culture represents the family business with a concentration of power. This power is radiated out from the centre by a key person to others in the family who then transfer the information on to other functions. As entrepreneurial company organized around an astute founder is a typical example. The culture is verbal and intuitive.

The task culture is characterized by a close liaison between departments and specialists in an organization that is involved in research and development activities. Temporary interdisciplinary project groups are organized around a task. It is a decentralized way of working but still formalized by the disciplines that must be joined.

Atomistic culture is characterized by the decentralized informal approach where independent experts joined together for mutual convenience, e.g. a group practice or a consultancy. These organizations reject formal hierarchies and are united in meeting the needs of their members.

Whilst it may be tempting to think of a company as fitting into one of the four types of culture, this is not always the case. Subcultures with their varying values exist in many organizations. These differences may be prominent between departments, geographic regions and head office. When classifying cultures, therefore, we need to be aware of subcultures.

In studying the performance of 80 companies, Deal and Kennedy (1982) found that the more successful companies were those that had

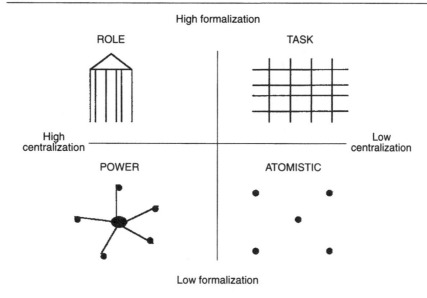

Fig. 18.2 Harrison and Handy's four culture roles.

strong cultures. A list of the characteristics of strong cultures that they identified are given below:

- had a widely shared philosophy of management;
- emphasized the importance of people to the success of the organization;
- encouraged rituals and ceremonies to celebrate company events;
- had identified successful people and sung their praises;
- maintained a network to communicate the culture;
- had informal rules of behaviour;
- had strong values;
- set high standards for performance;
- possessed a definitive corporate character.

Similarly Peters and Waterman (1982) listed as follows:
- the importance of enjoying one's work;
- being the best;
- people being innovators and taking risks without feeling that they will be punished if they fail;
- the importance of attending to details;
- the importance of people as individuals;
- superior quality and service;
- the importance of informality to improve the flow of communication;
- the importance of economic growth and profits.

18.6 CORPORATE AND QUALITY CULTURE

The concepts of culture and corporate culture have been introduced here on the assumption that there is an association between the quality concept and the corporate culture concept. As mentioned before, working with quality presupposes that you work with company's culture or with the elements of the company's culture that manifest themselves in relevant quality dimensions.

In recent years, the quality concept has attracted increasing attention and created a quality wave in management literature – a wave which introduced various books including *In Search of Excellence, Thriving on Chaos* and *Out of the Crisis*.

Pirsig (1974) has pointed out through the principal character – 'Faidros' – of his book that quality and culture are tied together. What excited Faidros was the whole idea that a concept like quality should even be subjected to a view. He realized that if quality by definition is kept undefined, then the whole field of aesthetics is wiped out immediately. Further, by refusing to define quality he had brought the concept outside the range of analytic thinking. If it cannot be defined, it cannot be subjected to intellectual rules either.

Pirsig (1974) pointed out that the removal of the quality concept will automatically reveal its importance. Of course, the world could continue to go round without it, he reasoned, but life would be so sad that one would hardly bother to live, 'Life would actually not be worth living at all.' The word 'worth' is a qualitative designation. Life would be completely void of any value and any purpose. Faidros concludes 'As the world obviously does not function normally without the quality concept, this concept obviously exists whether it is defined or not.'

According to Faidros, quality is neither objective nor subjective. He finally came to the conclusion that quality is neither a quality of the mind nor of the environment, but an experience. People can disagree on quality not because quality differs but because people have different experiences.

In a managerial context, it is necessary to give the quality concept more real values than it might seem desirable by others. Over time, great efforts have been made in this field but it was not until the last few years that the problem has been made the subject of a more varied discussion. A few decades ago, quality was considered synonymous with the concept of number of defects in a production process and it was related only to a very limited degree to the needs of the market.

Since then, quality has been developed as a concept of functional quality such as customer-felt quality, dual quality and total quality. One can say that the new quality concept now springing up is broadly a total assessment of the company's supply and demand (Figure 18.3), but with

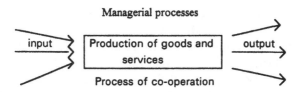

Fig. 18.3 Quality as a total assessment of the company's supply and demand.

the important addition that then it also becomes a question of the processes of production, management and co-operation involved in the supply and demand processes.

A view of the development of the theory of organization and management in this century shows a gradual movement from a narrow, rationalistic and instrumentalistic conception to a broader, more psychological and sociological viewpoint. A central part of this development is the concept of culture.

As mentioned earlier, it is the value of the concept of culture as a tool of control and change which has been at the centre of the interest in organizational theory in the concept of culture. By way of example, culture as a parameter of control has been emphasized in connection with the management of decentralized companies where traditional tools of control are not satisfactory but also in a large number of other contexts in connection with the management process itself.

Collin (1988) suggests that the organizational culture is a tool of change and he refers, among other companies, to Scandinavia Airlines Systems which has worked actively with the concept of culture and says: 'One must try to generalise the result in order to arrive at general knowledge about organisational cultures and the tools to be used for controlling and changing it. A conflict has arrived, however, as mentioned before, in the conception within the theory of organisations itself and between organisational theory and social anthropology.'

Within social anthropology it is a fundamental idea that cultures are very difficult to change, whereas the theories of organization and management emphasize the importance of culture as a tool of change. In other words: what explains the difference between unchangeable and changeable cultures?

In an attempt to understand the changeability and stability of culture Collin (1988) introduced the concepts of group-dynamic and internalized norms suggesting that culture may be of two essentially different types, depending on whether it is kept together by group-dynamic or internalized norms. The first type is relatively changeable, the latter quite resistant to change, which can be explained by the fact that the internalized control is a control where the driving force is in the person itself and where the person is controlled with no help from external influences, including pressure from group members whereas the group-dynamic control is linked up with the group. A characteristic feature of group control is that the dynamics for the group's processes of change often come from a leader or from a small number of leaders.

Collin (1987) also pointed out the two forms of cultural changeability that are both relevant in this connection. One is the possibility of changing a culture, i.e. changing the contents of the culture. The other might be called the question of change in cultures, i.e. the question of whether changeability in itself may be a value in a culture and thus part of the contents of culture.

From a management point of view, the establishment of a culture susceptible to change has advantages as well as disadvantages as compared with what might be called a conservative culture. This can be explained by the fact that the culture susceptible to change is by definition adaptable and puts up only little resistance to new processes if they prove to be expedient but lacks loyalty to the procedures.

Within organizational theory, cultural change is therefore a question of changing cultures as a rational process, beginning with a suspicion among the management of a organization that its culture is dysfunctional, continuing with a systematic sociological mapping out to understand whether this is really the case, followed by an effort to formulate a new, more adaptive culture and finally an effort to abolish the old and introduce a new culture.

Total Quality Management as a concept is a question of determining, developing and managing a company's quality. For this purpose, a number of tools and procedures have been developed, ranging from statistical techniques to, e.g. quality circles and they are all described in literature.

What is special about emphasizing the quality culture concept in this connection is an assumption that a considerable part of the literature so far on control and management of quality is too superficial. In real terms, a parallel can be drawn to French and Bell's (1978) organizational iceberg. By superficial is meant that a number of formal and real aspects of quality are treated but the more deep-rooted causal and explanatory factors remain hidden and subconscious. Various literature in this area has tried to penetrate some of the explanatory factors (see e.g. Peters and Waterman (1982), Peters (1987) and Waterman (1987)).

With a view to defining more precisely some of the cultural elements that are relevant in this connection, it has been found expedient to use Johnson and Scholes' (1984) model of influence (Figure 18.4).

This model is general and it deals with the total culture of the organization and thus points to a number of elements which together form the culture of the organization but, at the same time, the model also points to a number of the elements which in practice must enter into the concept of quality culture. A brief description of these main elements are as follows:

- Nature of the environment
  As mentioned in the model, the nature of the environment includes factors like values in the local society and values of organized groups. The increasing interest in quality seen in recent years may be regarded as an example of changes in value in society in general and among special groups.
- Type of company
  The type of company is a separate cultural factor. It is a question of the company's market situation, its products/technology and the trade or industry it is in. The market and competition situation are relevant for the company's quality situation and the same also applies quite traditionally to the product technology side.
- The special character of the company
  The special character of the company is made up of its history, size, management style and administration style. The subculture concept is often included under management culture. In this context, especially

Fig. 18.4 Main types of factors of influence determining the total culture of the organization.

in connection with the company's history, reference should be made to the importance of the different stages of growth or development to the culture of the organization and thus to the management situation (Schein, 1985).

- The special character of the employees
The special character of the employees is made up of the employees' values, attitudes, language, experience etc. and it is not unlikely that we will find elements of the company's quality culture in this complex field. This is where we find the values that substantially determine the actual/manifest quality of the company's products and services.

Management literature enumerates different methods of attacking change – methods that are relevant here. Collin (1987) has shown the relevance of rites, group-dynamic mechanisms, recognition of the effectiveness of norms and rewards and punishment to bring about cultural change. Schein (1985) enlists different types of processes of change: change as a general evolutionary process, change as adaptation, learning or a specific evolutionary process, change as a therapeutic process, change as a revolutionary process and change as a managed process.

18.7 WORKING WITH QUALITY CULTURE

We shall not elaborate on the different methods of attacking change mentioned above but use them as part of Total Quality Management.

One of the important aspects of the Total Quality Management process is that during the process one discovers new aspects of the goal. This requires: an ability to assess; situation consciousness; flexibility; ability to co-operate; and courage to enter the unknown. It also becomes clear that Total Quality Management processes are not simple, rational processes of solving problems but complex social processes of change.

The management idea underlying this formulation is that management consists in creating a framework that enables the employees to display their intelligence and creativity and, at the same time, ensure that it is done in accordance with the company's fundamental values and mission. This formulation is based on a holistic view of man, in this context aiming primarily at a view of the individual as a unique human being.

In the following, we will list some conditions, assumptions and views concerning Total Quality Management and try to outline the work method.

- There is no standard recipe for a good Total Quality Management process. Each single project must be planned and implemented on the basis of the real situation in the company in question.

- A Total Quality Management process cannot be implemented through a management decision. A TQM process implements itself concurrently with the involvement of employees and managers at different levels and the setting up of quality groups in the company.
- Every employee is in fact a quality and profitability centre him/herself and, together with others, forms one or more natural quality groups.
- When it comes to quality and profitability, the individual employee is the natural centre of creativity, initiatives, positive participation etc.
- The traditional decision-making structure in the company is not necessarily changed by a TQM process, which is partly because of the group phenomenon and partly because managers at different levels participate in relevant groups.
- A TQM process requires that each employee and each manager identifies his/her customers. In this connection it is of no importance whether this or these customers are other employees/managers or customers in the traditional sense of the word (Dahlgaard, Kanji and Kristensen, 1990).

We will now provide a brief account of a method for working with quality culture. Here the method is based on the assumption that the key question in connection with implementing TQM in practice is how to create quality consciousness in all employees.

It is believed that quality consciousness is achieved through visible results and actions with the individual employee. The prerequisites through quality consciousness are:

- To look at one's own quality situations through other people's observations, ideas and thoughts. Quality development must take place in a group situation where insight, experience and action can be created jointly.
- To motivate every individual in such a way that the framework acts as an incentive to quality development and gives the courage to make decisions and instil confidence into others with whom initiatives are taken.
- To create quality by means of a method going beyond the traditional problem-solving tools. This requires a willingness to work with quality questions in a deeper way, relying also on one's own attitudes and values. As a rule, quality levels are, for a given technology, the result of the norms, culture and expectations of individual employees.
- To set aside time and means and to mobilize persons who have the ability of developing and implementing quality initiatives. It must be clear to the individual employee that a quality improvement process is important to the company.

The work method to be indicated here is simple and has been used in practice in connection with quality work. The fundamental idea is that deep down in the value basis of an organization you find the source of understanding of an organization's special way of acting and taking decisions. Within social ecology, the term is used about the basic attitudes, values and principles on which a company bases its day-to-day decisions and daily behaviour. If we introduce the concept of quality in this context, we can then work with quality culture in practice. By working with quality policies an organization automatically becomes part of the TQM process. Here, the policy concept represents the formally adopted rules, procedures etc. for handling various questions and tasks in a company but without necessarily living by them in practice.

With reference to the model in Figure 18.5, we shall briefly outline the work method.

Field O: Observe present quality phenomena. Our starting point is the quality related questions in the organization. You might say that in field O (as a person or group of persons) in a company you wonder what is happening (or not happening) in two ways:

1. you wonder because you are curious to understand the quality situations and experiences etc.;
2. you wonder because you wish to find a new practice in certain quality areas.

It is important to note that at this level it is not a question of a formulated (and thus delimited) problem but merely a question, i.e. openings. Questions open up, whereas even formulating a problem represents a delimitation.

This leads to observations – experienced, observed situations, events that have taken place which a person can report about as fact. In principle it is all the types of situations in a company which in one way or the other are manifestations of quality dimensions.

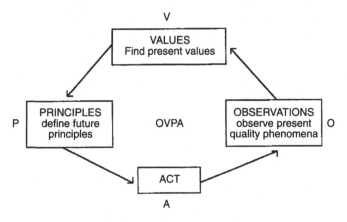

Fig. 18.5 The culture cycle.

In connection with a use of the work method, the activity in field O consists in reporting, e.g. in different group constellations, on these observed/experienced situations. The experiences are made as objective and vivid as possible. This is the company's present reality, or part of it. It is these realized pictures which, when using this work method, ought to be the starting point for working with the quality questions existing in the company.

Field V: Find present values. Field V is the next activity in the work method. The activity consists in maintaining single pictures from field O and questions relating to the experiences. In other words, in this activity you penetrate behind the experiences and into the layers of ideas, principles, values and basic assumptions explaining the pictures. This is what, in this context, is called quality policies which together form the whole or part of the company's quality culture. In practice, this activity, like the other phases/activities, will involve many people and require a considerable work effort which it is not generally possible, of course, to define more closely.

The result of working with the fields O and V is a number of statements or sentences characterizing the values surrounding quality existing in the company now.

Field P: Define future principles. The above is in itself valuable but when put into a managerial context, there will be against the background of the questions in field O, a wish for a change. Therefore, the activity in field V will typically be followed by an assessment of and decisions about the policies found and subsequently, in field P, desirable, future policies in the quality area are formulated, i.e. the desired changes in the company's quality culture are formulated. This is a work of visions that must be adapted to the company's other experiences of the future, fundamental ideas etc. The result is some future-oriented policy sentences representing wishes relating to future quality behaviour in the company. It is of decisive importance to the result of the total process that the company carefully takes a position on whether these policies are something the company really wants to work for including, in particular, whether they are attitudes that have the full support of the management.

Field A: Act. The last part of the quality management process reflected by field A is partly a decision on whether a realization of the new quality policies requires fulfilment of some special conditions which do not exist in the organization today and partly a detailed decision on the concrete actions to be initiated next, in order to work at changing the behaviour in the company in the direction of the new policies and maintaining those parts of the existing quality policies which are regarded as desirable to maintain and possibly extend.

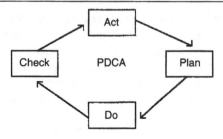

Fig. 18.6 The Deming cycle.

18.8 QUALITY CULTURE, QUALITY IMPROVEMENT AND TQM

It is a fact that the Deming cycle has become the basic work method for quality improvement. It consists of the phases shown in Figure 18.6.

This well-known model is a typical system model which works very well within a given cultural structure. Traditionally, however, it does not deal with phenomena of culture which means that it has a tendency to make the company stay within the given frames of activities.

We believe that culture has to be realized for quality and productivity within a given system. It is therefore relevant to supplement the Deming cycle with a culture side which continuously incorporates organizational values into the management of quality.

This can be done superimposing the culture cycle of Figure 18.5 on the Deming cycle to create an expanded Deming cycle. The result is shown in Figure 18.7.

The two cycles are connected in the action field and the Deming cycle is still the basic work method. In certain cases, however, the check activity will show so large a discrepancy that it is found necessary to

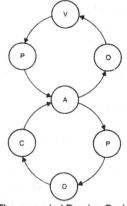

The expanded Deming Cycle

Fig. 18.7 The expanded Deming cycle.

consider a change in the culture and attitudes of the company. In that case the action leads to entering the OVPA cycle. From this a new cultural framework concerning quality emerges and the company is once again ready to use the PDCA cycle but on a new level.

As an example one could mention the well-known Nissan Corporation. Nissan has been a pioneer within quality assurance activities starting out, e.g. as early as 1966 with QC circle activities. In spite of good quality performance, i.e. good use of the Deming cycle, the company experienced profit problems in the middle of the 1980s that could not be handled within the traditional planning systems. A new top management realized that the culture surrounding quality had to be changed and the company entered into the phases described by our culture cycle. The result of this was a new definition of quality incorporated into an entirely new corporate philosophy: 'Our first commitment is to customer satisfaction. Through diligent efforts to develop new customers and expand our customers base, we are contributing to the ongoing progress and enrichment of society.' This philosophy was communicated to the workforce in different ways. Among other things the philosophy was printed on a small plastic card and distributed to every employee in the company.

According to Nissan the effect was tremendous. The culture of the company was changed dramatically and Nissan was back in a stable Deming cycle producing high quality goods but with a new definition of quality based on customer satisfaction. One notices that the main elements of this process have been the involvement of top management and the satisfaction of the customer which are the basic points given in the section on cultural change by Kanji (1990).

It will be seen that the expanded Deming cycle demonstrates an important distinction between traditional quality assurances and TQM. While QA usually operates within a given system framework, TQM operates on all levels of the company including the attitudinal. It is, however, not a total TQM cycle.

In order to make a total TQM cycle the model has to be expanded in the same way as Kondo (1977) did with the traditional Deming cycle. In what follows, we pursue this idea in more detail.

One of the important characteristics of TQM is the internal supplier–customer relationship. Each employee in the company has many suppliers and many customers and each has to be treated as if he or she were an external supplier or an external customer. Each employee knows the quality levels of the suppliers and the demands from the customers and he/she is continually trying to improve the quality of output in order to decrease the hidden factory and to increase customers' satisfaction. Such a successful implementation needs time and resources and many companies will never reach that level. There are many obstacles on

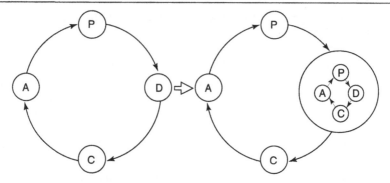

Fig. 18.8 The transfer of Deming's cycle to the 'do' level.

the path to success and you have to remove each obstacle before you reach the goal – TQM.

'Creativity in daily work' (Kondo, 1977) is needed by each employee in order to remove all the roadblocks. A necessary condition for creativity in daily work is that each supplier–customer relationship is controlled by its own Deming cycle and for the vertical supplier–customer relationships, e.g. relations between top management and middle management, a transfer of a part of the Deming cycle to the lower level is important. Such a transfer is described by Kondo as 'a transfer to the do level' and Figure 18.8 shows the basic idea of the transfer.

Normally there are no problems in transferring the Deming cycle to a lower level when you consider the relations between top management and middle management. The problems increase when you climb down the pyramid. Middle management too often acts as a dictator and is often not willing to transfer planning, checking and action activities to lower levels. However, management at all levels must understand that its employees are its customers. To obtain this a rotation in the culture cycle is needed. The expanded Deming cycle has to be implemented in all the vertical customer–supplier relationships from the top to the bottom in order to change the quality culture. Of course, top management is responsible for a successful implementation of the expanded Deming cycles at the lower levels.

Regarding the horizontal customer–supplier relationships a rotation in the culture cycle may be needed from time to time in order to improve the results and, in this way, satisfying the customers.

From the above, it is evident that a company which has successfully implemented TQM is characterized by a successful implementation of expanded Deming cycles at every level and in every customer–supplier relationship. Top management is responsible for such an implementation which is necessary for changing the quality culture of a company.

We believe that the proposed implementation strategy of the expanded Deming cycle has an inherent ability to change the quality culture. Through the implementation process both the group-dynamic factor (Collin, 1988) and the internalized norms factor will change the quality culture. The latter factor will gradually be effective when more PCA (plan, check, action) activities are transferred to each employee. The former factor, the group-dynamic factor, will immediately be effective when the network of supplier–customer relationships and the attached expanded Deming cycles are implemented. A successful implementation requires that the total concept is understood, accepted and utilized in every customer–supplier relationship all over the company. Of course this is not possible without the understanding, acceptance and active participation of top management.

In 1990 Ralph Stayer talked about the challenge of changing attitudes and performance of the employees of Johnsonville Sausage, a successful family business where he worked as chief executive. Stayer's primary concern was that of the gap between the potential and the performance of his employees. His people did not seem to care and continuously made costly mistakes. He became extremely anxious of his company's ability to survive any possible future competitive challenge with this low level of commitment and involvement.

His vision was to create Johnsonville as the market leader in the expensive sausage market. For this to happen, people had to take responsibility for their own work, product and company as a whole. As a result, the company products and service quality would improve, margins would increase, costs could be reduced and new markets could be entered into making Johnsonville ultimately less vulnerable to competition.

In order to understand the present position Stayer had an attitude survey carried out in the company. The results were not pleasing as Stayer found the attitudes of his employees to be only average and in line with large bureaucratic organizations.

The main problem was his management style although initially he was reluctant to admit this. Realizing that his business could not continue as usual, Stayer decided to make the change and imposed extra responsibilities onto his management team. After two years he managed to replace all three of the company top managers by appointing new managers who were strong enough to manage the required change took place.

Following this, Stayer started to change his management style, i.e. instead of making all the decisions himself he took on a coaching role. As a result, the individuals became responsible for their own problems, performance and quality. Also managers became providers of the resources in order to help people to do their jobs properly.

With the help of teamwork, the organization began to resolve quality problems and customer complaints. A system of reward was adopted to encourage people to seek new skills. A performance-based share incentive was implemented and teams were taking on the tasks of the managers, helping to reduce the hierarchical layers.

A systematic approach to educate the employees was developed and gradually the previous habit of no work-related education was replaced by work-related education.

In 1985 another sausage company decided to ask Johnsonville to take over part of a production plant that it was closing. This proposal naturally required a strategic decision and Stayer decided that this decision would be made by the process which all employees had to own. After several consultations the company decided to take the business and the Johnsonville employees rose to the challenge and overcame all the problems and difficulties successfully.

18.9 QUALITY LEARNING

18.9.1 INTRODUCTION

Learning can be defined as a process in which individuals can change their attitude to adopt a continuous development of basic knowledge and skills in pursuit of total professionalism.

The essential feature of an effective learning process is constant updating and continual feedback. Thus the effective learning process in an organization should be focused around the quality of feedback provided by the organization. Effective action must be organized around a range of systems and procedures to accomplish the goal.

Learning to learn involves the continuous development of various strategies and skills that support the process of learning in many different contexts.

The basic requirement of any effective learning process is, therefore, the desire to learn the skills, to implement them and to practise them in an appropriate context. However, continuous learning requires a sustained interest in learning over time and relates to the improvement in learning ability which is independent to the content being learned.

Experience shows that developing ideas for quality improvements is an investment which gives the highest return on resources. We believe that educational institutions have many opportunities for quality improvements which should be fully utilized. If employees (including teachers) and students are educated and trained in TQM, they have the joint capability to utilize these lost opportunities. Education and training is only one, albeit necessary, condition for the involvement of an educational institution's employees and students in continuous improvements.

However, continuous improvements also require leadership which is the foundation of TQM.

On the subject of the product of education, we agree with the definition by Brower (1994): The product of education is a person empowered to educate herself or himself – an educating person not an educated person.

In this modern world a person can never be truly educated. What a person learns within a limited time period, say, e.g. four years, will inevitably be more or less outdated within a few years. Put another way (Brower): The product of education is not a product at all; it is a process of never ending education. To be empowered in this way requires that the student gain from education:

1. knowledge of how to continue learning and developing for the rest of her/his life;
2. skills in continuing to learn and develop;
3. a state of mind and being that enables lifelong learning, that sees and feels self-guided learning to be natural, doable and fun;
4. a strong drive, a will, to continue learning and developing her/himself.

The key word in relation to continuous improvements is learning. In order to communicate this to his audience/readers, Deming changed the name of the improvement cycle (the Deming cycle) from plan-do-check-act to plan-do-study/learn-act. In the check phase of the improvement cycle, you have to study the results in order to understand what were the causes behind them. This learning process is the most important part of the continuous improvement process. Therefore, we will discuss the learning process.

In this section the authors will be discussing the goal, strategy, various learning processes, advantages and disadvantages of the continuous development of a quality professional.

18.9.2 CONTINUOUS LEARNING

There is a common misconception that learning in relation to working life at the professional level ceases when full-time education comes to an end. This may be at the first degree, masters or doctoral levels. The reality could not be further removed from this.

There are a variety of learning approaches but the major ones include:

1. studying for examinations for professional membership, e.g. quality management;
2. part-time study for masters and doctoral degrees by study and research, e.g. MSc TQM, MBA, MPhil and PhD in Quality;
3. learning at work.

It is this last approach that is the focus of attention in this section. It does not mean that these three ways of learning are mutually exclusive but the desire is to explore approaches to training and coaching in the workplace. Training in the workplace can follow many patterns: it can be *ad hoc* and uncoordinated with much of the responsibility put on the individual or it can be planned with some assessment of efficacy. This chapter looks at one learning model.

18.9.3 COMMON LEARNING

It is commonly assumed that learning is strongly associated with the teaching process when information is given by a teacher. The application of the assimilated information is then applied to appropriate tasks. This is not now thought to be the case. Most real learning is achieved via experience. This is on-the-job experience. There is a common learning cycle (Figure 18.9).

The essential feature is that of feedback; action is taken, the effect is noted and appropriate modification of behaviour follows.

If real learning is to be achieved then all stages of this cycle must be experienced.

The establishing of this learning cycle as a model of good practice for effective learning is the focus of this chapter. There are many issues relating to the facilitation/enabling of this learning cycle to be established in an organization but we must first look at how a start may be made.

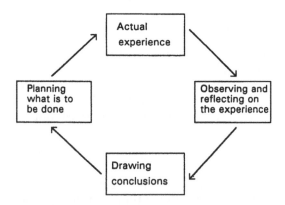

Fig. 18.9 Common learning cycle.

18.9.4 EFFECTIVE LEARNING

There is an obvious need to ensure effective learning. If learning is not treated seriously then there will be adverse repercussions for the organization concerned. An effective learning strategy is likely to encompass the following:

1. understand how and why people learn;
2. promote a healthy learning environment;
3. identify individual's learning needs;
4. prepare a learning plan with agreed objectives;
5. promote learning opportunities;
6. evaluate learning outcomes.

18.9.5 QUALITY LEARNING

We have talked a little about how adults learn through the learning cycle. If people are to really learn then each stage of the cycle must be travelled. There are many other factors involved in this process (some of which we will see later). What we need to do is to place this learning cycle clearly within the organization.

Within an organization there may be many equivalent cycles for areas of development. Here each cycle needs to be complete and unbroken for effective development to be possible. Take, for instance, the continuous quality learning process which includes all organizational activity.

The Continuous Quality Learning Cycle or Continuous Improvement Cycle (Deming, 1986) which helps to improve the quality of the organization can be described as shown in Figure 18.10.

In general, quality learning is a continuous process that can be broken anywhere in the learning systems of supply and customer service.

Here in the Deming cycle plan defines the learning process which ensures documentation and sets measurable objectives against it. The do executes the process and collects the information and knowledge required. The check analyses the information in a suitable format. The act

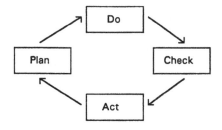

Fig. 18.10 Continuous improvement cycle (PDCA) (Deming).

obtains corrective action using quality learning techniques and methods and assesses future plans. At the end of each cycle the process is either standardized or learning targets are adjusted based on the analysis and the cycle continues.

The Continuous Improvement Cycle and the Learning Cycle can be superimposed, i.e. integrated in a planned, quality-improving strategy. To do that we need to consider the learner and how his/her needs should be considered and also look at the preparation of a learning plan.

18.9.6 LEARNING PLAN

Before a plan can realistically be drawn up both the learning needs of an individual and the desired learning outcomes for an individual need to be considered.

To identify the learning needs of an individual firstly the knowledge, skills and attitude required for a particular task or function to be performed successfully must be established. Against this list should be considered the knowledge, skills and attitude already possessed by the individual. This second list will probably be achieved by consideration of career history and known work record. The difference between these two lists is the learning need (or learning gap). Part of the process of the identification of learning needs should be open discussion with and the agreement of the individual concerned.

Learning outcomes define what (which tasks) an individual will be able to perform and how well they will be capable of performing these tasks as a result of the learning process. There should be a list of required outcomes in terms of behaviour and performance. The standard required should also be established so that the effectiveness and the amount of learning can be measured. There should also be a time horizon for this learning process.

The learning plan is thus, clearly, a bringing together of learning needs and learning outcomes. This plan, which is best formalized in writing, should be jointly agreed by both individual and trainer/supervisor. The plan should follow the learning cycle and so will consist of a list of desired outcomes together with a list of activities necessary for the desired outcomes to be achieved. There may well be resource and specific training needs identified at this stage. This can be viewed as the planning stage of the cycle. Once the learning experience has been completed than some reflection/assessment should follow. Hopefully there will have been appropriate consideration of the measurement of the desired outcomes. The final essential stage of the learning cycle is that conclusions based on reflection and/or assessment are fed into reformulating and refining the next planning stage of the learning cycle.

The process goes on and on and on . . . continuing and continuous learning.

18.9.7 CLOSING REMARKS

In this competitive business world, the traditional approach to quality is no longer desirable. The basic problem which prevents an industry from becoming a quality organization is connected with management and process. We believe that the best way of overcoming the organizational quality problem is through the practice of TQM. To practise TQM it is necessary to identify the basic activities affecting the organizational management and process. The approach to deal with these activities affecting management and process is therefore through education, training, research and quality learning.

Further the continuous development of a quality professional can be placed within the framework of a continuous improvement learning cycle. The implementation and monitoring of this learning model can be evaluated with the co-operation of a panel of employing organizations in the context of the professional experience.

18.10 CONCLUSION

There are situations when organizations have to change direction. Forward looking and dynamic organizations change before it becomes necessary to change. They anticipate the need to change. Sometimes the change occurs as a result of great success and the resultant need to shoulder much greater responsibility. In other cases it is not success but threat of failure or actual failure that compels organizations to reform themselves.

To effect a change it is essential to change the top management team and, through them, the layers below them, to a new way of quality understanding for continuous improvement.

TQM as management theory is a relatively new concept within organizational theory which may raise management theory up to a new level of understanding, relevance and consciousness. As regards the culture concept, it seems justified to conclude that we are dealing with a concept which it may be expedient to continue to work with within the theory of quality management.

It is interesting to note that business culture has similar characteristics to the culture of the country as follows:

- A culture which is lively and progressive can be found constantly evolving and changing whether it is a business or country culture.
- A progressive culture within a business or country readily evaluates and responds to stimuli.

- Like religious or political groups, business organizations also have the extreme culture, i.e. culture tries to preserve what is considered to be the true original set of beliefs.
- Large social migration sometimes creates hybrid cultures in a country in the same way we have seen the emergence of hybrid cultures created by the multinational companies.
- Changes in culture of an organization or a country occur when a leader provides stimulation with ideas that challenge tradition. Gandhi and Martin Luther did so with society at large.
- Behind all successful business organizations there have been leaders who revived and changed the culture of their organizations.
- In most cases cultural changes are based on retaining and developing what is good in an existing culture and adding to it new elements that will stimulate progress.
- A total rejection of all that exists can be devastating.

There is always a question of how fast an organization should try to change. The important thing is to change as fast as possible but certainly not as slow as organizations may find easy because it can run the risk of killing the organization. The companies that anticipate the need to change and respond to change not only survive but prosper in the future. Those who do not, die over a period of time.

In recent years the effect of cultural change has been manifested on several occasions at a national level often as a result of some catastrophe or disaster such as defeat in war or periods of economic upheaval. Well-known examples are the economic miracles of post-war Germany and Japan.

REFERENCES

Atkinson, P. (1990) *Creating Culture Change*, IFS, UK.

Braten, (1983) *Working with Culture Change*, Thorn EMI workbook, UK.

Brower, M.J. (1994) The paradigim shifts required to apply TQM and teams in higher education, in *Readings in Total Quality Management* (ed. H. Costin), The Dryden Press, New York, USA.

Collin, F. (1987) *Organizational Culture and Change* (in Danish), Copenhagen, Denmark.

Collin, F. (1988) Organizational culture as a means of change (in Danish), in *Philosophy of Production* (in Danish) (ed. U. Zeitler), Copenhagen, Denmark.

Dahlgaard, J.J., Kanji, G.K. and Kristensen, K. (1990) A comparative study of quality control methods and principles in Japan, Korea and Denmark. *Journal of Total Quality Management*, 1(1).

Deal, T.E. and Kennedy, A.A. (1982) *Corporate Cultures*, Copenhagen, Denmark.

Deming, W.E. (1986) *Out of the Crisis*, MIT, New York, USA.

Egan, G. (1994) *Re-Engineering the Company Culture*, Egan Hall, USA.

French, W.L. and Bell, O.H. (1978) *Organization Development*, New Jersey, USA.

Handy, C. (1976) *The Gods of Management*, Souvenir Press, USA.

Harrison, (1972) Understanding your organization character. *Harvard Business Review*, 119–28.

Hildebrandt, S., Kristensen, K., Kanji, G.K. and Dahlgaard, J.J. (1991) Quality culture and TQM. *Total Quality Management*, **2**(1), 1–16.

Kanji, G.K. (1990) Total Quality Management, second industrial revolution. *Journal of Total Quality Management*, **1**(1).

Kilman, R.H., Saxton, M.J. and Serpa, R. (1985) *Gaining Control of the Corporate Culture*, San Francisco, USA.

Kondo, Y. (1977) *Creativity in Daily Work*, ASQC Technical Conference Transactions, Philadelphia, USA.

Kroeber, A.L. and Kluckhohn, C. (1952, 1963) *Culture: A Critical Review of Concepts and Definitions*, New York, USA.

Laurent, A. (1990) *Corporate Culture*, Hampden-Turner Pitkus, USA.

Lorsch, J.W. (1985) Strategic myopia: culture as an invisible barrier to change, in *Gaining Control of the Corporate Culture* (eds R.H. Kilman, M.J. Saxton and R. Serpa),

Martin, H.J. (1985) Managing specialized corporate cultures, in *Gaining Control of the Corporate Structure* (eds R.H. Kilman, M.J. Saxton and R. Serpa).

Ouchi and Johnson (1978) *Working with Culture Change*, Thorn EMI workbook, UK.

Peters, T. (1987) *Thriving on Chaos. Handbook for a Management Revolution*, London.

Peters, T.J. and Waterman, R.H. (1982) *In Search of Excellence*, Harper & Row, New York, USA.

Pirsig, R.M. (1974), *Zen and the Art of Motorcycle Maintenance*, Copenhagen, Denmark.

Schein, E.H. (1985) *Organizational Culture and Leadership. A Dynamic View*, Jossey-Barrs, San Francisco, USA.

Stayer, R. (1990) How I learned to let my workers lead. *Harvard Business Review*, 66–8.

Tyler, E.B. (1871, 1958) *Primitive Culture: Researchers into the Development of Mythology, Philosophy, Religion, Art and Custom Vol.1: Origins of Culture Vol 2: Religion in Primitive Culture*, Gloucester, Mass., USA.

Waterman, R.H. (1987) *The Renewal Factor. How the Best Get and Keep the Competitive Edge*, New York, USA.

Milliken Denmark A/S case studies: leadership, participation and quality costing[1]

19

19.1 CONTEXT, IMPERATIVES FOR CHANGE AND OBJECTIVES FOR QUALITY MANAGEMENT

Milliken Denmark Ltd, located at Mørke, Djursland, is a 28-year-old producer and seller of washable rental mats, mops etc. plus soap dispensers, hand-soap, scent dispensers and assorted perfumes. Milliken Denmark is the European Headquarters for Milliken's Dust Control Organization.

Its customers are mainly laundries, cleaning firms and wholesalers in Europe and the Far East. More than 90% of production is exported.

Milliken Denmark Ltd is a subsidiary of Milliken and Co., a privately-owned textile and chemical concern domiciled in South Carolina, USA. Milliken and Co. is one of the world's leading textile concerns and also one of the largest.

19.1.1 CHARACTERISTICS OF THE ORGANIZATION

The firm has over 160 employees, of whom about 11 reside abroad (five in Belgium and six in the UK). Approximately 100 employees are

[1] This is a reprint of a case study written by J.J. Dahlgaard and K. Kristensen for the European Commission, DG III, as part of the European Way for Excellence Study. The authors thank the Commission and The European Foundation for Quality Management for permission to reprint the study. There are some overlaps between the case studies and the previous text in order to make the case studies as stand alone.

working within production and the remaining are working within administration and service (including management).

The sales turnover showed a stagnancy in the beginning of the 1990s, because of a taking over of the Japanese sales by a new subsidiary company in Japan.

19.1.2 CHARACTERISTICS OF THE MARKET DEVELOPMENT AND POTENTIAL

The development in mat coverage in Europe can be seen from Table 19.1. As can be seen the Nordic countries have the highest coverage and the south European countries have the lowest. For most countries the percentage increase in the coverage is higher than 100%.

The growth in the European mat business is due to two key factors: the growing standard of cleanliness demanded by the public and cost savings gained to the end user with a properly installed mat service. In the textile service industry, one thing all present and prospective customers have in common, is that they all have floors. Companies in this business therefore say that there is a potential mat customer behind every door.

The mat market can be divided into two segments: the rental industry market and the retail market.

The customers on the rental industry market are laundries and cleaning firms which have the relationship to the customers which are 'professionals', i.e. private and public companies of any type. The companies typically rent the mats from the laundries and cleaning firms. The total

Table 19.1 Actual development in mat coverage 1981 and 1993 (m^2 per 10 000 inhabitants and percentage increase)

Country	1981	1993	% increase
Finland	208	445	159
Denmark	205	397	93
Norway	128	258	101
Sweden	111	215	93
UK	81	115	42
Ireland	58	147	153
Belgium	41	138	237
Germany	59	110	86
Holland	30	91	203
Austria	26	79	203
Switzerland	31	57	84
France	6	36	500
Italy	–	4	–
Spain	–	2	–

market in Europe is approximately 1.3 million m^2 per year (1995). Milliken's market share of the rental market is more than 40%. The main competitors are a UK company, a US company and an Austrian company. The UK company has a market share of approximately 40%. Hence the rental market is an oligopoly.

The retail market is characterized by selling mats of a quality which is different from the professional market (i.e. mainly a lower quality). The total market is approximately 11 million m^2 per year. The market which Milliken goes for (high quality mats) is 2–3 million m^2 per year (1995), but this market is growing fast.

The customers are retail companies like furniture shops, building markets, department stores etc. Milliken Denmark started business on this market in 1993/1994 and their market share is growing fast.

19.1.3 IMPERATIVE FOR CHANGE

Milliken and Co. bought the Danish firm Clean-tex A/S in 1983, changing its name to Milliken Denmark Ltd. At that time, Milliken Co. was already two years into a quality improvement programme, so it was only natural that the Danish firm was drawn into this process and urged to start its own project.

Quality is Free, by Philip Crosby, was required reading for all managers and Crosby's 14-step programme was the first set of guidelines for Milliken's quality process, which in 1989 was further supplemented by Deming's 14-point programme.

During the whole period the owner (Milliken & Co., USA) has shown a strong, impressive and never weakening leadership for quality. Milliken's quality journey which is presented in sections 19.2 and 19.3 can be characterized by continuous change driven by this leadership.

19.1.4 OBJECTIVES FOR QUALITY MANAGEMENT

The objectives for quality management can best be described by quoting Milliken's business philosophy and the related quality, safety and environmental policies.

The Milliken philosophy:
At Milliken our culture is firmly based on the 'Pursuit of Excellence'.

As well as setting standards for the quality of our products and services, this philosophy also embraces the quality of our people. Each individual is called an Associate and each plays a vital part in achieving the Milliken goal.

Milliken has been working with all aspects of 'Total Quality Management' for the past thirteen years, and is now recognized as a leader in this field.

This dedication and hard work was recognized when, in 1989, Milliken received one of the highest awards for quality; the Malcolm Baldridge Award which was presented to Mr. Roger Milliken by the President of the United States at that time, Mr. George Bush. After having received the European Quality Prize in 1992 Milliken Europe received in 1993 the European Quality Award.

Milliken's quality policy:
Milliken and Company is dedicated to continuous improvements of all products and services through the total involvement of all associates.

All associates are committed to the development and strengthening of partnerships with our external and internal suppliers.

We will continually strive to provide innovative, better and better quality products and services to enhance our customers' continued long-term profitable growth by understanding and exceeding their requirements and anticipating their future expectations.

Milliken's safety policy:
The safety and health of all its people are of primary importance to Milliken and Company.

Milliken will devote resources to train its people to perform their jobs safely, to ensure equipment can be operated in a safe manner, to eliminate workplace hazards and to comply with applicable safety and health laws and regulations.

Milliken believes that all injuries are preventable, all health risks are controllable and management is accountable.

Milliken's environmental policy:
Milliken and Company is committed to operating our plants and facilities in complete compliance with all applicable environmental regulations and to operate in a manner that protects the quality of our environmental and the health and safety of our associates and the public.

We are committed to strive for a goal of zero waste generation to all media – land, air, water – to be achieved by continual improvements in all our operations. This goal will guide the conduct of our manufacturing operations, the development of new products, and our interaction with our suppliers and customers. Recycling of material is an integral part of this on-going effort.

We are committed to encouraging our families, our associates and our communities, through education and leadership to conserve our natural resources and protect the environment in our daily lives.

We reaffirm our commitment to work with local, state and federal authorities to develop effective environmental solutions that meet tests of practicality and feasibility.

19.2 HISTORY OF QUALITY MANAGEMENT

19.2.1 IT STARTED WITH MEASUREMENTS

Milliken Denmark's great fortune was that its parent company had a couple of years' lead and was thus able to set an example. The group management showed the necessary leadership and from the start one thing was emphasized over and over: 'Before you start to change anything, find out where you are now!' Or, put another way: The quality process starts with measurements. What the Danish organization was being told, in fact, was that the firm's future operations should be based on facts, not beliefs and opinions. This was echoed by Peter Hørsman, managing director, who declared that, from now on, guesswork was out, adding that one measurement was better than 10 opinions.

(a) Employees' safety

As can be seen from the safety policy, Milliken gives top priority to employees' safety. The firm's basic principle is that all accidents can be prevented. Every safety problem is followed up until an acceptable solution has been found. The following anecdote illustrates this.

Each year throughout the 1980s, the American division president would pay Milliken Denmark a one-day visit. The top management had about eight hours to tell him everything about the business, their plans, visions, investment hopes etc.

A few days before one of these visits, one of the cleaners slipped on some ice in the car park and broke her ankle. This episode took up fully three hours of the eight hours of the president's visit, because he would not let management get away with passing it off as an unfortunate accident. Management had to draw up plans to make sure that similar accidents could be prevented in future.

Every four weeks for the past 12 years now, management has sent reports about safety conditions to the group management, even though there has not always been anything to report. Milliken keeps statistics on accidents which result in sick leave, on minor accidents where sick leave has not been necessary and Milliken Denmark has also been required to keep statistics on irresponsible behaviour which could have led to an accident.

(b) The company barometer

The 'Company barometer' is an annual customer satisfaction survey. A sample of customers are questioned by a bureau on a wide range of things connected with how they rate collaboration with Milliken Denmark and its competitors. If the survey shows that Milliken's competitors have come out on top, or if Milliken has achieved a lower score than in previous years, then corrective measures are taken. This measurement is regarded as the most important measurement of all.

The experiences at Milliken are that you can achieve an improvement of almost 50% the first year simply by measuring and following up regularly – in more or less every area.

(c) Customer satisfaction and Hoshin planning

The following seven business fundamentals are evaluated in the customer satisfaction survey:

1. quality
2. cost
3. delivery
4. innovation
5. morale
6. environment
7. support.

Each of these seven parameters is evaluated on a scale from 1 to 10 and a comparison with the most important competitors is made. These measurements are input to the strategic planning process (Hoshin planning process) where strategic teams evaluate the results in order to start the process of establishing new objectives, targets, strategies, measures, etc. in order to secure continuous improvements in customer satisfaction. For this purpose they use specially designed forms which have proved to be a valuable tool for securing that the planning for improvements will also result in improvements.

On each of the above parameters the customers have evaluated Milliken's quality between 8 and 9, and compared to the most important competitors Milliken's overall quality level is approximately 0.8 higher. This is the definite proof that Milliken's TQM journey which has lasted for more than 10 years has been a very valuable one.

(d) Keeping delivery dates

The third area which Milliken Denmark has paid particular attention to from the start of its quality process is keeping delivery dates. Every morning at 9 a.m., all office staff are informed about how successful they have been in fulfilling the delivery deadlines promised to customers. If there have been any delays, a full account of why they have occurred is given.

Each week Milliken has to report to the European division manager and each month to the group management in the USA. Excuses such as 'the delay was due to a subcontractor' do not count. The goal is 100% delivery on time and 'the score' is over 98%. In the USA, the manager of any company (there are over 50 companies in the group in the USA alone) which comes under 97% has to present himself at the monthly board meeting and explain the action he has taken to prevent it happening again.

When analysing the measurements of on time delivery Milliken has, for several years, used a control chart which has been a valuable tool giving signals when the delivery process is out of control. Figure 19.1 shows the average results from 1986 to 1993 and the control chart for the years 1994 and 1995. Comparing 1995 with 1994 it is seen that the delivery process has become more stable with an average around 98%.

(e) Other measurements

Apart from the things mentioned above, which Milliken's group management is especially concerned about, Milliken Denmark measures many things, e.g. employee satisfaction, number of credit notes, employee education, the amount of time it takes to process designs,

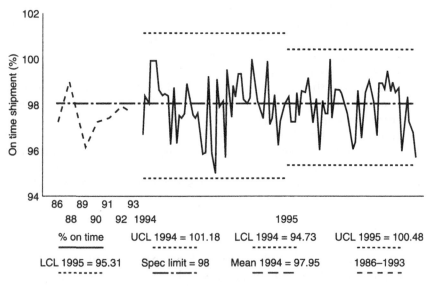

Fig. 19.1 On time shipment 1995.

number of guests, all kinds of waste, composition of inventories, number of complaints about goods and services etc.

19.2.2 QUALITY IMPROVEMENT TEAMS

Milliken Denmark is one of the Danish companies which was able to motivate employees to form quality improvement teams in the 1980s and still succeed with this 'philosophy of work'.

The team activities started in 1989 with the so-called 'workshop groups', i.e. quality improvement groups established in production. Table 19.2 shows how many workshop groups operated in 1989 and 1990. From the end of 1991 the team activities extended to become cross-functional and more focused on removing causes (specific or common) from the various business processes. As seen from Table 19.2 Milliken's TEAM REGISTRATION classify improvement teams into the following four different types of teams:

1. supplier action teams;
2. customer action teams;
3. corrective action teams;
4. process improvement teams.

It is interesting to see the relatively big variation in the 'percentage of associate participation' from 1991 to 1994. This variation is due to the fact that the organization used the year 1991 to prepare for 'team-building'. The associates were educated and trained in various team-building tools (see below) and after that (in 1992) campaigns for team-building activities were running. The results of these activities can be seen in Table 19.2.

One learning point from the team activities in 1992 and 1993 is that there was a tendency to start up too many teams at the same time. Management had difficulties following up and giving feedback to the teams and the organization as a whole experienced some difficulties finding the necessary time for this valuable but also time consuming

Table 19.2 Milliken's Team Registration

	1989	1990	1991	1992	1993	1994
Total number of teams	23	53	58	53	71	76
Percentage of associate participation (%)	32	69	13	85	77	44
Supplier action teams	–	–	6	3	4	4
Customer action teams	–	–	23	17	23	14
Corrective action teams	–	–	13	24	23	9
Process improvement teams	–	–	16	9	21	49

activity. It is Milliken's experience and belief that the team-building activity from 1994 and onwards has found 'the optimal level'.

(a) The 2 × 7 tools for quality improvements

To make the team activities as effective as possible, all employees have been trained in the use of the seven quality tools, thus enabling team members better to analyse and document the project they are working on. Now all employees have become familiar with cause-and-effect diagrams, Pareto analysis and flow charting. It is Milliken's long-term goal that all employees will be able to use these tools, together with run-charts, scatter diagrams, histograms and control charts.

Today, management routinely uses affinity diagrams, tree diagrams and matrix diagrams – three of the seven planning tools (the seven new quality tools). These three diagrams have been a great help in giving them an overview of large-scale projects or problems. Management has also acquired knowledge of and training in the use of the other four planning tools.

(b) Strength of error cause removal teams

After impressive results of the team activities in 1990 and 1991 management realized the strength of addressing problems by teams. Milliken had experienced several times management's confusion that problems which were brought to the management's attention through the suggestion system were not always solved, even after implementation of a solution. We call the suggestion system our Opportunity For Improvement (OFI) process (section 19.2.3).

The person who submitted the suggestion was pleased but the colleagues working on another shift did not always see the problem or they did not like the solution. The consequence was often a new suggestion (a new OFI) which suggested going back to the original solution or another solution.

The similar situation happened frequently between departments on the sales and administrative side. Sub-optimization within a department happened often. A department solved a problem for itself and created a problem for another department.

Milliken's parent company had for many years organized its error cause removal activities in teams – and suddenly the management of Milliken Denmark understood why. From 1992/93 all problems in Milliken Denmark were addressed and solutions implemented by teams – the few which are not are seldom solved.

The team members are persons who have an interest in a proper solution of the problem. Most of the teams are therefore cross-functional teams.

19.2.3 THE SUGGESTION SYSTEM

(a) Rediscovering the suggestion box

In 1987 Milliken rediscovered the much-maligned suggestion box. All employees were invited to suggest ways of improving the firm. There were only a few suggestions to begin with. Nobody felt they had any contribution to make – not if they had to write it down and send it to management at any rate.

People had all sorts of excuses, which were really down to their being unaccustomed to expressing themselves in writing, feelings of inferiority, spelling errors and illegibility. The breakthrough came at a staff meeting where the managing director convinced them that he really needed their suggestions. Apart from this, their suggestions would be a good way of letting him know what employees thought could improve the firm. And, since he was often away on business trips and therefore could not get round to all employees as often as he would like, he offered to share his secretary with them.

So twice a week, Inge Høj, management secretary, did the rounds of all production employees and the result was overwhelming. She got one good suggestion after the other on everything from organization of the workplace, through product improvement, to changes in machinery and processes, plus many minor suggestions which, though not terribly significant, were no doubt good solutions to daily irritants.

After about a year, these bi-weekly visits became unnecessary – by now employees had overcome their reluctance to put pen to paper.

Now the number of suggestions has grown to over 4700 a year and a whole organization has grown up to deal with them.

All approved suggestions are rewarded with a small prize, the size of which has only a minor relation to the importance of the suggestion for the company (see below). Basically, Milliken believes that the OFI system is in the interest of all employees to ensure a strong firm, giving them greater job security and the chance to earn more. This belief also reflects their conviction of employees' collective responsibility for the continuing existence of the firm. It is realized that not all employees share this belief but it is also realized that it is management's responsibility to help them appreciate this.

(b) The suggestion process and error cause removal

Milliken has found the OFI system indispensable complementing the error cause removal process.

Many opportunities for removing root causes of errors or for process improvements are brought to the management's attention through the suggestion system. Forms are readily available for everyone throughout the plant and offices and many ideas which come during discussions and process review activities are captured immediately on an OFI form.

On the OFI form the submitter (or the OFI committee) is asked to classify the suggestion into one of eight alternative OFI types which are equal to six of the seven business fundamentals evaluated in the customer satisfaction survey (section 19.2.1(c)) and later on used as input to the strategic planning process called Hoshin planning plus safety and energy.

The eight OFI types are shown below:

1. quality improvement
2. cost reduction;
3. delivery;
4. innovation;
5. safety;
6. morale;
7. environment;
8. energy.

The close relation to the seven business fundamental's supports the Hoshin planning process. It happens frequently that the management asks the whole organization to support a certain activity with their ideas. Examples of this could be the drives which Milliken has with intervals to improve the safety in the plant and to reduce the environmental impact of their activities. The organization responds with many ideas about how this could be accomplished and all the ideas feed into the error cause removal team activity.

The OFI process also plays a very important role as a communication tool on a smaller scale. When Milliken has a problem area it establishes an error cause removal (ECR) team of four to six employees to address the problem. Many employees outside the team are normally affected by the problem or they are aware of it and they often have an opinion on what the cause is and how it can be solved even if they are not members of the team. The OFI system has proved to be an excellent vehicle for carrying the ideas of the employees to the ECR teams.

(c) The suggestions received

The suggestions received can be classified into three categories:

1. About 20% are rejected as unsuitable.
2. About 30% are minor suggestions.
3. About 45% are good suggestions which can make a difference to day-to-day activities.
4. About 5% are really good suggestions which can make all the difference to our competitiveness.

Table 19.3 Statistics of Milliken's suggestions

	1989	1990	1991	1992	1993	1994	1995
Received suggestions	1512	3625	3586	3689	3269	3747	4729
Approved suggestion (%)	87	79	85	80	85	92	88
Employee participation (%)	71	100	95	90	93	88	79
Number of suggestions per employee	8	16	18	20	16	20	26
Annual saving due to suggestions (1000 kroner)	1415	598	1222	780	3504	734	1565

Table 19.3 shows statistics of proposals from 1989 to the end of 1995.

The annual savings cover only the suggestions of OFI type number 2. The gain from these ideas has, amongst other things, been able to finance a brand new factory and an administration block with a modern auditorium.

As can be seen from Table 19.3, the suggestion system runs very smoothly. The programme has become a natural part of everybody's daily work. The reasons for that are several.

One reason is that new employees are given a sponsor and the first contact the new employee will have with the suggestion system is through this sponsor. The sponsor is usually a manager from another department and the manager's responsibility is to make it easier for the new associate for the first couple of weeks in the new company and to help him/her to submit his/her first suggestion (OFI). The sponsor simply asks if there is anything the new associate has seen which he or she thinks may have an opportunity for improvement.

Milliken's attitude to the importance of helping the new employees become acquainted with the suggestion system can be understood by reading the following quotation from Mr Ejvind Jensen:

A company should be especially attentive to suggestions from new employees, because a new employee's power of observation isn't yet reduced due to routines and principles. It is very important that the commitment from new associates isn't suffocated with remarks like 'we don't work like this'. Instead we point out that we expect to hear from them what we can do better according to their point of view. This goes for all associates, whatever their function or position in the company.

This attitude and the resulting 'sponsorship for suggestions' are examples of Milliken's 'Leadership for Suggestions'.

Another example showing Milliken's 'Leadership for Suggestions' is that managers (including top management) are also very active in submitting suggestions for improvement to the OFI system even if they are

Table 19.4 Reward guidelines for OFI suggestions

	Points	Savings (kroner)
'Normal' OFI	1–5	1000–25 000
OFI improving safety	Min. 3	
Other OFI	10–15 15–20 20–25	25 000–50 000 50 000–75 000 75 000–100 000

not rewarded for that. Only ordinary associates are rewarded for participating in the OFI programme.

(d) The reward system

The reward system is very simple and unbureaucratic. It is based on
points where every point is equal to 25 kroner. The minimum reward is
1 point (= 25 kroner) and the maximum reward is equal to 25 points
(= 625 kroner).

The reward guidelines followed by the OFI committee are shown in
Table 19.4.

It is important to realize that the rewards are very small compared to
the savings. The size of the rewards does not seem to be a motivator for
the impressive number of suggestions.

'Leadership for Suggestions' and recognition have been the most
important factors used when Milliken succeeded in building up its
suggestion system.

(e) The OFI organization

The OFI organization is divided into two parts with the quality manager
as the process owner. One part of the organization is for production
associates and the other part is for the administration associates.

The reasons for having the quality manager as the process owner are
the following:

1. The quality manager is the person in the company with the best
   overall view of quality improvements in all departments.
2. It is important to have a top manager as process owner. This sends out
   a clear signal of the importance of the OFI programme.
3. The quality manager has the needed authority to make important
   decisions.

The OFI Committee Administration meets every morning at 9.00 a.m.
and the OFI Committee Production meets every afternoon at 13.00 p.m.
The meetings last about one hour and the number of OFIs dealt with

varies from 10 to 30. In the afternoon meetings three associates from production participate voluntarily. Every six to eight months these three positions are reported vacant and those who are interested are encouraged to apply as new members. It has become very popular to become a member of the OFI committee.

The administration of the OFI programme is handled by the managing director's secretary who is responsible for the registration of the OFIs and to help her she has an especially designed computer database.

Every month a list is produced containing the scores (number of OFIs and number of points) of all the associates. The list is distributed to all departments and put on the notice boards.

A project manager and a blacksmith are more or less permanently engaged in implementing the suggestions – to the mutual benefit of both employees and the company.

The success of the OFI system is the result of 'Leadership for Suggestions'. One example which is the result of Milliken's 'Leadership for Suggestions' is the standard feedback time to the associate who has submitted the suggestion. This standard is very low. The reason why the OFI committee holds meetings every day is to be able to give quick feedback. The goal is to give feedback within 24 hours and in case an OFI is circulated for comments the submitter receives a provisional response within 72 hours.

19.2.4 EXPERIENCES WITH ISO 9001

(a) ISO certification failures

The last months of 1988 were a milestone in the history of Milliken Denmark. This was when the quality assurance system finally obtained an ISO 9001 certification. Twenty office staff had spent 4000 working hours over 10 months in documenting the system.

The documentation process was extremely important, since it gave Milliken the opportunity of looking into every nook and cranny in the company. There were overlapping areas of responsibility in several parts of the firm and, what was perhaps worse, other areas where there was no precisely defined responsibility at all. Co-ordination at management level during this phase undoubtedly speeded the quality process along.

The management group thought that they would end up with 'quality management', but they found that an ISO certification is more about the quality of management. They understood that they had to demand integrity and responsibility from all managers if the certification was to be more than just a pretty diploma on a wall.

The management underestimated the interest and involvement of shop floor workers in the documentation phase. Management was so caught up in things that there was not the time to tell them what sort of certificate Milliken were trying to get, what lay behind such a certificate, or how they would be affected by it. Employees were fobbed off with assurances that, as far as they were concerned, it would be 'business as usual', the only difference being that now it would be in the name of a formal quality assurance system.

Once the press conferences and receptions were over, management was accused by employees of having pulled a fast one. Management was put in the same category as the Emperor's New Clothes. This was not felt fair in the management group, of course, because during the lifetime of the company Milliken had won over 40% of the European market for rental mats. But management had clearly failed in its educational role.

(b) The awakening of the organization

Milliken Denmark has realized that if measurements are the first step of the quality process, then the education of personnel is the second and the most important one. The American group management realized this early on and by the time Milliken Denmark was incorporated into the organization, it was already company policy that everyone in management should have at least 40 hours of relevant supplementary education a year. Milliken Denmark has more than lived up to this, e.g. managers clocked up almost 100 hours of supplementary education in 1991.

This policy expanded relatively quickly to include all staff workers, though at the end of the 1980s it was still hard to see how all these hours of education had contributed much to an understanding of the quality process.

The management group had tried for years to push the ideas and thoughts of the quality process down the organization but it had proved extremely hard to translate this effort into changed behaviour or a greater understanding of the firm's intentions.

By a coincidence in 1989, Milliken became aware of the courses offered at various AMU centres (government supported Labour Market Education Centres) and management quickly realized that there was a chance to mobilize the grass roots to break through middle managers and administrative personnel. The management group expected that if both top management and production workers put pressure on administrative personnel and middle managers, then they might be able to get the process back on course again.

Milliken developed a very positive relationship with the AMU centre in Djursland and on the centre's recommendation, they sent groups of four staff workers and eight hourly-paid workers on five-day courses in quality consciousness. In all, 15 groups were sent and the mix of white and blue-collar workers proved to be very beneficial to the success of the process. Suddenly, they all became aware of each other's professional and human qualities. The middle managers found out that the blue-collar worker was an expert in his field, while the blue-collar worker realized that management did not have ready-made solutions to all the problems.

For a whole week they talked about quality in the abstract and in relation to their common place of work. The organizational pyramid was broken down and everybody learned something from the other.

Not all engineers or other highly-educated employees were overjoyed at the prospect of spending a week at an AMU centre but this problem soon disappeared when the managing director himself spent a week there and reported that the course was good both for the firm and the individual.

Willingness to take on work outside normal demarcation areas was overwhelming. At one time, Milliken had over 40 teams at work solving problems and some of the results they achieved were truly remarkable.

Today, Milliken's policy is that all employees, whether they work on the shop-floor or in an office, must have at least 40 hours of relevant supplementary education a year.

It has gradually become the experience and belief that the quality process is sustained by three things: by a management which sets an example by its own behaviour, by the education of all employees in the process and finally, by an appreciation of the results achieved by employees.

(c) Zero-defect philosophy and ISO 9001

The Milliken management embraced the zero-defect philosophy relatively early on (1986), the reasoning being that they felt they should be just as much able to demand zero defects from themselves and from the employees as we expect from pilots, surgeons, bus drivers etc.

Discussions about this philosophy have often petered out in a simple exchange of opinion, with one side rationalizing that to err is human, while the other side claims that errors can be avoided. However, the management soon realized that the interesting thing about the zero-defect philosophy, is not the goal of 'zero defect' but the process which ensures fewer and fewer defects every year.

But it was only with the ISO certification in 1988 that Milliken finally found a 'tool' to help prevent defects. This tool was the 'correction report', the purpose of which is to systematically describe defects and ensure that their causes are eliminated. Since 1988 about 1000 correction reports have been written, each of which has eliminated at least one source of error.

These correction reports have also made management realize that it is not only employees who make mistakes – sources of errors are often built into machines and processes. Management has also sat through futile discussions where employees' main concern has been to shift the blame as far from themselves as possible.

The managing director settled this problem once and for all by saying that any defects which occur are his fault and his fault alone. In return, he expects any associate to tell him about 'his' mistakes and how they can be avoided in the future. This has dramatically shortened the length of discussions and reoriented them towards considering how similar defects can be prevented in future.

(d) Standardization, KAIZEN and innovation

KAIZEN is a Japanese word which, roughly translated, means 'small, continual changes for the better'. Innovation stands for 'new thinking, revolutionary, breakthrough'.

There have been several product developments at Milliken Denmark which can be described as innovations and these have raised the products and the company up to new technological and economic heights. Unfortunately, they are also rare occurrences.

Such breakthroughs have created enormous interest in the past, both in the company and in the market. But even if the competitors soon catch up, Milliken's top management has experienced that its own interest in continuous improvements wanes after a while, with the result that the lead it has built up is lost again.

The management has realized that through standardization it will be able to hang on to and consolidate the leads it has built up. Management has realized that as soon as a new standard has been established it should immediately be challenged by means of KAIZEN. There is now a common agreement that this not only produces incremental advances but also ensures that these advances are not lost through lack of attention. Furthermore, it raises the standard, so that the next breakthrough occurs at a higher jumping-off point than the previous breakthrough brought the firm to.

The suggestion system and the error cause removal teams are both used actively to challenge the standards documented by the ISO system, thereby creating 'small changes for the better' and ensuring that when the next breakthrough comes, it occurs at a higher jumping-off point than before.

(e) Process owner and process employee

In 1991 Milliken realized something else. The management group and the other associates had been struggling for a long time with problems caused by the hierarchical nature of the organization, where authority and responsibility were shared among department managers. This structure did nothing to promote problem-solving in the firm, because problems were rarely limited to only one function or department. As a result, from the customers' point of view, problem-solving in the departments had been less than satisfactory over the years.

By focusing on processes, management came to realize that everything they do is part of a process and that each process can be divided into innumerable sub-processes. Management has realized that each process must have a 'process owner' who has the authority and budgetary authorization to change the process and in the process itself there are process employees, who influence the process but who are not entitled to change it. It was emphasized that each process employee has both a right and a duty to make suggestions for improving the process.

Milliken has now assigned process 'owners' to all identified processes and their authority overrides department managers in those departments the process crosses. This realization has helped to reduce pressure on individual process employees when the demands of process change have been especially great. The Milliken associates are much more aware now of who the process owner is and who the process employees are and these roles are a far cry from the usual rigid organizational hierarchy.

The management and other associates at Milliken Denmark have also learned that processes have inbuilt variations (normal) and that they can be affected by outside variations (abnormal). Management has learned that the quality improvement process should start by concentrating on reducing the normal process variations and that it is wrong to adjust the machines if they find that the variations can be traced to specific causes.

19.2.5 THE EUROPEAN QUALITY AWARD

Milliken European Division, of which Milliken Denmark is a part, participated in the competition for the European Quality Award in 1992 where they won the European Quality Prize. In 1993 they won the award.

The self-assessment framework of the European quality model greatly helped Milliken to obtain a much better overview of all its quality related activities including the management process.

One of the key learnings the company realized from the 1992 participation was that it needed to look at its process management. Management learned the importance of following the Plan, Do, Check, Act cycle for continuous improvements and to ask itself the question whether the process itself was designed to generate the results it was striving for.

19.2.6 CONCLUSION

Milliken's quality process has been under way since 1984 now and has taught management a number of things. One is that the quality process requires patience and endurance. Another is that progress is often of the two-steps-forward-one-step-back kind and that the best remedy when you are starting to lose heart is to compare the from today with what it was a couple of years ago. This is invariably a good pick-me-up.

Milliken's management has learned that there is no alternative to the quality process. Today, nearly all firms operate in markets where supply exceeds demand and where it is often difficult to tell one manufacturer's products from another. The only possible winner in such a market is the firm which offers goods and services of the highest quality at competitive prices.

The problem of how to secure both the highest quality and, at the same time, also secure competitive prices has a lot to do with the problem of how to measure and reduce the cost of poor quality. Section 19.3 is devoted to that problem.

19.3 MEASUREMENT OF QUALITY COSTS (THE RESULTS OF QUALITY MANAGEMENT)

19.3.1 SOME THEORY AND DEFINITIONS

In relation to TQM it is well-known that the level of quality will be improved by investing in the so-called quality management costs. These consist of:

1. Preventive quality costs. These are costs of activities the aim of which is to prevent quality defects and problems cropping up. The aim of preventive activities is to find and control the causes of quality defects and problems.
2. Inspection/appraisal costs. The object of these costs is to find defects which have already occurred, or make sure that a given level of quality is being met.

'Investment' in the so-called quality management costs will improve quality and result in the reduction of so-called failure costs.

Failure costs are normally divided into the following two groups:

1. Internal failure costs. These are costs which accrue when defects and problems are discovered inside the company. These costs are typically costs of repairing defects.
2. External failure costs. These are costs which accrue when the defect is first discovered and experienced outside the firm. The customer discovers the defect and this leads to costs of claims and as a rule, also a loss of goodwill corresponding to the lost future profits of lost customers.

We know now that a large part of failure costs, both internal and external, are invisible, i.e. they are either impossible to record, or not worth recording. We know too that, for the same reasons, a large part of preventive costs are also invisible. This leaves inspection costs, which are actually the most insignificant part of total quality costs, inasmuch as these costs gradually become superfluous as the firm begins to improve quality by investing in preventive costs.

Investing in preventive costs has the following effects:

1. Defects and failure costs go down.
2. Customer satisfaction goes up.
3. The need for inspection and inspection costs go down.
4. Productivity goes up.
5. Competitiveness and market shares increase.
6. Profits go up.

This is why we can say that 'quality is free' or more precisely 'the cost of poor quality is extremely high'.

But how can we reduce the cost of poor quality when most of the quality cost elements are invisible? Well, the first step is to define the total quality cost (Campanella, 1990):

> The sum of the above costs [prevention costs, appraisal costs and failure costs]. It represents the difference between the actual cost of a product or service, and what the reduced cost would be if there was no possibility of substandard service, failure of products, or defects in their manufacture.

This definition is a kind of benchmarking definition because you compare your cost of product or service with a perfect company – a company where there is no possibility of failures. We have never met such a company in this world but the vision of TQM is gradually to approach the characteristics of such a company.

In practice we need other kinds of benchmarks as the perfect company. Such benchmarks will gradually be built up when you start measuring the most vital elements of the total quality costs. The following sections will show how Milliken Denmark succeeded with that process.

19.3.2 HOW IT STARTED

The group management asked Milliken Denmark's top management to find out how high the quality costs were. To avoid any long arguments about how these should be defined, they made it simple by pointing out four accounts from the accounting records. These four accounts contained costs of complaints and claims, costs of taking goods back, write-offs in production, plus the costs of sending products two or more times through the production process.

The definition of the costs on these four accounts were the following:

1. Discounts. This is an internal failure cost element. A failure has been built into the product but it is found before shipment to the customer. The customer is offered a discount in order to accept the failure.
2. Allowances. This is an external failure cost element. A failure has been built into the product and the customer finds the failure. An allowance is negotiated. If the customer does not accept the shipment the allowance is equal to the amount of invoice.
3. Returns. This is an external failure cost element. If a customer does not accept a shipment because of a failure caused by Milliken the customer may decide to send the shipment back. Returns are the freight of returned shipments.
4. Reworks. The cost to repair a product may be either internal costs or external costs depending on who finds the failure.

These four main accounts contained the sum of failure costs coming from many more detailed accounts showing what product and what place (departments, functions etc.) the detailed registrations were coming from.

The group management wanted to establish a simple quality cost system without arbitrary cost allocations. The quality cost system was not intended to compromise all the quality cost elements. The intention was to construct a simple thermometer which could measure if the patient was sick and also of course how sick and what disease.

It was the experience from other companies in the Milliken group that these four cost categories comprised the major quality cost elements and so the group management wanted to compare the quality costs from these four accounts between the different companies.

The group's companies already had these figures but if any were missing, the instructions were quite clear: reconstruct it or estimate its size. 1984 was chosen as the base year and the management has closely followed the trend in these four figures every four weeks.

19.3.3 THE QUALITY COST THERMOMETER

In 1984, the quality costs measured as the sum of the above quality cost elements were related to the production volume (measured as the number of square meters produced) and given an index of 1.00. This index became Milliken's quality cost thermometer and the company has followed the trend in this index from 1984 until 1994. The advantage of using index figures and not actual figures is that index figures are free of the distortions due to periodic changes in production volume.

Thirteen times per year for more than 10 years the index has been presented to the top management team at Milliken Denmark and twice a year the index has been presented to the top management at Milliken, USA. Goals for the index have been established every year and 'error cause removal teams' have been established in order to reduce the index.

Parallel with the activities of the error cause removal teams (see below) bottom-up activities (QC circles as well as individual improvement activities) gradually became more and more widespread. These activities were supported by the suggestion system which was gradually developed to become more and more effective. In 1995 the number of suggestions per employee had increased to a level of 27 suggestions per employee (per year).

In 1985 the index was reduced to 0.49 and the following years showed a reduction to 0.19 in 1986 and 0.12 in 1987. Management almost immediately felt, on the bottom line, the effects of these 'gold digging activities'. The index in 1991 was 0.07, or put another way, Milliken has achieved savings of 93% measured on the index, which represent more than five million kroner a year. In 1994 the target was 0.05 which is well below Milliken's world benchmark. Table 19.5 shows the development of the index from 1984 until 1993.

(a) Error cause removal activities

When a team is established with the purpose of addressing a problem with quality costs (or any problem) the team members' first activity is to create a shared view on the problem.

Measurements of non-conformance related to the problem are normally available for the team and what is missing in terms of measurements for illustrating the magnitude of the problem is organized by the team.

The key measures available today are, e.g. quality opportunity costs indexes (section 19.3.4), delivery on time reports, customer satisfaction indexes, complaint registrations, employee satisfaction indexes etc. which, in most cases, give a clear signal when there are problems. Milliken Denmark also has a series of measures which are directed towards the performance on the individual job, workstation or department.

Table 19.5 The development of the quality cost index at Milliken Denmark from 1984 until 1993

Year	84	85	86	87	88	89	90	91	92	93
Index	1.0	.49	.19	.12	.09	.09	.09	.07	.04	.06

A review of the relevant measurements is the starting point for any error cause activity (ECR) in Milliken Denmark and the team hereafter follows the five-step procedure which is described in section 19.3.5.

The team establishes thereafter its goals in accordance with the objective for the team. Valuable input for this part of the process can, in many situations, be obtained from the customer satisfaction surveys and from the strategic planning process.

Finally, the team starts to plan how to accomplish the goal and the objective. It is Milliken's experience and belief that if this planning process is done properly the probability for success will be high. The learning point is obvious. It is more easy to implement a carefully developed, detailed plan than it is to bring a fragmented, uncompleted plan to completion.

19.3.4 THE OPPORTUNITY COST CONCEPT (THE NEW THERMOMETER)

In 1992 Milliken realized that it needed a new method to measure the quality costs. Management increasingly felt that it was difficult to motivate the employees to go on with the quality cost reduction process. The index had been reduced so much that people felt – and also said – that the possible cost savings were not worth the efforts. For that reason management decided to extend the number of quality cost accounts from four to eight and at the same time also to change the way Milliken measured the quality costs. The management felt it was time to introduce the opportunity cost concept when measuring the quality cost elements.

The following eight quality cost accounts have been used since 1993:

1. Quality discounts (internal failure cost) or price reductions when selling second quality.
2. Reworks/replacements (internal failure cost).
   a. Reworks because of failure found before delivery.
   b. Replacement when it is not possible to do rework – hence new production has to be initiated in order to satisfy the customer.
   The failure cost is measured as 'full costs', i.e. it is the sum of variable cost, indirect material cost, depreciation, other fixed production cost and contribution to administration cost. A common quality cost standard has been set up within the different product groups.
   The philosophy of this 'full cost measuring system' is the following: 'In each square metre produced we have budgeted with a saving for payment of the fixed costs. When doing reworks or replacements we have lost this opportunity.'
3. Final inspection cost (internal failure cost).
   The costs include variable costs (wage cost, material cost etc.) and contributions to fixed production cost and depreciations.

4. Down-time cost (internal failure cost).

The causes for down-time cost are mechanical breakdown of machines, lack of raw materials, preventive maintenance, planned machine stop because of holidays etc.

The costs are calculated on a 'full cost basis', i.e. they include wages, depreciations and other costs calculated by using the machine time lost in the bottleneck process.

5. Returns and allowances (external failure cost).

a. Returns are calculated as full costs including freight.

b. Allowances – return pay to customers because of complaints.

6. Quality adjusters (external failure cost).

The total cost of support services for handling customer complaints. The costs are based on the total expenditures of the support services departments and other identifiable sources including salaries, benefits, travel etc. discounted for any proactive service to the customer purely to enhance relations. The costs calculated are based on the time used for handling complaints.

7. Write downs (internal or external failure cost).

The causes for write downs are obsolete fabrics, obsolete yarn, over-runs etc.

8. Waste (internal failure cost).

The costs include materials as rubber, textiles, paper etc. In 1991, 390 tons of wasted materials were sold to waste dealers. The waste is calculated as the difference between purchase price and waste price. The total waste cost is the biggest cost element in the new quality cost system.

19.3.5 EXPERIENCES WITH THE NEW THERMOMETER

Milliken Denmark now has two years of experience with this new quality cost system. In 1993, management found out that even though it has worked intensively with quality cost reductions since 1984 and achieved world class results there were still many opportunities for quality cost reductions. This was realized when constructing and working with 'the new thermometer'.

The new thermometer (the new index) was calculated as the sum of the eight new quality cost accounts divided by production volume. The sum of the eight new quality cost accounts represented a substantial amount of money.

The start temperature (index) was set equal to 100 in 1993. In 1994 this temperature was reduced to 99 and the target for 1995 was 84.

As shown in Figure 19.2 the target for 1995 was not achieved.

One learning point with the new system is that it took some time for the organization to learn how to understand and utilize the new

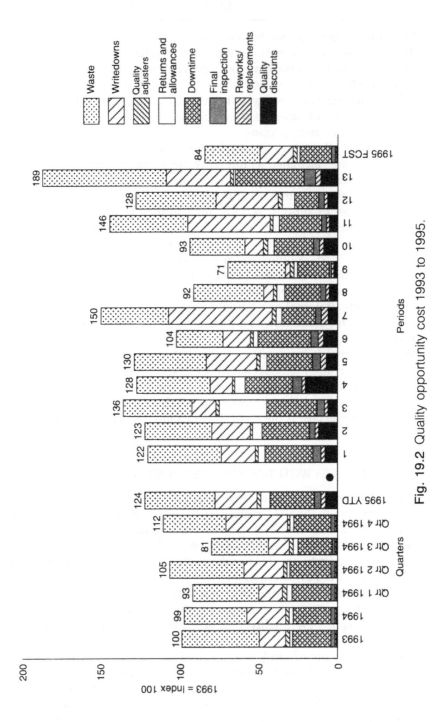

Fig. 19.2 Quality opportunity cost 1993 to 1995.

measurements. It was realized that the quality of the measurements in the pilot period (1993–1994) was lower than the quality of the measurements in 1995 when the measurements became more comprehensive and detailed. People are now more careful in the measurement process than they were in the pilot period. This is the main reason why the results for 1995 do not look as satisfactory compared to the previous two years and compared to the goal.

(a) Conclusion

The new quality cost measurement system by which Milliken tries to calculate the real failure costs by using opportunity costs has given management a very powerful signal that it still has some big problems to work on. This signal would not have been so powerful in the old quality costing system.

19.3.6 STEPS IN USING THE QUALITY MEASUREMENTS

When reducing quality costs the teams used the following five-step procedure.

- Step 1: Pareto diagram of the total failure cost is set up.
  For each four-week period the measurements are collected and analysed. A Pareto diagram is constructed showing the eight quality cost categories. The category with the highest costs is selected for further analysis (Appendix 19.A). Process waste is selected as an example here.
- Step 2: Pareto diagram to identify 'the vital few' is set up.
  A new Pareto diagram is constructed showing the elements of the quality cost category selected in step 1 (Appendix 19.B). One or more of the most vital elements are selected for 'error cause removal', i.e 'a Business–Hoshin Implementation Plan' is developed. Tufted fabric and rubber trim waste is selected.
- Step 3: The 'Business–Hoshin Implementation Plan' is set up.
  The 'Business–Hoshin Implementation Plan' is developed by using Milliken's 'Hoshin forms'. The strategy and tactics are decided and responsible persons are chosen. A review of progress is done in each period of four weeks.
- Step 4: The Hoshin plan is checked.
  'Check of Hoshin' means that the total plan is checked at the end of the 'Hoshin Period'. A graph is constructed showing the trend in quality costs for the chosen cost element. An example in Appendix 19.C shows a slow reduction in 'rubber trim waste' since 1985. It is also shown that YTD 95 (year to date) periods are near (but above) the goal for 1995.

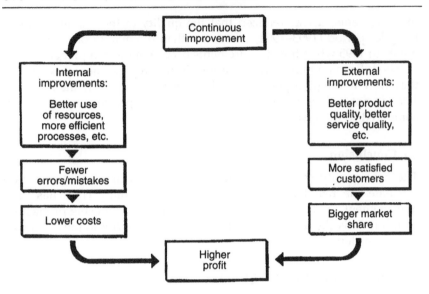

Fig. 19.3 Continuous improvements and their consequences.

- Step 5: Presentation to top management.
  The results are presented to top management after each four-week period and each quarter the results are presented to top management in Milliken and Co., USA, together with presentations from other Milliken companies. Figure 19.3 above shows a typical graph presented at this meeting. The results are discussed and knowledge is spread in this way between Milliken companies all over the world.

19.3.7 ECR/OFI/COST OF QUALITY

At this point it may be appropriate to ask the question whether it is possible to measure in financial terms the total impact of Milliken's error cause removal process and the Opportunity For Improvement process (sections 19.2.2 and 19.2.3)?

The answer to this question is that Milliken does not have any measurements which can split the results in the impact of the error cause removal process and the impact of the Opportunity For Improvement process on the financial results.

It is an important learning point that the measurable effects of the two processes have been on both the 'internal improvements', i.e. on 'better use of resources, more efficient processes etc. . . . ' and on the external improvements (Figure 19.3).

The aim of the internal improvements has been to reduce costs and to remove dissatisfaction. The aim of the external improvements has been to increase the quality of products, services and associates in order to keep or increase market share. Both effects will in the long run increase the company's profit. It is obvious that there has been a synergy between the two aims and also between the activities which have been completed at Milliken Denmark during the 12 years which the case study covers.

The important learning point is that one process cannot thrive without the other. Milliken Denmark has learned that there is a high element of synergy between the two processes which has had effects on both the number, the size and the type of improvements.

19.4 CONCLUSION

The conclusion and learning points from Milliken's experiences with the continuous measurement and reduction of quality costs are the following:

1. A quality cost measurement system is a valuable tool in helping to identify the most vital areas which must be improved.
2. When starting to measure: keep measurements simple and measure only the most vital failure costs!
3. Have a continuous focus on the results!
4. Establish functional and cross-functional error cause removal teams which have the responsibility to identify the causes behind the results and to propose and implement solutions which will 'kill the causes'!
5. The effect of points 3 and 4 above will typically be a reduction in the measured quality costs of 50% per year in the first three years, i.e. a reduction to 10–15% of the start level.
6. After the first three years progress will not be so easy. Now it will be increasingly important to rely on 'everybody's participation'. Suggestion systems should be set up with clear and simple criteria for recognition and reward. Standards for quick response are imperative. The suggestions complement ideas for improvements generated by permanent and *ad hoc* error cause improvement teams.
7. The quality cost elements to measure (the cost accounts) should be analysed for comprehensiveness. New cost elements may be included and the opportunity cost concept may be applied in order to assure continuous reduction of the total quality costs.
8. A continuous reduction in the total quality costs demands that the quality cost system is an integrated part of the total management concept: Total Quality Management.

Perhaps the most important learning point has been that the new quality costing system has made it clear for everybody in the organization that even after 10 years of continuous reductions in failure costs to a world class level there are still many opportunities for improvements.

If Milliken Denmark is to continue to be a world class company it has no choice other than continuing, finding and implementing these opportunities for improvements.

APPENDIX

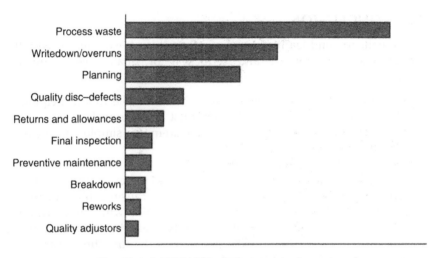

Fig. **19.A.1** 1995 YTD quality opportunity cost.

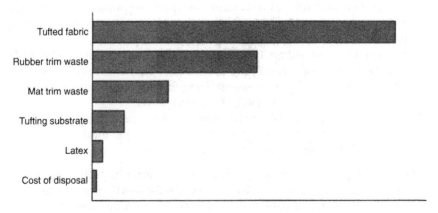

Fig. **19.B.1** 1995 quality opportunity cost: process waste.

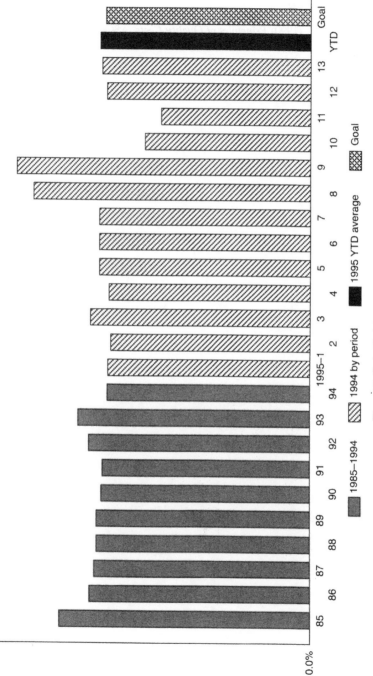

Fig. 19.C.1 Rubber waste.

REFERENCES

Campanella, J. (1990) *Principles of Quality Costs*, ASQC, Milwaukee, USA.
Crosby, P.B. (1982) *Quality is Free*, The New American Library Inc., New York, USA.

International Service System A/S case studies: the winning hand[1]

20

20.1 CHANGING FOR THE FUTURE – ADHERING TO OUR CORE BELIEFS: PREFACE BY GROUP CHIEF EXECUTIVE WALDEMAR SCHMIDT

When I took over as President and CEO of ISS on October 1, 1995, I also took on the task of changing ISS to prepare it for the challenges of the next century – without abandoning the core beliefs that made ISS what it is today.

Throughout our development, we have had the firm belief that the leader of the professional cleaning industry must take on the responsibility to develop and lift the whole industry to be successful in the long-term.

This has brought about enhancement of the esteem and image of our operatives through the development of professional equipment and methods, training schedules and the creation of career paths for service professionals. And last but not least, improvement of pay and work conditions. Competition has been forced to follow similar paths.

Focus on the customer and high business ethics has been and is ISS's foundation for building respectful relationships with customers.

Cutting corners, compromising quality and using unethical – even unlawful – business methods have earlier been practised by some in the industry, to be able to cut prices and achieve short-term progress.

[1] This is a reprint of a case study written by J.J. Dahlgaard and K. Kristensen for the European Commission, DG III, as part of the European Way for Excellence Study. The authors thank the Commission and The European Foundation for Quality Management for permission to reprint the study. There are some overlaps between the case studies and the previous text in order to make the case studies as stand alone.

However, we firmly believe that by an ethical business conduct and by investing in people, methods, quality and service development together with our customers, we create a win–win situation for all parties that leads to sustainable growth and profitability. This is a model that our serious competitors have adopted.

Building of these core beliefs, where are we heading?

20.1.1 THE ROLLS ROYCE OF CLEANING

Today, the ISS Group's core business is cleaning and this will continue to be the case in the future. We pride ourselves in being the 'Rolls Royce' of the industry, because we have invested over the years in quality, training and systems, all of which now differentiate us in our markets. We also had the courage to expand internationally over the years, so that today we are in 32 countries, a fact which gives us considerable competitive advantage for servicing international accounts.

One of the key strategic issues we must now address is that of the emerging demand in some geographical markets, particularly the USA and the UK, for facilities management. Whilst I do not see ISS becoming a facilities management company, I do believe that we must have the capability to offer a wider range of services if so required. Facilities management is a rather vague discipline at the moment. There are no clear definitions. However, we need to be flexible and open-minded and seek ways of broadening our service package in those markets and segments where the demand is real, either through strategic acquisitions, or through partnerships.

20.1.2 MULTI-SERVICE AND MULTI-SKILLING

ISS Mediclean, our UK hospital service company, is an excellent example of the success we can achieve by extending our services to respond to specific market opportunities. When it was acquired in 1989, Mediclean was a hospital cleaning company. Today, it is a true hospital service company, offering cleaning, catering, portering and car park management. It even helps hospitals turn their canteens into profit centres by handling everything from the redesign and construction of their facilities to the management of the service!

20.1.3 WE NO LONGER CLEAN EVERYTHING FOR EVERYBODY

We used to think that we were in the business of cleaning everything for everybody. We now believe that there is a more strategic approach to identifying which markets and customers we want to do business with. By breaking the market up into segments, or groups of customers which share common characteristics, we can choose which segments are most likely to yield the turnover and profit which we need to achieve our financial goals. We can then identify and target the customers within each segment we want to do business with. The most attractive accounts are 'key accounts', because their contribution to the Group's health and wealth is particularly significant – either in turnover or in profit terms, or because they are strategically important for other reasons. Key accounts and non-key accounts usually need to be treated in different ways to ensure that resources are allocated most cost-effectively.

20.1.4 A GLOBAL/PAN-EUROPEAN SERVICE PARTNER

Another trend which will influence our strategic thinking is the small but significant demand which is emerging for global service agreements. As the world becomes increasingly more competitive, some multinational corporations are seeking to reduce the number of suppliers they deal with worldwide, in order to achieve cost and quality efficiencies. ISS sees a major opportunity in this trend. We are uniquely positioned to offer such corporations a global/pan-European service, because we often operate in many, if not all, of the countries in which they operate. Our entry into nine Far Eastern countries further underpinned our spread.

20.1.5 NEW MARKETS

We still need to reinforce our geographical presence. There are some other major markets in the Far East which we need to be in, such as Japan, in order to serve our key accounts and benefit from the growing trend in outsourcing. Canada and Argentina are other countries we must penetrate. As far as our European coverage goes, our only major gap today is Italy, and plans are afoot to remedy this.

As far as new service markets are concerned, elderly care will offer increasingly attractive opportunities in some countries. The ISS 'Care Concept' has already begun in Sweden and is in its early development phase in Belgium and the UK.

20.1.6 FUNDAMENTAL MANAGEMENT PRINCIPLES

Since ISS launched comprehensive management training in the mid 1970s, several principles have guided our culture and management practices, amongst which are the Team Planning Process, the Unit President Concept and Total Quality Management.

These principles will continue to guide our thinking. However, we will not stand still. The strategy of setting up dedicated operating companies for specific market segments, which we implemented in ISS Europe, will be rolled out elsewhere when appropriate, for it is the cornerstone of a targeted and market-driven culture. Dedicated operating companies with their own business plan, budget, balance sheet and profit and loss and which have a management team which can 'talk the customer's language' are undoubtedly the best vehicles for developing specialist markets, as results have shown.

Whatever we do, we will be driven by the market and our customers. There is no doubt that if we are successful in signing global agreements we will need to ensure that we have management and operational structures which can provide a consistent and 'seamless' service across borders.

Global key account management is a major component of this and will be one of the most exciting challenges which ISS will address in the near future.

However, as I stated above, there will be no fundamental changes in the principles of ISS. We will continue to strive for excellence, to build our organization on the foundation of decentralization, training, quality and technical superiority and thus deliver what we have promised to our customers, our employees and our shareholders.

20.2 CONTEXT, IMPERATIVES FOR CHANGE AND OBJECTIVES FOR QUALITY MANAGEMENT

20.2.1 CONTEXT: THE COMPANY

International Service System A/S (ISS) is the largest cleaning company in the world today. It operates in more than 30 countries all over the world and employs more than 120 000 employees.

The company was founded in Denmark in 1901 by a lawyer and began its activities as a small security company providing guard and other security services to business especially in the Copenhagen area. It was not until 1934 that ISS began its cleaning activities and at that time it was mainly as an add-on to the security service.

ISS began its internationalization in 1943 by setting up a Swedish operation and this was followed by a Norwegian operation in 1952. Both of these operations were mainly cleaning activities because it proved to be very difficult to export the security side of the company, mainly due to the fact that within this area customers preferred a local supplier.

The real expansion of ISS, at that time actually called DDRS (Det Danske Rengørings Selskab A/S), started with Mr Paul Andreassen's being appointed managing director in 1962. He was a 34-year-old engineer working as a technical expert at Scandinavian Airlines and with him modern times came to ISS. He was both an efficient manager and an entrepreneurial leader – a very rare combination – and under his leadership from 1962 to 1995, ISS grew from a rather modest Danish company to a recognized multinational company. In 1962, ISS had a turnover of 50 million kroner and 2000 employees. In 1994, the turnover had grown to

14 232 million kroner and the number of employees was, as previously mentioned, more than 120 000. Financial information about ISS has been included in Table 20.A.1.

The 35-year leadership of Mr Paul Andreassen may be divided into four phases. When he first arrived at ISS the main thing was to turn the company into a professional business. Hence the idea was to introduce professional management to the company. This led to a strong system of standards for cleaning with a very efficient outcome. The market had, however, started to demand more and ISS realized that the way forward was to provide value-added services. Management focus was then turned to the concept of service management and the two together proved to be a very successful combination for ISS.

In the middle of the 1970s it was realized that the company had grown so much and had become so diversified that it was necessary to standardize the planning process. A new system of strategic planning, the team planning process, was developed and through this third phase ISS could safety continue its growth by application.

At the end of the 1980s the fourth phase of management was introduced. Mr Andreassen realized that continuous improvement was the only way forward for ISS. This called for a more holistic management system and to this end the philosophy of Total Quality Management was adopted. In what follows the development of the quality process from the late 1980s to 1995 will be described with special emphasis on the measurement side.

20.2.2 IMPERATIVE FOR CHANGE: THE CHALLENGE OF THE WINNING HAND

The discussions concerning a modern quality project at ISS started at the end of the 1980s where it had become clear to the executive management board that changes had to take place in the management style and business performance if ISS were to continue its success as an efficient and competitive supplier of services to the world market.

The result of the modern quality revolution of Japan and the USA had started to make an impression on the ISS top management and furthermore the basic ideas of quality management were not very far from the general viewpoints of management held by Mr Paul Andreassen. Way back in November 1979 quality had been discussed at the yearly TMC (top management conference) and Mr Andreassen had at this time stated that organic growth of ISS could be obtained by an improvement circle starting with quality. 'Improved quality leads to satisfied customers and satisfied customers lead to increased turnover and increased profit', was the message to the participants of the TMC. This point of view was followed up in 1908 with a big poster where Mr

Andreassen was photographed in the same position as the army general announcing that 'your country needs you'. Mr Andreassen pointed to the employees of ISS and said: 'I want you to think quality.'

In order to clarify the situation a planning group was formed to discuss the future. The planning group headed by Mr Jan Rasmussen, then vice president of human resources, chose to characterize the possible stages that a company may be in relation to the market at three different points of time: the 1980s, the 1990s and year 2000. The result of this characterization which was called 'the winning hand' is shown in Table 20.1.

It will be seen from Table 20.1 that the possible stages have been characterized as:

- the admission criteria
- the finals
- the winning hand

and for each stage it was asked: what are the requirements to reach this particular stage?

To be a player at the market-place for cleaning in the 1980s the company needed to be cost-effective. This is obvious because the profit margin in the cleaning market is very small and if you are not efficient you will very soon be history. To become part of the so-called choice set you should in addition to cost-effectiveness be able to deliver on time, or to be more specific, you should be able to deliver where and when your customer wants. To achieve this was not enough, however, you should also be able to deliver a quality service on top of the others and this is where the ideas and practice of service management came in.

Moving into the 1990s and more companies have become able to handle the traditional ideas of service quality and even more companies are both cost-effective and able to deliver on time. This means that in order to be

Table 20.1 ISS and the winning hand

	1980	1990	2000
The winning hand	Service quality	Quality of relationships Management by facts	Innovation Continuous improvement
The finals	On time	Service quality	Quality of relationships Management by facts
The admission criteria	Cost-effectiveness	Cost-effectiveness On time	Cost-effectiveness On time Service quality

a player you now have to be both cost-effective and able to deliver on time. To reach the finals you should, in addition, provide service quality but this is no longer enough to become the chosen company. New requirements showed up in the 1990s and when ISS did this work it was already clear from the experience made by other companies that these requirements probably could be characterized as follows:

- quality of relationships
- management by facts.

Talking about quality of relationships it was expected that one of the ways to improve business performance was to focus on all types of relationships in the company: relationship to customers, relationship to vendors, relationship to suppliers and the internal relationship of the company's employees. By improving the quality of these relationships you would be able to improve the total quality of the company's services and hence business performance.

But as Roger Milliken once said 'a team without a scoreboard is only practising' It is not enough to talk about quality of relationships. If you really want to improve, you must measure both your position and your rate of improvement and this will call for much more focus on facts. People must be trained differently and taught how to manage by facts.

Moving on to the year 2000 the expectations of the ISS working group was that quality of relationships and management by facts had become standard equipment for many competitors in the market. In that case the only way to remain at the top of the class was to implement the ideas of continuous improvement in the organization and to create a basis for innovativeness.

It appears from the discussion above that the conclusion of the working group prior to any quality initiatives was that a future management system would require the following focus areas:

1. quality of relationships;
2. management by facts;
3. continuous improvements;
4. innovation.

With this conclusion as a starting point it became clear that the ideas of TQM were very similar to the requirements of ISS. TQM focuses on more or less the same things. Management by facts and continuous improvements are usually considered to be cornerstones of TQM and furthermore TQM focuses on the customer and the employee and these are of course part of the idea of quality of relationships.

Following this it was not difficult to understand that the ISS top was motivated to embark on a quality journey. To begin with it was decided to start the journey in the Scandinavian division called ISS Scandinavia (see the organization chart in Figure 20.A.1), headed by Mr Sven Ipsen, who appointed two VPs to be in charge of the process, Mr Flemming Schandorff and Mr Poul Poulin, but even if Mr Sven Ipsen was not directly involved in the structuring of the process he never left it and he was fully aware of the necessity of top management involvement.

20.3 HISTORY OF QUALITY MANAGEMENT

20.3.1 MANAGEMENT INVOLVEMENT

The planning group headed by Mr Schandorff and Mr Poulin was in no doubt that it was necessary to start the quality journey by involving management at all levels and that the best way to do this was to start an education programme for the managers. In order to get some help with this they contacted the authors and asked them to join the planning group.

After some discussion it was decided to start with the first three layers of management in the Danish division of ISS Scandinavia A/S. The result of this was that approximately 160 managers at different levels were included in the first wave of education. It was of course realized that this was only the beginning of the education required but it was the idea that the first wave should somehow be exploratory and set the guidelines for the future work.

Today it is generally accepted that a TQM process starts with a self-evaluation and today we have a number of instruments for this purpose, e.g. the EFQM model. At the time the ISS process started, systematic self-evaluation was not all part of the normal routine of process improvement in companies and hence it was quite a revolution when the planning group suggested that the basis of the management education should be a self-evaluation done by all participants according to the criteria of the Japanese Deming Prize. The reason for the choice of the Deming Prize was that at the time the EFQM model, which probably would have been chosen today, did not exist and experience with the American Baldridge Award was minimal. On the other hand the authors were familiar with the criteria of the Deming Prize and furthermore had access to a great deal of internal material from the Japanese Union of Scientists and Engineers which could be of a very big help when formulating questions and benchmarking the results.

The basis of the self-evaluation was a questionnaire divided into three parts:

A. Key questions for a service company.
B. A number of questions structure according to the 10 headlines of the Deming Prize.
C. Perceived quality problems, the perceived causes to these problems and the suggested solutions.

The first two parts consisted of a very structured set of closed questions while the last part was open-ended. This meant that the analysis of the questionnaire was divided into two parts but still combined. The first part was a standard statistical analysis while the second part first consisted of an interpretation of the many answers to the questions in Group C and after this a coding of these answers in order to make a combined statistical analysis possible.

The questions in group A – the key service questions – are shown below:

1. Do we have a broad understanding of the service policy of ISS?
2. Have we established specific goals?
3. Do we always consider our customer to be the king?
4. Do we have a continuous identification of our problem areas?
5. Do we have a continuous evaluation of our progress?
6. Do the employees know the requirements of our customers and can they explain these requirements?
7. Do we have a willingness to perform market research in order to identify customer requirements and our competitive position?
8. Are you (the management) the perfect role model for your employees?
9. Do we know the barriers preventing us from providing an excellent service? If so, are these barriers systematically removed?
10. Is focus on the customer the main theme for the training of our employees?

As already mentioned, the questions for the second part of the self-evaluation were structured according to the Deming Prize. Within each headline a number of statements were formulated and the managers were asked to indicate the extent of which the statement was fulfilled. A few examples of the statements are given below.

1.4 The quality policy is regularly maintained on the basis of collected information about quality.
3.3 The staff understands the idea of variation in relation to quality.
4.1 The company has a system for the collection of data on customer satisfaction.

The areas and the corresponding number of statements – the Deming Prize headlines – are shown below:

1. Policy and strategy (7).
2. Organization and operation (6).
3. Education and training (6).
4. Collection and use of data (7).
5. Analysis (4).

6. Standardization (3).
7. Quality control (6).
8. Quality assurance (7).
9. Effect of quality initiatives (3).
10. Planning for the future (4).

The entire analysis was conducted not only for ISS but also for a small independent company belonging to another part of the service industry. The reason for this was that it was expected that a number of managers would be reluctant to accept the results and especially the implications of the results with reference to ISS being very special. A reaction like this was well-known from other situations within ISS and also from other companies and hence the planning group decided not to make an excuse like this possible.

Based on the results of the empirical study which are shown together with their consequences in the following section an education programme for the managers was constructed. It was decided to split the education into four blocks as follows:

1. day one training combined with a company visit to Milliken Denmark;
2. private study of material distributed on day one;
3. day two training at ISS University approximately one month after the day one training;
4. a one-week visit to Disney World and participation in the Disney service quality training programme.

The contents of the two days of training are shown below:

Day 1:
1. The ISS quality profile: identification of problems.
2. What is quality (in general and ISS specific)?
3. What is TQM?
4. Quality culture – possible changes.
5. The economics of quality – visible and invisible quality costs.
6. Milliken's experience.

Day 2:
1. The ISS quality profile: problem-solving.
2. Deming's 14 points – stations along the way.
3. Measurement of quality.
4. Product development.
5. Quality tools.
6. Team-building.
7. Quality improvements and strategic quality management.
8. Implementation – how do we get started?

As mentioned already this training programme was only intended to be an introduction. At the end of the programme it should be decided how and to what extent the education of the rest of the employees should be carried out. In this connection it should be remembered that ISS is a very large company with more than 120 000 employees in more than 30 countries. Furthermore, ISS is a very diversified service company with activities spanning from simple daily office cleaning to very complicated care service activities. This means that education and training of the staff is a complex task which requires very careful and detailed planning.

20.3.2 THE RESULTING QUALITY OBJECTIVES AND QUALITY POLICY

The results of the self-evaluation study provided a wealth of information for the future process and it also proved to be very motivating for the quality work because for the first time there was an overall picture of the quality situation in the company. A picture not provided by some remote expert but a picture provided by those who had the daily experience in the company. This made a major difference concerning the acceptance of the results it showed.

Furthermore it showed that it would be a very good idea to have a validation sample to compare the results with. First of all it prevented the 'not-invented-here-syndrome' which has already been mentioned but it also made it possible to put the results into perspective.

In Table 20.2 some of the results from the Deming Prize evaluation are reported. Both ISS results and validation sample results are shown as index numbers. These numbers have been constructed from the original

Table 20.2 Results of Deming Prize evaluation

	Index of performance	
	ISS sample	Validation sample
1. Quality consciousness – planning for the future	> 80	> 80

2. The organization of quality management
  – quality assurance
  – standardization
  – policy
	50–60	40–60

3. Quality techniques
  – analysis
  – control
  – education and training
	40–50	20–40

4. Information about quality
  – collecting and using information
  – effect
	< 40	< 20

four-point rating scales using statistical techniques. The higher an index number, the better the performance within the reported area.

The grouping of the individual Deming Prize areas has been done by use of a quality management technique called matrix data analysis. This technique is part of the so-called seven new management techniques and it helps to provide an overview of large data sets. It should be mentioned that the headings of the groups do not come from the Deming Prize. Instead they are the result of the discussions in the planning group.

The results showed two main things. First of all it was clearly indicated where the managers actually saw the problems and secondly it could be seen that structurally ISS was no different from the small service company shown in the validation sample.

There was no doubt that the managers claimed to be motivated for the quality process. This is seen from the high score in the quality consciousness area. This holds good, actually, for both companies. But apart from this they evaluated that the organizational area was their best even if it was not too good. On the other hand the collection and use of information about quality-related topics was seen as rather poor.

In addition to the overall Deming Prize evaluation, an in-depth discussion of the perceived problem areas was made, which led to the identification of seven 'problem areas' that were to be taken up in connection with the training and which should also be the basis of the formulation of a future quality policy. The seven 'problem areas' are given below together with their suggested solutions. The numbers in parenthesis are the percentages of answers to the areas in question.

Identified 'problem areas':

1. Lack of definition of quality and lack of understanding of customer requirements (63%).
2. Too large variability in product and service (23%).
3. Inefficient internal communication (21%).
4. Functional errors (20%).
5. Delivery problems (19%).
6. Internal deliveries (15%).
7. Add-on services to the customers (9%).

Suggested solutions:

1. Definition of quality standards (57%).
2. Definition of standards for education (56%)
3. Definition of standards for internal procedures (42%).
4. Programmes for employee motivation (39%).
5. Improvement of internal communication (25%).
6. Systematic market surveillance (14%).
7. Improved instruction of customers (11%).

All these elements were summed up in a conclusion for the future work in the quality area. This conclusion was divided into three areas as follows:

1. ISS needs a systematic quality policy, especially standards for quality both internally and externally.
2. ISS needs systematic education in the quality area, including the education of collaborators.
3. ISS needs a systematic information procedure for:
   - customers
   - competitors
   - processes
   - employees.

With this as a starting point the education of the managers was carried out as explained in the previous section. Furthermore, a smaller group, consisting of the managing directors of the individual companies belonging to the ISS Scandinavia group, met on a two-day seminar in order to work out quality goals and quality policies for the group. The results of this work are shown in the following points.

ISS quality goals:

- Our goal at ISS is for customers to receive products and services which fully live up to their requirements and expectations and, in addition to this, a unique service.
- To achieve this, ISS will involve customers and employees in a continuous process, the aim of which is to develop products and services with an ever-increasing level of quality while at the same time strengthening employees' quality consciousness.

ISS quality policies: 'focus on the customer':

- Customers define what satisfactory quality is.
- Customers have a right to products and services which fulfil their expectation of total quality.
- Customers are entitled to personal and individual service.
- Customers' satisfaction is of the utmost importance and is therefore measured at fixed intervals.

ISS quality policies: 'focus on employees':

- Every employee has an influence on and is responsible for quality.
- Employees' commitment, knowledge and ability are crucial to the firm's total quality.
- Internal communication and marketing are just as important as external.
- Education and personal development are necessary for the fulfilment of the firm's quality goals.

- Employees at all levels must be treated with respect in accordance with the agreed personnel policy.
- A condition for the continuing attractiveness for ISS as a place of work is mutual respect for each other and each other's work.
- Employees' satisfaction is measured at fixed intervals.

ISS quality policies: 'guarantee and quality of delivery':

- Maintaining satisfactory quality demands continuous quality improvements. This means that no matter how good present quality is, it can always be better.
- All high-quality work is performed by the firm's employees who are customers and suppliers in the processes which produce goods and services to the firm's customers.
- The best method of achieving quality is to prevent defects and problems instead of discovering or correcting them after they have occurred.
- Measuring and reporting defects, problems and improvements at fixed intervals are a condition for continuous quality improvement.

It is obvious that the ISS management has clearly adopted the principles of TQM. Focus on the customer, focus on the employee, the concept of internal customers, continuous improvement, everyone's participation and last but not least the focus on facts are all elements which are found in the quality policy.

The key areas for the future work coming out of the analysis are very close to the ones coming out of 'the winning hand' discussion at the beginning of this chapter. To summarize they were:

1. quality of relationships:
   - customers
   - employees
   - vendors;
2. management by facts;
3. continuous improvements.

In what follows we see how these areas were taken care of, focusing especially on management by facts. We are not going to handle the other two areas in detail in this chapter. To give an idea of the quality of relationship, however, Figure 20.B.1 and Tables 20.B.1 to 20.B.3 summarize the discussion that took place in this area.

20.3.3 THE VEHICLE: ISS UNIVERSITY AND ISS QUALITY INSTITUTE

The results obtained for ISS Scandinavia A/S were found to be promising for the future development of ISS and henceforth it was decided by Mr Sven Ipsen, CEO of ISS Scandinavia and his working group that it was a good idea to give a one-day presentation together with some basic TQM training to the remaining ISS top management: Mr Paul Andreassen, CEO of ISS, Mr Waldermar Schmidt, CEO ISS Europe, Mr Henrik Slipsager, CEO ISS North America and Mrs Lise Friis, financial director of the ISS Group.

Following this, the top management decided that it would be a good idea to have a special vehicle for driving the total quality process. The idea of a quality institute was formed and Mr Jan Rasmussen was appointed managing director. Inspiration for the quality institute was taken from several places but especially the Renault Quality Institute was chosen as a benchmarking partner. The institute was set up in Copenhagen close to the ISS head office and the board of directors comprised the top management committee of ISS plus one of the authors of this book (Kai Kristensen).

Shortly after the creation of the ISS Quality Institute a decision was made to collect all ISS development activities under the same umbrella. The ISS University was formed with the Quality Institute as an important part. Mr Jan Rasmussen became managing director of the university which as a whole has become a very important factor in driving the entire quality and development process of the company. The ISS University, its components and its mission are described below.

(a) The ISS University

ISS University A/S is the ISS Group's international learning and development centre. Primarily, it is an in-house resource which supports ISS operating companies. Through continuous development and the transfer of best practices, the ISS University helps the operating companies to win and retain profitable service contracts. ISS employees, existing/potential customers, academics and specialists from all over the world come together at the ISS University to develop service management techniques, service concepts and TQM.

The ISS University was established as a response to the continuous change and increasing complexity in the markets where ISS operates. Furthermore, the ISS University was established to enhance the continuing development and the transfer of 'best practices' between ISS companies worldwide.

Success in service as previously mentioned is synonymous with the development of employees and support systems. That has been the underlying philosophy of ISS for many years. Seeking new methods, being alert to new opportunities and achieving results are driving forces of the ISS culture.

The ISS University plays an important role in demonstrating that ISS is capable of handling any challenge better than any other company in the service business. The ISS University has expressed its mission as follows:

- To position ISS – at any time and place – as the leading option for the quality-conscious customer.
- To assist and support ISS companies in winning and retaining service contacts with a high value added to the customer.
- To develop and maintain methods, tools and processes to assist the development of human resources and the continuous improvements of ISS services – in accordance with the needs of the operating companies.
- To strengthen effects of synergy and innovation by facilitating the transfer of expertise across ISS worldwide networks – those which currently exist and those to be established.
- To create a 'home-from-home' for colleagues and customers.

The ISS University has to contribute substantially to creating the best conditions for development and new thoughts internationally within ISS. The driving forces in this work are a number of central questions where the ISS University looks for the answers in co-operation with the operating companies:

1. Customer focus. How does ISS create an in-depth understanding of the needs and expectations of its customers and how does ISS ensure these are built into ISS service concepts?
2. Focus on results. How does ISS 'translate' customer needs and expectations into the function and quality of ISS services – and then into specific operational goals and results?
3. Monitoring results. How does ISS measure and monitor the achievement of goals and results to produce meaningful, action-oriented information that can be used by employees, management and customers?
4. The delivery system. How does ISS develop and maintain a cost-effective delivery system which helps achieve goals and results based on the most up-to-date techniques and methods?
5. Human resources. How does ISS develop and manage human resource and how does ISS create a working environment that motivates employees to deliver services which match customers' expectations?
6. Organization and management. How does ISS apply organizational and managerial principles and strengthen an organizational culture which supports customer focus and profitability improvements and also ensures the full commitment of human resources?
7. Innovation and continuous improvement. Which management tools should be deployed to ensure continuous improvement in quality and

productivity and to create the best possible framework for innovation together with ISS's customers.

The ISS University has concentrated its efforts on four key activity areas – areas in which ISS believes it can benefit from an international development. The key activity areas are:

- TQM – the ISS Quality Institute;
- service development;
- management development;
- hotel and a conference centre – the ISS University Hotel.

The ISS Quality Institute

The ISS Quality Institute was established in January 1992 to undertake the long-term development of TQM and quality assurance as well as ensuring ISS's ability to respond quickly to the demands and wishes of its customers. Examples of activities at the ISS Quality Institute follow.

Quality training Quality training is targeted at top and middle management as well as supervisors and operatives. The contents and methods taught to each group are the same – only the structure is different. In some cases, quality training has been adapted to specific contracts and the training has included key persons, employed by the customer.

An important part of quality training is the training of quality facilitators who support the quality training in their own companies and thereafter facilitate the ongoing TQM improvement process. The ISS Quality Institute is responsible for enabling the operating companies to start the TQM process and to maintain it. The training is a vital part of this work.

Five-Star Programme The Five-Star Programme is a career progression programme, designed to ensure that talented operatives can progress to team leader and supervisory status. The goals of the training programme are to:

- reinforce TQM in the service delivery system;
- provide quality management to the front-line staff;
- offer an attractive career path for service professionals.

The programme highlights subjects such as customer relations, understanding of ISS, job skills, cleaning systems, personnel management, quality control etc. The programme is adapted to each country and each company. The ISS Quality Institute staff work as advisers when starting up the programme in the operating companies.

Systems for quality measurements TQM demands a fact-based approach to quality service development. It does this by systematically examining every aspect of the customer/vendor relationship. The ISS Quality Institute works alongside the operating companies to develop methods which measure quality. As this work must be done in co-operation with the operating company, the ISS Quality Institute and the customer, it produces a fruitful dialogue between ISS and the customer. As customers increasingly demand responsiveness to their changing needs, the need for differentiated quality measurements is constantly changing and expanding.

The ISS Quality Institute also trains users in the measuring systems developed and assists in the implementation of such systems to the extent required by the operating companies concerned.

The ISS Quality Institute provides help to any operating company considering upgrading its methods to provide the best possible service to the individual customers. This includes the development of a so-called TQM service contract which means applying the concepts and principles of TQM to an existing or new contract, aimed at improving customer satisfaction.

Quality benchmarking One way to become the 'top of the class' or to pinpoint and implement 'best ISS practices' in a specific area, is through a benchmarking project. The ISS Quality Institute provides support for operating companies engaged in setting up and performing benchmark projects. The ISS Quality Institute is also developing a database of ISS benchmark studies through contact with external sources. That means that the Institute is well-placed to help establish contact with the most appropriate benchmark partners – those already using 'best practices'.

Customer retention programmes A significant aspect of TQM can be described as 'listen to the customers' voice'. The ISS University has developed a standard package which focuses on the issues involved in customer retention. The ISS University assists in putting customer retention programmes in place.

The customer retention package is a total system which incorporates:

- Planned and structured contacts between several levels within the customers' organization and their ISS counterparts. The points of contact would cover systematic listening, co-planning, co-management and joint control.
- Planned and structured follow-up and reaction processes to ensure the information and facts gathered are put to good effect.
- A financial analysis method of assessing the contract's life cycle.
- A programme to develop the ISS personnel on the contract and their counterparts with the customer.

- A method to match measurement systems to customer expectations and so form the basis for contacts, follow-up and quality assurance.
- An activity-based cost management system.

ISS team planning process The ISS team planning process (TPP) is the term for the strategic planning process in ISS – it has been an important and integral part of the ISS way of management since the end of the 1970s. It is the responsibility of the corporate planning function at the ISS University:

- To make sure that the ISS organizations use the TPP in a structured manner to develop strategic plans which will enhance ISS's competitiveness and commercial success.
- To ensure that the TPP remains an important management tool in ISS, by developing the process and introducing best practice methods, models and software for structuring the planning base, strategic analyses and strategic and operational decision making and producing guidelines and workbooks which reflect this.
- To help the organizational units adopt and adapt the process by training ISS managers to understand the process and coaching selected teams in using the tools.
- Working with the total quality management function to ensure that TQM and TPP are developed and integrated to become the core of the total ISS management concept.

ISS service development

Alongside the increasing internationalization of ISS, the demand for cohesive co-ordination and development of joint service concepts increases. The ISS University has therefore established international service development committees, responsible for identifying shared improvement points and implementing best practices. The committees cover food hygiene services, hospital and health care services and airport services. The choice of these three services has been made as they are identified as services with a strategic potential.

In the committees, the managers in charge of the different services meet. Also, a representative from the ISS University and one from ISS headquarters are present. This composition ensures that both operations and the overall service development benefit from the work of the committees. Furthermore, ISS headquarters and the ISS University can allocate resources to projects whenever needed.

ISS management development

It is the responsibility of the ISS University to ensure international management development. The ISS University offers a variety of training and development programmes. These programmes are aimed at managers and potential managers at all levels. All training and development programmes are developed continuously in line with the needs of the operating companies. Examples of programmes are as follows.

International Management Course (IMC) Once a year, the ISS University offers a training programme for newly-appointed line and staff managers – the International Management Course (IMC). The IMC introduces ISS management concept and principles and provides participants with an understanding of professional service management and the language of ISS management. The course aims to create international networks and provide participants with a thorough understanding of 'The ISS Way', i.e. the basic characteristics of ISS as a service enterprise and the ways the enterprise should be managed.

Management and middle-management training The management and middle-management training programmes aim to give the participants the tools to perform their job as better leaders as well as reinforcing 'The ISS Way'. On an individual level, the training deals with the leader's function and responsibility within his/her own organization. It provides the tools with which to organize and implement changes within individual companies. At the organization level, it aims at developing networks which support the co-ordination and synergy in the workplace.

The training programme for higher-level middle-managers is performed in co-operation with other big companies, so that participants and teachers are mixed. This mix gives participants a unique opportunity to understand their own culture by comparing it to other companies.

Top management programme The aim of the TMP is to obtain greater synergy between the ISS operating companies in mutually developing service management and service concepts. The programme provides training that will impact upon the individual and his/her organizational abilities as well as improving overall management abilities.

The Sales Academy The Sales Academy has been established to help the ISS sales force to reach an understanding of the entire sales process and its mechanisms.

The Sales Academy offers an introductory sales training for newly employed sales people within ISS. The purpose of the sales training is to give newcomers a basic introduction to sales work at ISS, to ensure selling methods match ISS standards and strategies.

The Sales Academy also offers five training programmes for experienced sales personnel and sales managers. Every step of the sales process is taken into consideration: sales psychology, cost-benefit arguments (how to illustrate to the customer the cost and benefits of using ISS service), analysis of customer needs, telephone canvassing (how to get the first appointment with a potential customer) and how to successfully finalize sales negotiations.

The ISS University Hotel

To host all the development activities and training programmes it is vital that the University has its own hotel and conference centre. The ISS University Hotel is the place where the majority of the development activities takes place. It has 54 bedrooms and seven VIP/customer suites, several conference rooms, two auditoriums and all the facilities expected of a professional, modern conference centre. The Hotel is located – like the rest of the University – 25 km north of Copenhagen, Denmark. The idea is to create a 'home-from-home' for the guests whether they are ISS employees or ISS customers.

20.3.4 DEVELOPMENT OF A MEASUREMENT MODEL

As seen from the quality policies and again reflected in the description of the ISS University, measuring quality and monitoring results are cornerstones of the development process. This particular area was one of the first to be taken up by ISS. Through research and development a very good procedure of quality measurement has been created. In what follows this system will be described.

(a) Development of a theoretical model

It was realized that modern measurement of quality should be closely related to the definition of quality. As mentioned earlier many times the ultimate judge of quality is the customer which means that a system of quality measurement should focus on the entire process which leads to customer satisfaction in the company, from the supplier to the end user.

It was also realized that a basic point behind the creation of customer satisfaction is leadership and that a basic aspect of leadership is the ability to deal with the future. There is a clear tendency that leaders in general are much more focused on short-term profits than on the processes that may be in statistical control.

The result of this may very well be an increase in the variability of ISS's performance and hence an increase in quality costs. In this way 'the short-term leader' who demonstrates leadership by fighting fires all over the company may very well achieve quite the opposite of what he wants to achieve.

To be more specific, the working group at ISS was of the opinion that 'short-term leadership' may be synonymous with low quality leadership and the group was quite sure that in the future it will be necessary to adopt a different leadership style in order to survive – a leadership style which in its nature is long term and which focuses on the processes that lead to the results, rather than the results themselves. This does of course not mean that the results are uninteresting *per se* but rather that when the results are there you can do nothing about them. They are the results of actions taken a long time ago.

All this is of course much easier said than done. In the modern business environment leaders may not be able to do anything but act on the short-term basis because they do not have the necessary information to do otherwise. To act on a long-term basis requires that you have an information system which provides early warning and which makes it possible for you and gives you time to make the necessary adjustments to the processes before they turn into unwanted business results. In the ISS view this is what modern measurement of quality is all about.

In order to create an interrelated system of quality measurement it was decided to define the measurement system according to Table 20.3 below, where measurements are classified according to two criteria: the interested party and whether we are talking about processes or results.

As appears from Table 20.3 it was decided to distinguish between measurements related to the process and measurements related to the result. The reason for this is obvious in the light of what has been said above and in the light of the definition of TQM. Furthermore it was decided to distinguish between the 'interested parties': the company itself and the customer.

Traditional ISS measurements have focused on the lower left-hand corner of this table, i.e the business result, and ISS has built up extremely detailed reporting systems which can provide information about all possible types of breakdown of the business result. However, as mentioned above, this type of information is pointing backwards and at this stage it is too late to do anything about the results. What is needed is

Table 20.3 Measurement of quality – the extended concept

	ISS	The customer
The process	Employee satisfaction (ESI) Checkpoints concerning the internal service structure	Control- and checkpoints concerning the internal definition of product and service quality
The result	Business results Financial ratios	Customer satisfaction (CSI) Checkpoints describing the customer satisfaction

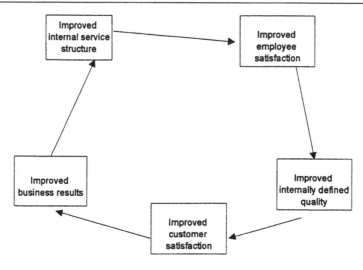

Fig. 20.1 The ISS improvement loop.

something which can tell ISS about what is going to happen with the business result in the future. This type of information is found in the rest of the table and it was especially believed that the four squares of the table are related in a closed loop which may be called the improvement circle. This loop is demonstrated in Figure 20.1 below.

This is particularly due to an increase in customer loyalty stemming from an increase in customer satisfaction. The relationship between customer satisfaction and customer loyalty has been documented empirically several times. From a benchmarking with Rank Xerox, Denmark, it was reported that when they analysed customer satisfaction on a five-point scale, where 1 is very dissatisfied and 5 is very satisfied, they observed that on the average 93% of the customers who were very satisfied (5) came back as customers, while only 60% of those who gave a 4 came back.

The expected relationship between business results and customer loyalty on one side and customer satisfaction on the other was considered very important information for the ISS management. This information provides early warning about future business results and as thus provides the ISS management with an instrument to correct failures before they affect the business result.

The next logical step will be to take the analysis one step further back and to find internal indicators of quality which are closely related to customer satisfaction. In this case the warning system will be even better. These indicators which in the table have been named control points and checkpoints will of course be company specific, even if some generic measures may be defined. At ISS the name chosen for these measurements was quality standard index or QSI.

Moving even further back we come to the employee satisfaction and other measures of the process in the company. It was expected that these were closely related to the internally defined quality. This is actually one of the basic assumptions of TQM. The more satisfied and more motivated employees you have, the higher the quality in the company.

Based on this theoretical model and the reflections related to it, it was decided for each ISS unit to introduce four levels of reporting:

1. employee satisfaction index (ESI);
2. quality standard index (QSI);
3. customer satisfaction index (CSI);
4. profit before tax (PBT).

PBT was of course well defined, but the other areas had to be developed. It was decided to develop a general model for ESI and CSI in co-operation with one of the present authors (Kristensen), while QSI should be developed individually at the units of ISS.

Before going into detail with the development work however it was decided to first have a try with a simple measurement system in the USA in order to get some experience with the internal acceptance and use of a quality measurement system.

(b) A first try in the USA

For the first try in the USA it was decided that the system should be cheap and simple. Data should be collected from internal sources and the reporting system should be very easy to understand. It was decided to follow the eight-step process below:

1. identify measurement areas;
2. identify data sources to use;
3. develop measurement index;
4. develop reporting format;
5. research and clean up data sources;
6. begin reporting quality data;
7. develop secondary reports to further define errors;
8. develop action plans to improve quality.

Four areas of measuring quality were chosen in accordance with the classification above. As a representative of customer satisfaction, credit memos were chosen. As representative of internal efficiency the number of manual payroll checks was chosen and as representatives for employee satisfaction it was decided to use the number of workers' compensation claims and the employee turnover.

Data sources for each area were defined and careful instructions were given as to the calculation of the quality index in order to prevent discussions later on.

The results were very promising with rapid improvements in all areas. It was concluded that measurement was a necessary basis for continuous improvements and it was decided to continue the development of quality measurements. In his progress report to the Executive Management Committee Mr Henrik Slipsager, then CEO of ISS North America, concluded as follows:

1. definite relationship between quality and profit;
2. corporate office needs to maintain the focus;
3. focus creates action;
4. actions create improvement;
5. improvement creates better profit;
6. better profits create happiness!

(c) Measurement of customer satisfaction at ISS

(d) Theoretical considerations

It was first decided to assume a very simple delivery system in which the goods and services are delivered directly to the end user and where ISS can obtain customer satisfaction information directly from the end user. The group was, of course, fully aware that this was a simplification that should be relaxed later on but in order to get acceptance for the system it was decided not to complicate matters too much. Furthermore, it was assumed that the goods and services are evaluated by the customer on N different parameters concerning importance of and satisfaction with each parameter. The rate of importance (weight) of the ith parameter was named w_i and the individual satisfaction evaluations were named c_i and both were measured on an appropriate rating scale. The customer satisfaction index (CSI) was then defined as follows:

$$CSI = \omega_1 c_1 + \omega_2 c_2 + \cdots + \omega_N c_N \qquad (20.1)$$

Furthermore it was assumed that the revenue from customer satisfaction may be described as some function of the CSI. This function is, of course, assumed to be an increasing function of CSI – the larger the CSI, the larger the revenue.

In addition, it was assumed that the cost of obtaining customer satisfaction is a quadratic function. What the assumption means is that it becomes more and more expensive to increase customer satisfaction when customer satisfaction is already at a high level.

Based on these assumptions it was suggested that the company should balance its quality effort according to the rule:

$$\frac{c_i}{\omega_i} = \frac{c_j}{\omega_j}$$ (20.2)

According to this simple rule which can easily be implemented in practice the degree of fulfilment (i.e. the score divided by the weight) should be equal for all quality parameters in the company.

An even simpler presentation of the result can be made as follows, if a few theoretical assumptions are met

$$c_i = \omega_i$$ (20.3)

This type of result will make it very easy to report the outcome of the customer satisfaction study in a graphical way.

The practical procedure

At first a seven-step procedure was chosen for the conduction of CSI analysis. This procedure was rather simple and has been refined several times since the first start. Today the ISS Quality Institute and the ISS Telemarketing Service recommends a 12-step procedure where the inclusion of loyalty and segmentation is very new:

1. determination of the customer and the process leading from ISS to the customer;
2. pre-segmentation of the customers;
3. determination of relevant quality attributes (parameter);
4. choice of competitors (if necessary);
5. design of questionnaire;
6. sampling;
7. post-segmentation of customers based on results;
8. determination of quality types;
9. construction of quality maps;
10. determination of cost points;
11. determination of sales points and customer loyalty;
12. determination of corrective actions.

Steps 1 and 2: The first crucial step is to determine the customer and the process leading from the company to the customer. In certain simple cases we have a situation like the one described above, where the company delivers goods and services to the end user and gets information back concerning the satisfaction.

In most cases, however, the situation is more like the one described in Figure 20.2, where the delivery consists of a chain of so-called middlemen before the goods and services reach the final customer.

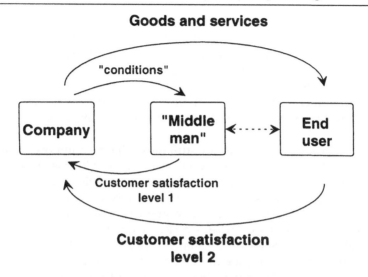

Fig. 20.2 Dual customer satisfaction.

It is, of course, crucial that from the start it is well-known what the delivery system looks like. It may lead to very wrong conclusions if one forgets certain parts of the chain as the following example illustrates.

In New York, ISS had contracts on the cleaning of large building complexes with a large number of tenants in each. The level of cleaning and the prices were discussed not with the individual tenants but rather with a building manager who decided everything in relation to the contract with the cleaning company. At the beginning ISS never really considered the individual tenants as their customers, instead they focused on the building manager. For a long time this went well. From time to time ISS called up the building manager and asked him about his satisfaction and usually he was satisfied because ISS of course lived up to the contract. After a time, however, the tenants became more and more dissatisfied with the services they received. In the first case they did not say anything to the building manager, instead they gathered and decided that they wanted another cleaning company to do the job. A spokesperson went to the building manager and told him that they were not satisfied with ISS and he was left with no other choice but to threaten to fire ISS who of course could not understand this, because, as far as ISS knew, it had lived up to the contract and its customer was satisfied. ISS learned its lesson, however and in the future never just considered the middleman as its customer. Instead the company went out all the way to the end users and asked them about the satisfaction and it used this information not just to improve its own services but also to keep the building manager informed about the situation.

At this stage it should also be decided if customers should be segmented. In most cases customers do not constitute a homogenous group. Different segments will require different treatments. Hence it will usually be necessary to split up customers in groups based upon the information which is already used within marketing, e.g. size of customer, private or public customer, location, etc. In this case we can come as close as possible to the individual customer with the corrective actions.

Step 3: Determination of relevant attributes is the next important step. It was decided that this takes place in co-operation with the customer. In too many cases one sees companies themselves defining what is relevant to the customer. This is a very bad idea because experience shows that very often companies only have a vague impression of what is really relevant to the customer. There is a clear tendency to define quality in technical terms instead of consumer terms. From this follows that customers should participate in defining the relevant attributes and the best form of doing this is usually by setting up focus groups.

Steps 4, 5 and 6: In this group of steps the sampling takes place but first of all it must be decided whether competitors should be included in the analysis. In many cases it will be a great advantage to have competitors in the analysis but this will of course make the entire customer satisfaction analysis somewhat bigger. Furthermore it may complicate the analysis because in some cases it will be difficult to find respondents who know both the ISS company in question and the competitors.

Depending upon the decision concerning competitors, a questionnaire must be designed. The size of the questionnaire should be kept to a minimum in order not to annoy the customers. At ISS it is recommended that the number of parameters should not exceed 30. It goes without saying that the questionnaire must have a professional layout and, in the case of business-to-business research, a contact person must be identified.

Steps 7 and 8: Before constructing quality maps it will usually be a good idea to go through the collected material in order to let the data speak. First of all it is very useful to find whether there are other segments in the material than the ones already defined. This can be done by using a variety of statistical tools. If significant groupings are found these groupings will also be used when reporting the final results. Furthermore it is useful to find out whether the parameters may be segmented into meaningful groups.

Steps 9, 10 and 11: The following step will be to introduce the quality map. This map is based upon the theoretical result above in which the

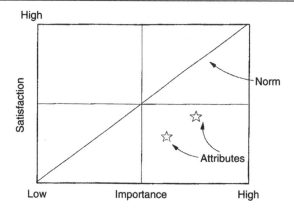

Fig. 20.3 A quality map.

optimum was found when the importance is equal to the satisfaction for each parameter. An example of such a map is given in Figure 20.3.

The map is constructed by plotting importance on the horizontal axis and satisfaction on the vertical axis. To reach optimum profit the developed theory then shows us that the parameters should be placed on the principal diagonal of this map.

Very often, however, it has proved to be a good idea to relax this a little. Instead the map is divided into squares by dividing each axis into two, using the average importance and the average satisfaction as dividing points. These four squares are then used for decisions concerning actions. The two squares with either high/high or low/low are of course the squares in which the parameters have a correct placing. The other two squares are more problematic. If the importance is high and the satisfaction is low, the company is faced with a serious problem which may lead to loss of customers in the future. Similarly if the importance is low and the satisfaction is high, the company has allocated its resources in a wrong way. Being good at something which the customers do not appreciate means loss of money. Instead these resources could be used for improving the situation in the high/low square.

The reasoning above of course depends upon the assumptions made in the theoretical development. A very important assumption is that the costs of improving the satisfaction of a parameter is equal for each parameter. If this is not the case we have to establish a cost index for the individual ISS company and use this index as a correction factor for each parameter. Then the horizontal axis will no longer be the importance of the parameters but instead the importance per unit of the costs.

Another way of improving the analysis will be to introduce 'loyalty points' in the analysis to see if there are any differences between the importance established in the interview with the customer and the loyalty established from a different set of questions. This difference will usually reflect a difference between short-term and long-term importance of the parameters.

In practice, the loyalty points are constructed by using a series of questions concerning the loyalty of the customers towards the company. Will they buy again, will they recommend ISS to others and similar questions. Using these questions it will then be possible to determine by use of statistical techniques the (short-term) loyalty effect of each parameter. This information helps the ISS manager to choose among the individual improvement areas.

The procedure reported here reflects the state of the play at ISS in November 1995. However the procedure is subject to constant development and the ISS Quality Institute together with the ISS Telemarketing Service (now ISS TeleResponse) are working closely together with marketing specialists and statisticians in order to improve the methodology.

Parallel with the development of a customer satisfaction measurement procedure, a procedure for the development of employee satisfaction has been developed. The theoretical model is exactly the same as the theoretical model for customer satisfaction. The only difference lies in the sampling procedure – in other areas the CSI methodology is followed.

Both the customer satisfaction procedure and the employee satisfaction procedure are documented in manuals from the ISS University in which the process is described and questionnaires are shown together with a reporting procedure. Furthermore time schedules and cost are described.

20.4 SOME RESULTS

ISS now has a very large number of results concerning measurement. In what follows we will show the results of the first CSI study made according to the theoretical developments from the Quality Institute and its associates. After this some results documenting the ISS's improvement circle will be shown.

20.4.1 ISS DARENAS A/S

In order to begin the process of customer satisfaction measurement one of the seven companies belonging to the Danish section of ISS was selected for a pilot implementation. The company, ISS Darenas A/S, is mainly a sales company selling cleaning machines and other cleaning materials but it is also undertaking consultancy concerning different aspects of cleaning. Typical customers are other companies or the public sector.

In this particular case it was decided to use the following seven-step procedure when implementing the system. This procedure was the first one suggested by the working group on CSI and it is the one which has now been refined into the 12-step procedure given above:

1. Define the relevant quality characteristics, i.e. the total set of characteristics creating customer satisfaction.
2. Define the relevant customer population and the relevant segments to be used when reporting the results.
3. Obtain the sampling frame.
4. Construct the questionnaire and decide upon the scales to be used for measuring customer satisfaction.
5. Carry out the survey.
6. Compute the relevant statistics.
7. Communicate the results.

(a) Step 1

In co-operation with the top management of the company the quality characteristics were divided into five main groups each containing specific characteristics. The resulting 10 quality characteristics were as follows:

Administration
1. Switchboard
2. Service in connection with placement of orders
Delivery
1. Number of residual orders
2. Number of errors
Products
1. Assortment
2. Product quality and documentation
Consultants
1. Knowledge of products
2. Observance of agreements
Repair
1. Quality of repair
2. Waiting time.

The main problem in connection with this step seemed to be keeping the list down to a manageable size. Initially the list contained more than 75 items but after lengthy discussions all parties agreed upon the list above.

One experience from the work done at this stage is that it is very important that there is a consensus of opinion about the list of quality characteristics. Otherwise people may reject the results at a later stage.

Furthermore, one should be very careful when preparing the list because once the list has been agreed upon it should not be changed since one of the basic ideas is to compare results from one period to the next.

(b) Step 2

In step 2 it was first discussed whether the company was going to concentrate on the existing (or known) customers or whether it was going to sample the total potential market. The latter case was considered preferable but not feasible. Owing to this, it was decided to start out with the known customers and optimize the procedure with these before turning to the ultimate goal, i.e. a full-scale market measurement.

In the present case it was decided to sample from a population of known (i.e. past and present) customers. This was based partly on cost considerations and partly on the assumption that it would be very difficult to obtain valid information in this particular case from people who had never done business with the company.

When reporting the results of a CSI study, results should, as mentioned above, be broken down on relevant segments, segments possibly calling for different treatment. In the present case the following segments were decided upon: 1. the number of years the customer had been with the company; 2. line of business; 3. location; 4. financial importance.

(c) Step 3

The sampling frame will of course depend upon the chosen population. In the present case the company had records of all past and present customers for a period of two years. These records were used as a sampling frame with reasonable success apart from the fact that information about past customers had not been updated.

One particular problem was the contact person. It is very important that you get the right person to answer your questions. The right person of course being the person making decisions concerning the product or service. In this case the records did not contain sufficient information about this and a lot of effort was expended in order to shape the records in such a way that sampling was facilitated in the future.

(d) Step 4

Construction of the questionnaire did not cause any problems. With regard to scales a balanced five-point rating scale was used for both importance and individual quality ratings. After sampling all quality measurements were rescaled to a number between 0 and 100.

Table 20.4 CSI study for ISS Darenas 1992

Quality characteristics	c_i	Weighted c_i
Switchboard	87.3	144.2 (10)
Placement of orders	90.0	111.2 (9)
Residual orders	83.9	104.9 (8)
Delivery errors	87.4	103.9 (7)
Assortment	85.4	87.7 (6)
Product quality and documentation	90.1	83.7 (3)
Knowledge of products	86.8	82.3 (2)
Observance of agreements	91.3	86.8 (5)
Quality of repair	85.8	79.9 (1)
Repair waiting time	85.2	85.1 (4)
Total customer satisfaction index	89.1	–

(e) Steps 5 and 6

The survey was carried out as a traditional telephone survey with a sample of approximately 300. An independent market research bureau called Markeds/Consult A/S carried out the interviews and the name of the client was not revealed until after the questions concerning the relative importance of the individual quality characteristics had been answered. The basic results are shown in Table 20.4.

The weighted c_i values are the original satisfaction measures divided by the number of parameters as well as the weights. The reason for this scaling, which does not affect the optimality criterion, is that in this case the weighted average of the weighted satisfaction values will be equal to the arithmetic average of the individual satisfaction values. (Note that the figures in the table have been slightly changed in relation to the original ones. This means that it is not possible to calculate backwards in order to obtain the weights!)

(f) Step 7

Both weighted and unweighted satisfaction values are reported. In connection with the weighted satisfaction values, a rank is given. The lower this rank, the higher the priority concerning improvements in the area. Remember from the theoretical discussion that in order to obtain optimal allocation, resources should, in principle, be moved from areas with high to areas with low weighted satisfaction.

The two indices have different purposes. The unweighted index was communicated to the individual areas and used for individual inspiration and motivation while the weighted satisfaction was used by management to allocate resources to the areas. In practice, a total reallocation is, of course, not possible; instead the numbers show the order in which quality improvements should be carried out.

In the present case the total CSI is 89.1; a number which will not have much meaning before some kind of comparison is made possible. This will of course be the case when sampling is done on a regular basis. The aggregate figure was reported to the top management of the ISS Group.

Contrary to the aggregate CSI the individual measurements caused immediate action. The c_i values were made public and discussed in detail at a series of meetings where relevant breakdowns of the material on the segments mentioned previously were available. Furthermore task forces were created within each area in order to discuss and suggest quality improvements.

As mentioned the weighted satisfaction values were both communicated to the individual areas. Instead they were used by the management to pick out areas for immediate action. It was decided that the repair area should be improved. Not just through the created task forces but also through an increase in resources, due to the obvious importance of this area. Furthermore, it was decided to start up an information programme in order to improve product knowledge and to improve product documentation.

20.4.2 DOCUMENTATION OF THE ISS IMPROVEMENT CIRCLE

As reported, the whole idea behind the new measurement system was to create a system of early warning within the ISS Group. It was expected that improved employee satisfaction would lead to improved customer satisfaction which again would lead to improved profit before tax.

Due to this it was of great interest to study whether this hypothesis could be documented in practice. First of all the entire system rested upon this assumption and furthermore it would be of great internal value when promoting the ideas within the Group.

An indicator of the relationship has been established at ISS Servisystem in Denmark, where employee satisfaction and customer satisfaction have been measured on a regular basis for some years now. In order to verify the hypothesis of the improvement circle, employee satisfaction and customer satisfaction were measured for 19 different districts in 1993. The results were measured on a traditional five-point scale and the employee satisfaction index and the customer satisfaction index were both computed as weighted averages of the individual parameters. The results are shown in Figure 20.4.

These interesting figures show a clear linear relationship between employee satisfaction and customer satisfaction. The higher the employee satisfaction, the higher the customer satisfaction. The equation of the relationship is as follows:

$$CSI = 0.75 + 0.89 \, ESI \qquad R^2 = 0.85 \tag{20.4}$$

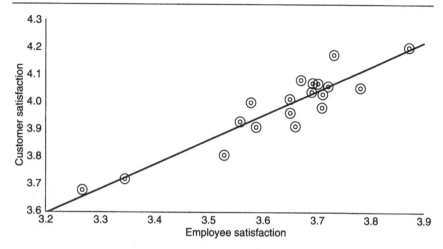

Fig. 20.4 Relationship between ESI and CSI at ISS Servisystem.

The coefficients of the equation are highly significant. Furthermore we cannot reject a hypothesis that the slope is equal to 1.

It appears from this that a unit change in employee satisfaction more or less gives the same change in customer satisfaction. One cannot of course just from these figures claim that this is a causal relationship but, combined with other information, ISS believes that this is strong evidence for the existence of an improvement circle like the one described previously. To ISS, therefore, creation of a measurement system along the lines given in Figure 20.1 is necessary.

Only in this way will management be able to lead ISS upstream and thus prevent the disasters that inevitably follow the fire-fighting of short-term management.

20.5 CONCLUSION

The quality process at ISS is now well under way. In some areas it may even be concluded that the level is an example of genuine European excellence. The way, e.g. that ISS has tackled the problem of measurement by combining well documented theoretical results with true practical sense in a continuous improvement process should be an example for other European companies.

The fact that ISS today lives quality can be seen from, e.g. the annual report for 1994. In this it stated:

Total Quality Management and Certification under ISO 9000 are just two of a number of quality-related concepts which have become household words in all ISS contexts. The trend is clear:

continuous quality improvements have become a business prerequisite – not just for ISS but also for its customers. ISS gives high priority to quality, and many of the Group's activities now incorporate new systems which document quality.

Later on in the report under the heading of the creation of competitive advantages it stated:

Quality: With the setting up of ISS Quality Institute and the Group-wide implementation of TQM-programmes, ISS has responded to the market's demands for continuous quality improvements. The pivotal element is training and education for all staff categories. Quality management is based upon regular measurements of satisfaction among customers and employees. The aim is to optimize customer satisfaction by an unfailing ability to meet or, even better, surpass their expectations of the services delivered.

It appears that quality and TQM are not buzz-words at ISS. They have simply become part of excellent management. Furthermore, in the future, quality and TQM will serve as the background for development of new business ideas. ISS is on the way to becoming a mature TQM company in which the basic idea is management by return on investment in prevention.

APPENDIX A

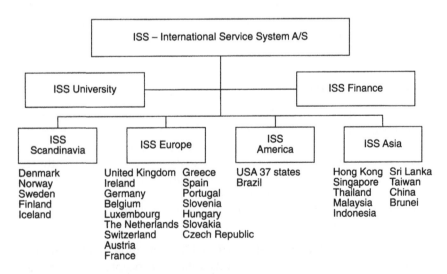

Fig. 20.A.1 The ISS Group (including ESGO).

Table 20.A.1 Financial overview of ISS

	1992 (kroner)	1993 (kroner)	1994 (kroner)	1994 (US dollar)
Consolidated turnover	11 356.0	13 307.0	14 232.5	2339.7
Staff costs	(8326.5)	(9994.5)	(10 805.9)	(1776.4)
Cost of goods sold	(783.6)	(875.2)	(873.3)	(143.6)
Other operating costs	(1379.0)	(1460.7)	(1621.3)	(266.5)
Depreciation	(329.9)	(343.7)	(298.8)	(49.1)
Operating costs	(10 819.0)	(12 674.1)	(13 599.3)	(2235.6)
Operating profit	537.0	632.9	633.2	104.1
Amortization of goodwill	(60.7)	(84.2)	(101.8)	(16.8)
Interest receivable and similar income	77.5	61.4	44.3	7.3
Interest payable and similar charges	(180.0)	(186.4)	(155.2)	(25.5)
Interest receivable/(payable), net	(102.5)	(125.0)	(110.9)	(18.2)
Profit on ordinary operations	373.8	423.7	420.5	69.1
Other income	35.1	247.8	128.7	21.2
Other expenses	(31.9)	(78.3)	(98.3)	(16.2)
Other income/(expenses), net	3.2	169.5	30.4	5.0
Profit before tax	377.0	593.2	450.9	74.1
Tax on profit for the year	(105.9)	(130.8)	(151.6)	(24.9)
Consolidated profit	271.1	462.4	299.3	49.2
Minority interests	(5.2)	(0.7)	(10.9)	(1.8)
ISS consolidated net profit	265.9	461.7	288.4	47.4

APPENDIX B

Fig. 20.B.1 Quality of relationships.

Table 20.B.1 Key areas for future work at ISS: customers

From	To
Nuisance	Customers to satisfy
Break down sales resistance	Listen to, meet needs, co-operate
Vendor's specifications	Customer's specifications
Acceptance of contract losses	Concern about contract losses
High-pressure sales talks	High quality to sell service
Let customers discover defects and fix them	Prevent defects, detect and correct them
Delays	On time
Vendor defines what quality is	Customer defines what quality is
Pricing for short-term profit	Pricing for lowest cost of high quality
Customer complaints sometimes corrected	Continuous customer contacts
Employees indifferent towards customers	Employees trained in how to satisfy the customer

Table 20.B.2 Key areas for future work at ISS: vendors

From	To
Many vendors. Selected for lowest prices	Selective. A few high-quality vendors
Often remote relationship	Close, co-operative working relationships
Rare 'technical' assistance	Advise on specifications and solutions
Some rating of vendors	Vendor 'partnerships'
Try to meet specifications	Co-operation to see that specifications are met and work
Inspection	Joint 'early-warning' systems
Sporadic, businesslike communication	Planned dialogue based on measurements and new direction

Table 20.B.3 Key areas for future work at ISS: employees

From	To
Autocratic management	Participative management
No criteria for recruitment	Selective recruitment
'People don't like to work'	People like to work if properly led
Keep employees in the dark	Keep them informed
Personal growth is ignored	Growth is planned and stimulated through career progression programmes
Grievances are ignored	Grievances are resolved
Suggestions are ignored	Suggestions are invited
Errors are accepted	Errors are prevented through training
Training is absent or sporadic	Training for continuous improvement
Very limited recognition	Recognition is emphasized

Index

Page numbers in **bold** refer to figures and page numbers appearing in *italic* refer to tables.

For Product Safety Concerns and Information please contact our EU
representative GPSR@taylorandfrancis.com Taylor & Francis Verlag GmbH,
Kaufingerstraße 24, 80331 München, Germany

Printed and bound by CPI Group (UK) Ltd, Croydon, CR0 4YY
08/05/2025
01864388-0001